We Cannot Escape History

BY

JOHN T. WHITAKER

New York

THE MACMILLAN COMPANY

1943

Fellow citizens, we cannot escape history. . . . The fiery trial through which we pass will light us down in honor or dishonor to the latest generation. . . . We shall nobly save or meanly lose the last best hope of earth.

ABRAHAM LINCOLN

Annual Message to Congress, December 1, 1862

CONTENTS

WE CANNOT ESCAPE HISTORY

I

MY DEAR BROTHER

FOR my brother, Captain Lawson Spires Whitaker, U.S.A. You walked up the gangplank of the troopship as I would expect my brother to go. Around the corners of your mouth there was the flicker of a smile, diffident yet proud; and with the bright excitement of the eyes this shy smile lighted up your whole countenance. As I stood on the blacked-out dock it seemed to me that your face shone above the rail of the darkened liner. Yours was the eager look of a young man who has a rendezvous with destiny, whose nation in his own generation faces a situation unique in modern history.

To you the inevitability of our war was plain enough. One year before Pearl Harbor you volunteered. "Somebody's got to be willing and ready to fight," you said, "until the country as a whole wakes up and gets armed and learns how to win." You believed we could win when the other countries were going down before the Axis and when at home we heard the voices of defeatism. But you thought we would have to learn how. Western civilization failed to learn how when Genghis Khan first introduced *Blitzkrieg*. The Mongol Hitler carried the whole of his army on shaggy little ponies, feeding his men mare's milk and butter made from it, to avoid the impediment of baggage, so that no army learned to match the momentum of his impact. In the end no nation stood before the Mongols from the China Sea to the Danube. The offensive had gained a new speed and mobility, and civilization went down before the Western World could catch its breath. This was precisely the situation with which Hitler and the Japanese war lords confronted us when they

1

introduced mechanized armies supported by a preponderance of aircraft. They achieved an overwhelming speed and momentum—first with the most men—and they confronted us with fire superiority at the point of impact. For they held the strategic initiative.

You were no military man, but you saw this thing as clearly as the Major General of Marines to whom I introduced you. He talked sense, that general. Do you remember how he put it? "I'm in my fifties and no man in his fifties is going to win this war," said the general. "I represent the old-fashioned way. I don't know how to beat the tank and the dive bomber. I only know that somebody can beat them. The Germans aren't invincible. It is my job at my age to lead an American division in uneven battle until some younger officer finds out how to beat the tanks and the dive bombers. He will find out from my mistakes in the field and from the lives which my men will not have sacrificed in vain."

You were no professional soldier, like the general, but you knew that we faced a long war and the danger that our allies would be destroyed one by one as we ourselves moved from one disheartening defeat to the next. Could we overcome the ten-year head start in the arms race? Could we prevent our enemies from making us an isolated and have-not power? Could we gain the initiative and take the offensive or were we always to be pushed back, outnumbered on the fronts of our enemy's choosing? You understood because you confronted the problem of the survival of America rationally and methodically just as you had studied the problems of medicine. I remember when you felt that it would be possible to perform a certain kind of operation on the human heart. You learned later that a man named O'Shaughnessy was experimenting in England. You dropped everything else and went over and persuaded him to let you work at his side. You sought neither position nor money; you wanted to master the technique of a new operation. You learned how to do an operation—not yet publicized—which can save millions of lives. And poor O'Shaughnessy died at Dunkirk. This silver-haired giant, with only a mild rationalization of his loyalties and his duties, need never have left the hospitals of London. But he volunteered to go into the field and he died on the beach at Dunkirk with a Bren gun in his hand, a Colonel of the Medical Corps who met the problem of the dive bomber standing up and with a borrowed Bren gun roaring.

Some may think that such a death for one of the world's great surgeons was needless. Not you. You went up the gangplank to the troopship the way O'Shaughnessy went and for the same reasons. Why study to save a million lives if they are to exist only in Herr Hitler's kind of world? You are a young man, but you are wise in the accumulated experience of our civilization and our democracy. I know that you fear many things, but death is not first among them. Civilization can get on without the operation which O'Shaughnessy taught you. It is doomed without O'Shaughnessy's spirit.

In conquered country after conquered country our enemies have been snuffing out this spirit of freeborn and freedom-loving men. Hitler wrote in *Mein Kampf:* "The greatest of spirits can be liquidated if its bearer is beaten to death with a rubber truncheon." This declaration, written soberly by the Fuehrer, is a succinct statement of the Nazi way of life and it is subscribed to by the Japanese war lords, who have murdered all liberal statesmen who stood against them. Rising in their armed might, lawless and violent, our foes threaten the extinction of everything we have lived by—the Greek discovery of the dignity of man, the Christian revelation of compassion, the Roman rule of law, the Frenchman's intellectual integrity, and our own evolving Anglo-Saxon theory of equality of political, social, and economic opportunity. This is our heritage and it gives us our unity as free men. The unschooled simple man shares in it as truly as the scholar who goes to the original Greek or Vulgate. When

Emerson lent Plato's *Republic* to the farmer the simple man read with understanding and, returning it, said, "This book contains many of my ideas." Indeed! It is this heritage of free men believing in human progress for all classes which bound Emerson and the simple farmer together and it is against this unity that our foes fight.

Out of a parvenu perversion of Nietzsche and Hegel and Spengler came Hitler, the leader of a *Blut und Boden,* or blood and soil, mentality of monopoly which knows how to achieve unity only through suppression—suppression of the individual at home, suppression of other peoples abroad. How startlingly similar these Germans are to the Japanese, their "honorary" Aryans, who invented *Bushido.* Venerating the code of feudal loyalty—though *Bushido* is found in no dictionary before 1900—the Japanese military leaders achieved national unity by an expedient as direct as Hitler's. They murdered every liberal statesman who opposed the acquiescence of the masses in their program of conquests undertaken in the name of the God-Emperor. The National unity of Germany and Japan—by these methods—could be achieved only at the expense of their neighbors and upon their assumption that we were decadent. The Italians, also schooled to the antidemocratic ideal, have been persuaded for two decades of the decline of the Anglo-Saxon empires—persuaded, of course, by a leader who held forth the promise that these empires could be plundered as ancient Rome was plundered. Count Galeazzo Ciano, Mussolini's son-in-law and foreign minister, laughed at the notion that the United States —unprepared either in armaments or in national psychology —could stand against the Axis. "But time is on the side of the democracies," I argued. "Yes—if there is time enough!" Ciano retorted.

If Ciano is right and there is not time enough for a people caught flat-footed to reverse the preponderance of power and fight through to victory, then a book like this is useless, for they—not we—survive. But you asked me to write this book.

You and I both believe that in the end the democracies will prevail. But you said that our generation would have fought in vain if, having won the victory, we failed to understand and to make secure the things for which we fought. As a foreign correspondent I went abroad just before Japan startled us with the first Axis aggression in 1931 and, witnessing the betrayal of the League of Nations, I watched the democracies fail thereafter to halt the Fascist conquest anywhere until—surpassed in armed strength and daring everywhere—we stood at bay within a war-encircled globe, fighting not for our ideas alone but for our very existence. You said that through this tragic decade which extended from Manchuria to Pearl Harbor there must have been lessons—lessons which, though unheeded in peacetime, might be pondered by a people at war. You asked me to search through my observation of our allies and our enemies for the things which we must know about the world in which we live if we are to survive the war and win the peace.

And so this book is for you, a worthy heir to the men who fought at Kings Mountain, on the plains of the Republic of Texas, and at bloody Shiloh. "In the strength of our forefathers we go, not in their tracks. Their stars we follow, not their dead campfires."

II

WHOM DOES THE ARMY OBEY?

My mother wrote about the roses, for she had planted the bushes by the dozen and she loved them. "The unseasonable heat has brought the roses out in profusion and the darkies—bless them—are too lazy to prune properly," she said. My father was concerned as usual about repairs, "the inescapable minimum of painting, plumbing, and wallpapering which must be done every spring despite depression, taxes, and tenants who are behind in their rents." My young brother, glad to be home from medical school, swam all day in the country-club pool. There was also news about the kinfolks because to Southerners they matter. I reread my mother's letter, ordered another glass of the tart Swiss wine, and watched the *Dents du Midi* turn red in the Alpine glow. Seated on the shore of Lake Geneva, I thought of America and it seemed both far away and very near. Homesickness for the faces of loved ones and for the familiar ways of my own land swept over me. That homesickness now seems fateful. For since that Saturday afternoon—June 30, 1934—our world has never been the same.

That was the day when Hitler carried through the counter-revolution. That was the day of the purge which made the second World War inevitable. Adolf Hitler's action, four thousand miles from my home, was destined to affect my mother's roses, my father's property, and my brother's career just as it condemned me to live almost continuously from that day onward in the presence of physical violence. A few minutes after I had pocketed my mother's letter the Swiss extras were out. "Roehm and Schleicher killed . . . Terror

6

in Berlin." I took the airplane and went into Germany for the New York *Herald Tribune* to help John Elliott, the resident correspondent, cover the story of how Hitler, backed by the militarists, destroyed the revolutionary elements in the Nazi party and handed Germany back to the same reactionary forces which had taken Kaiser Wilhelm II to war.

On the excuse of inspecting a labor camp Hitler had gone to Westphalia and there he entered an airplane for Munich at the unlikely hour of 2:00 A.M. The Chancellor's associates struck with equal stealth. While Hitler himself went for Captain Ernst Roehm, Chief of Staff of the *Sturm Abteilung* (S.A.), others dispatched Gregor Strasser, who had been Hitler's first assistant. Thus Germany was rid of Roehm, the soldier who personally led the 2,500,000 S.A. storm troopers, and Strasser, the revolutionary who enjoyed the fanatical loyalty of the old guard of the Nazi party. A nice discrimination was shown in the further killing of four S.A. *Obergruppenfuehrers* (major generals) and twenty-two brigadiers and colonels of the S.A. In a matter of hours the revolutionary leadership of National Socialism was wiped out. Hitler had shot his earliest collaborators and his two warmest friends—Roehm being the only man who addressed him with the intimate "thee" and "thou." Simultaneously the killers struck down every forceful personality capable of taking Hitler's place. They murdered General Kurt von Schleicher, the former Chancellor, together with his wife, and General von Bredow, formerly of the Ministry of War. They murdered Dr. Erich Klausner, leader of "Catholic Action," and a dozen other important Catholics. Two former Chancellors escaped—Franz von Papen, by a fluke, after two of his secretaries were shot, and Heinrich Bruening, who told me later that friends had persuaded him to slip the Dutch frontier twenty-seven days before.

It was this purge—or "blood bath," as the Nazis called it— which made the present war the inescapable historic necessity of the twentieth century. "The German people are like other peoples; there are good Germans and bad Germans," as my friend Count Karl von Pueckler expressed it. "But the bad Germans contrive to rule and the good Germans always obey." This was the tragic meaning of the purge of June 30, 1934. The German leaders elected the traditional military solution of the problems of the Third Reich—instead of revolution—staking the destiny of their country once again on the gamble of world conquest. Twenty years and two days after the assassination at Sarajevo, the Germans turned the clock back to 1914 and their decision made another world war inevitable.

Hitler had come to power in Germany in January of 1933—a year and a half before. The nationalistic-minded reactionaries had handed the chancellorship to Hitler. Hindenburg and Papen had called in the ridiculous little corporal just when the Nazi strength seemed checked. This action had bewildered observers. "How could the conservative Hindenburg—the aged Junker of the previous war—offer the chancellorship to a violent rabble rouser and hoodlum?" they asked. They had forgotten the estimate of the Junker made by Lord D'Abernon, the former British Ambassador, who wrote: "The President, Hindenburg—essentially a soldier—instinctively distrusts anything but force." Hitler represented force—the rubber truncheon and the blazing pistol—so he was called to be Reich Chancellor. Hindenburg and the other conservatives felt that they could hold Hitler in line, channelize his force, in short, against their Socialist and Communist enemies alone. But Hitler's Nazis surprised even the Hindenburgs by their exuberant violence. They burned the Reichstag to disenfranchise the Communists—whom they blamed for the fire—in order to gain their seats in the Reichstag and enjoy a full parliamentary majority. By this reckless expedient Hitler, having been made Chancellor, became dictator. In all of German history no man or group had ever achieved such unbridled authority.

Hitler and the National Socialists had got the power—

unprecedented power. But what were they going to do with it? "Where do we go from here?" had become the cry, not only of the German people, but also of the Nazi leadership. For, having promised all things to all men, the Nazis were divided among themselves. There were two main cleavages. Hitler's popular support rested on the lower middle class and he had promised the little storekeepers, the clerks, and the petty civil servants that he would cut up the great estates of the Junkers and smash simultaneously the great banks, the chain distributors, and the department stores. Hitler had made these promises to the "little man"; but his dictatorship, like the chancellorship they had given him, depended upon the favor and consent of the generals, who were allied by marriage with the Junkers and the industrialists. To the generals the essence of the Nazi movement had been Hitler's attack against the Versailles victors and his pledge to regenerate the Reich militarily. To them Hitler had promised to carry through that totalitarian reorganization of the German nation outlined even before the termination of the last war in a memorandum by General Quartermaster Erich Ludendorff. Ludendorff's elaborate plan provided state and military control of family life, marriage, childbearing, education, housing, health, and even amusement. Germany was to become a new Sparta, one great solemn-faced barracks. This total organization for total war could not go forward, however, if there was to be a social revolution diverting the national wealth to welfare rather than to armaments. The purge of June 30 was destined, therefore, to resolve the struggle between the military, the landowning Junkers, and the great industrialists on the one hand and the lower middle class and the hungry millions on the other. The old feudal system and the promise of the new revolutionary democracy were deadlocked.

The struggle was fundamental and it had been fought out before. England and the other democracies had become democracies only when their armies had been made answer-

able to the people through the people's parliament. The
Kaiser and his war lords, however, had retained autocratic
power. The political backwardness of the Germans had
enabled them to make the state ultimately responsive to the
military caste, not to the people. "Wherein lies the real
power?" asked Delbrueck in *Regierung und Volkswille*. "In
military strength. The question, therefore, by which to
determine the essential character of the state is always the
question 'Whom does the army obey?'" A revolution in
the nature of the German state had been averted in 1914.
Then the German Socialists were moving steadily toward a
majority in the Reichstag. They were pacifists. Had the
first World War been delayed a decade, the Socialists might
have achieved power and asserted the sovereignty of the
Reichstag over the war lords and the Kaiser. The great
world conflagration of 1914–1918 might thus have become
neither necessary nor likely. The German militarists were
certainly not uninfluenced by this impending revolution
when they judged the moment propitious in 1914 to launch
that war. In 1934 Germany was again at the crossroads.
How were her leaders to solve the problems of an industrious
and virile people whose density of population was 348 to the
square mile as against 36 to the square mile in the United
States? The Nazi radicals wanted a redistribution of wealth
through the confiscation of the great properties and the
socialization of the great industries—a little man's revolution.
Switzerland was the perfect example of the little man's state.
Without raw materials, foodstuffs, or colonies, the Swiss
consistently enjoyed the highest standard of living in Europe.
But that way lay the abandonment of the rearmament program, the assertion of state control over the great monopolies,
and the destruction of the military and Junker classes. The
generals preferred the way of war.

The political strength of Hitler in this moment of decision rested on the 2,500,000 S.A. members. These storm
troopers were the street-fighting hoodlums who had brought

Hitler to power. Organized by Captain Roehm, these Brown Shirts served as the Nazi party army. They had beaten the Communists and terrorized the public. As Hitler's private army they were rivals to the Reichswehr—the army of the German state—a professional elite recruited by the conservative Junker class. The S.A. rank and file hated the directors of the great department stores and the industrialists and landowners, who were the support of the Reichswehr. The S.A. had made and won a revolution. Its members believed that to the victors belong the spoils. Their social program was increasingly toward the left. Hitler himself characterized this wing of the Nazi party as virtually Communist when he said that "a national-Bolshevist rising was being prepared."

For some years, even before Hitler came to power, I had gone into Germany to attend Nazi meetings organized by the S.A. The same pattern ran through every. meeting. There were almost always, for instance, five speakers. The first attacked the Treaty of Versailles; the second attacked the rich, the third the Jews, the fourth the foreigners—any foreigner, every foreigner—and the fifth held forth promises. The technique of the promise-making was too obvious. It was so simple that the responsible elements in Germany failed to take the Nazi movement seriously, just as they had underestimated Hitler—a ridiculous little figure who mouthed kitchen German through a Charlie Chaplin mustache.

"Do you want bread?" the fifth speaker would scream.

"Yes," roared back the claque and with it the crowd.

"Then vote for Hitler," said the speaker.

"Do you want shoes? . . . Vote for Hitler."

After eighteen months in power the Brown Shirts were asking Hitler to fulfill the party promises. "What about the bread—what about the shoes?" they asked. They had had enough semimilitary discipline and Spartan self-denial. Now they wanted state ownership of the factories and great properties and social legislation for the masses. They could watch the big-shot party leaders indulge themselves with big estates, big cars, and big blondes. Men like Goering and Goebbels lived like steel magnates, and the rank and file— still without spoils for themselves—began to say openly that the Nazi leadership had sold out to the reactionaries and the generals. An open rupture had come between Hitler and his first assistant, Gregor Strasser, the National Socialist who was also a socialist. This obstreperous radical wanted something done for the masses and he demanded that the promises be fulfilled.

Now Hitler was and is the most intelligent Nazi of them all. He knew that he could not keep the promises and the power too. He understood the basic nature of the totalitarian revolution. Had he not defined National Socialism as "the mass in movement"? His technique was one of keeping the millions on the run, inchoate, inarticulate, and confused. A demand that he should give the people the good things of this life enraged him. He fumed at idealistic socialists and thought of the masses only as an instrument of power. Hitler had recorded his attitude toward the people: "Man is congenitally evil. He can only be controlled by force. To govern him everything is permissible. You must lie, betray, even kill, when policy demands." Hitler's notion of "policy" and its exacting demands was best explained to me by Mussolini, who boasts that he showed Hitler the way and schooled him to totalitarian revolution.

In a private conversation Mussolini said to me, "The masses are easily persuaded to any view, thanks to the modern techniques of the press and radio. But it is hard to hold the masses to a given view. Public opinion, if left volatile, is likely to react, crystallize, and harden into a point of view not at all pleasing to the leader. The public, therefore, must be kept uncertain and confused except in moments when the leader asks for its applause. Let me illustrate. If the Italian public begins to agitate a policy which I myself have secretly planned I will denounce it. I will put through this policy only when I have killed public demand for it. I do not desire that public opinion should come to feel that it has a power of its own."

This is a vital technique—the debauching of public opinion—and Hitler no less than Mussolini knows that without it the power of the secret police is insufficient to maintain a dictatorship. It is his understanding of this which has made each dictator (of necessity) lead his people from one costly and nerve-racking adventure to another. In this fashion they made the Italian and German peoples docile in risky moments and taught them to react only in applause for an accomplished coup. It was the conscious application of a studied technique which is necessary in any country that lacks what Ferrero calls a "legitimate" government.

Hitler was afraid, therefore, to give the German masses the higher standard of living he had promised them. He knew that if he gave them bread they would want butter. If he gave them shoes they would want automobiles. And then they would want universities and golf and country clubs and the forty-hour week and all the "good things of life" which characterize what Hitler calls "soft, decadent, effete, bourgeois, capitalistic democracy." With an improved diet, leisure from work, and automobiles for holidays, the German people would have time to think. Hitler knew that you had to give the Germans a sense of want, a sense of grievance, a sense of crisis. He knew that he had to move them from one crisis to another at high tension, trying on the nerves, evocative of that hysteria which lies deep, if dormant, in the German soul.

Hitler knew that if he gave the Germans time to think they would overthrow his dictatorship. He could not afford politically to give them bread and shoes. For a totalitarian revolution consists in essence of a wartime economy in peacetime and depends upon the dictator's ability to persuade or coerce the people to sacrifice their normal way of life to the exigencies of a state of emergency. The German General Staff, for different reasons, held like views. The generals had already worked out with the Junkers and industrialists a common program both for their class and their Third Reich. By June 30, 1934, Germany's secret rearmament was already in second gear. The generals wanted the arms, and the industrialists and the Junker families, from which the generals came, wanted the armament boom. War? They were not afraid of it. They had never regretted the great war of 1914–1918; they had only regretted losing it. The war had been a good thing for the Junkers. Prices for their agricultural products had reached all-time highs and they had kept the wages of the farm hands low and had been spared by inflation the hardship of the mortgages. It was the middle classes which the inflation had destroyed. These stolid middle-class elements of the community had been stripped and then maddened by the economic consequences of the war, but now this queer chap Hitler had caught their imaginations. Hitler led them around by some potent magic which dramatized their failures, shifted the blame to others, and promised victorious regeneration. The military were content. If they could persuade Hitler to stop this agitation for social reform and to dissolve the S.A., all would be well. The Nazis were not going to be allowed to take over the factories or to cut up the Junker estates. If an end could be put to this nonsense, Hitler would be the perfect German Chancellor. His ideas of a totalitarian state made it possible to mobilize all the resources of Germany and to herd the people into a single barracks square. The generals could put Germany on a war footing in peacetime.

Captain Roehm and other left-wing leaders of the S.A. did not see eye to eye with these monocle-wearing dandies of the Reichswehr, or professional army. What was the Third Reich? It was the creature of the Nazi revolution. Who had made the revolution? The street fighters of the S.A., the organization which had been the private army of the Nazi party. Very well, then, the thing to do was to make the party army the national army. The S.A. numbered 2,500,000. The Reichswehr numbered only 250,000—though limited to 100,000 by the military clauses of the Versailles Treaty. By feeding the S.A. into the expanding conscript army, Germany could be given a great people's army—a national army under the leadership of men like Captain Roehm, who represented the have-not masses of Germany instead of a few Prussian families.

There was never any evidence that Captain Roehm or Gregor Strasser plotted revolution. We correspondents never found any convincing evidence, and Hitler and Himmler and Goering and Goebbels certainly worked hard to persuade us of their guilt. I am convinced that Hitler anticipated the possibility of action by the radical group and struck with his customary surprise tactic.

It is possible now to print for the first time the true story of Roehm's murder. It was given me by Captain Roland von Strunk, one of the four men of the *Schutzstaffel,* Himmler's S.S., or black-shirted elite guard, who were present when Hitler confronted Roehm. Captain Strunk gave me the story some years later. I knew Strunk in Austria when Dollfuss was murdered and during the Ethiopian and Spanish wars. A career officer in the German Imperial Army, Strunk was born a "gentleman"; but, falling on evil days, he had become a Reichswehr spy, an S.S. officer, and a Nazi secret agent. I had been puzzled by his behavior during the Spanish Civil War. Several times he had refused to let me accompany him to fronts where German specialists served with Franco's troops—even though I had nursed him through a mild case of shell shock and felt certain that he trusted my discretion. A year later when we happened to find ourselves together in Africa I asked him about this. He explained that on any one of these visits German Gestapo agents with the troops might have shot him in the back. "You as a witness would have been shot too. They would have had the Spaniards say that we had been killed in action. Ha! Ha! They would have even given us medals—posthumously, of course." Then Strunk told me how he lived under sentence of death because of his part in the June 30 purge. The other three S.S. men who had witnessed Roehm's death had already been killed one by one, and Strunk was certain, he told me, that his turn had come. A year after this conversation he was murdered in Berlin—by a curious coincidence the day before I returned to that city. The *Voelkischer Beobachter*, which he served ostensibly as a correspondent, printed his picture on the front page and explained with mocking regret that he was the victim of a duel.

"After we surprised Roehm at 6:00 A.M. in Wiessee—twenty miles from Munich—he was brought into the presence of the Fuehrer," Strunk said. "Roehm was in a very disadvantageous position, ridiculous in his nightgown. Hitler charged him with a plot 'to murder me, your Fuehrer, and members of the German General Staff.' Drawing his own revolver, Hitler handed it to Roehm. 'You are a traitor. I give you the easiest way out.'

"Roehm's eyes blazed. He strode up and down the room, stamping his bare feet in fury. Then he stood before the Fuehrer, his face thrust almost into Hitler's face. 'Mein kleiner Adolf,' said Roehm, 'it is thee, not I, who has betrayed the National Socialist party. Strasser and I have been steadfast. Thou, Adolf, hast run with this one and that one and deceived us one and all. Through all these years I have been unswervingly loyal to the party and to thee.'

"Roehm thrust the revolver in Hitler's face. 'If this is to be murder, commit the murder thyself. Thou hast no courage to shoot me with thine own hand. I am not guilty of treason as charged. I will not blow my brains out like a coward.'

"It was a terrible scene to behold. Hitler cringed before the scorn of Roehm. He began to fall back and Roehm pursued him slowly around the room. Holding the pistol by the muzzle, Roehm shook the butt in Hitler's face. The Fuehrer suddenly burst into tears. He began to sob. He sank to the floor, his face in his hands, his hair hanging down over his face. Burly and savage, Roehm was ridiculous and incongruous in his nightgown but strode round and round the seated Fuehrer, laughing and upbraiding him.

"We carried Hitler out of the room. He lay down in a darkened bedroom for four hours. Roehm was dressed and escorted into Munich. Later, on direct orders of the Fuehrer, we four S.S. men shot Roehm. Roehm stood with his chest thrown out, his arms at his sides, a sneer on his lips. Each of us fired one bullet."

Strunk shrugged his shoulders as he told me this story. "We four S.S. men fired four shots. I knew and my fellow officers knew that they were four shots for us as truly as for Roehm. We four had seen the German Fuehrer stared down by Roehm, sobbing on the floor, his hands and his hair over his face."

How many others went down before the guns of Himmler's S.S. men we may never know. Pooling our efforts, several American and British correspondents drew up a list of four hundred and seventeen whose deaths were known to us personally or could be verified. Others have estimated that not less than one thousand men and women were murdered in the bloody days which June 30 ushered in. Some two weeks later I still heard the volleys of firing squads within the squares of three Berlin barracks alone. The Nazis took a ghoulish delight in this purging. They cremated some bodies and sent the ashes parcel post collect to the victims' families. In one instance they decapitated a man, sent the head to his widow in a sack, and charged her for the sack.

This was in the eighteenth month of Nazi rule and at that time there was still a normal or, if you prefer, sane element in the German community. The good German *Hausfrau* and her heavy-jowled, unimaginative, but hard-working husband were shocked. Had the German military not supported Hitler his movement would have been destroyed then and there. The average German had deplored, but been complacent about, Nazi savagery before June 30. After all, the Nazi hoodlums had murdered Communists until the purge. To the middle- and upper-class Germans this had been dog eat dog. But in the purge the Nazis turned their guns against the bourgeoisie. The S.S. murdered good Catholics and generals like Schleicher and Bredow. The night Hitler took the rostrum to answer for the purge he had lost the sympathy and support of the German nation. Hitler's future, the future of the German people, and indeed the future of the world rested in the hands of the German generals. And —unhappily for Germany and the world—the generals knew what they were about.

In anticipation of the purge General Werner von Blomberg had made a remarkable declaration on behalf of the generals. Speaking June 28—two days before the purge— he offered the army's blanket endorsement of what Hitler was about to do. Traditionally the Reichswehr played a passive role politically, employing its power only for a veto in the last resort. Blomberg startled Germany, however, by declaring: "The time has passed when selfish interests can indulge at will in prophecies about the 'Reichswehr Sphinx.' The Reichswehr is now serving a government which it endorses wholeheartedly. If foreign voices for obvious reasons are reviving old tunes, it shows that they do not comprehend the fundamental changes that have taken place in Germany."

Hitler and the people knew, therefore, that he had the support of the Reichswehr when he rose to justify himself before the German nation for a "blood bath" unprecedented in civilized times. When Hitler began to speak in the Kroll Opera House before his own regimented, brown-shirted Reichstag, I left the auditorium and went into the street.

I wanted to study the reaction of some of the millions of Germans who would listen to the Fuehrer. The applause of the Reichstag boomed out over the radio, punctuating the speech of Hitler; but it was not echoed back by the millions who listened in public squares, theaters, and open-air restaurants. The crowds were curious and sullen—the "smart" crowd in the Wilhelmsplatz like the workmen in the eastern Sport-Palast. The multitude plainly wanted to know how many men were shot on June 30, and why; how many more men were to be shot, and why. I think I shall never hear again anything so eloquent as the silence of those crowds. Over the radio came the applause of the Reichstag; the roar halted the rush of impassioned, almost hysterical words with which Hitler in past speeches had inflamed the passions of the whole German people. A man here and a women there applauded, grew conspicuous, and fell silent. Hitler's millions heard him in silence and without cheers. In the Siemensplatz there was no applause, and the Alexanderplatz, which once surged with Communists, was empty before Hitler had spoken twenty minutes. In the Sport-Palast couples drifting away were intercepted by storm troopers and sent back to their seats.

I watched the small family groups seated around tables in Schloss Park—working-class families. As Hitler's staccato bursts of speech became more impassioned, the look of sullen resignation became more plain in their empty faces. They were not free to order beer while der Fuehrer was speaking, and der Fuehrer was speaking for hours. One man continually lifted his empty beer glass, looked at it, suddenly recalled the occasion, and put it down furtively. A middle-aged couple with a young girl between them sat stiffly attentive. As Hitler spoke of Roehm's death, saying that it was better that Roehm should die than that thousands of revolting storm troopers should be killed, this man caught his wife's eyes. They stared at each other wide-eyed, their faces immobile. Then the man shook his head, almost imperceptibly; and the woman made a clucking sound, patted the braid of her daughter's hair, and hugged the little girl to her. These Schloss Park working people had the kind of unhappy faces which do not meet another's gaze but are always looking into tabletops or off into space.

But I was wrong in believing that at last the demagogue had lost his people. Hitler's oratory is meaningless to a foreigner, but it is potent magic to a German. Before my eyes Hitler regained the German masses. He spoke to some innermost recess of the German soul in a speech typical of his technique. Like a man in sackcloth and ashes, he evoked the mood of the 1918 defeat, pictured Germany's subsequent ills as due entirely to incompetent and timid Chancellors, and painted a horrendous picture of Communist disorders as the alternative to his own regime, which already was talking up to foreigners who hate Germany. Through all this there was a pseudoreligious note: man's original sin and the agony of hell. Then the orator moved toward a note of hope or redemption. The Nazi excesses of graft and lawlessness for which Hitler himself was responsible were ascribed exclusively to Roehm and the S.A. It made Hitler sick merely to contemplate them and, of course, there would now be no repetition. Then he grew bolder, moving toward his equally effective trick of picturing himself as the fearless and audacious leader who would bring the German people out of the slough of despond to victory.

"If anyone reproaches me," he shrieked, "and asks why I did not resort to the regular courts of justice for conviction of the offenders, then all that I can say to him is this: 'In this hour I was responsible for the fate of the German people, and thereby I became the supreme justiciar of the German people'!"

It was better that a few score be killed than that Germany should be plunged into general bloodshed, Hitler concluded. A new light came into the eyes of his listeners. Stability! Power! Victory! Something deep inside this distressed and misled people grasped at Hitler's promises of a victorious and all-powerful Germany. The speech had done the trick. Meaningless to anyone not German, Hitler's oratory had touched something that Wagner calls forth from the sentimental emotionalism and uncurbed romanticism of the Germans.

Observers in Berlin took too much satisfaction from the liquidation of the S.A. Slowly, painstakingly, methodically, this private army was stripped of its shining boots and its Sam Browne belts. My office was near the Columbushaus and I watched the Brown Shirts go in to have their dossiers checked. They went in with fear in their eyes. Sometimes they stayed a few hours, sometimes a few days. Some never came out alive. We imagined that they were carried away in the trucks that meshed gears and raced motors every night in the roped-off back alley. This great street-fighting army of 2,500,000 men was destroyed as a political or a military instrument.

Liquidating the S.A.? Hitler became the prisoner as well as the leader of the German generals. He built up, of course, the S.S. and the Gestapo, his own elite guard and secret police organizations, and they served to terrorize many an individual general. The generals knew and Hitler knew, however, where ultimate sovereignty lay. There were disagreements between Hitler and the General Staff. Sometimes Hitler won and sometimes the staff won. Both knew that in a crucial moment of showdown the army would prove stronger than the S.S. and the Gestapo—stronger, that is, if the issue were really crucial, if the generals stood united, and if it came to a question of machine guns against truncheons. Thus began the new structure of the Germany which from June 30, 1934, was dedicated inevitably and irretrievably to war. There was an excruciating balance between Hitler and the military, between the party and the great industrialists, but the ultimate veto power rested with the army's superior numbers and superior arms. The Nazi party, for all its great power, never again interfered with or crippled the preparation for war. That is why and how Germany became a military rather than a revolutionary state.

Hitler found politically minded "yes-man" generals and he gave them rapid advancement. Blomberg, whom I first met in Geneva during "disarmament" days, is a typical example. Blomberg was Hitler's man; but when he broke the code of the military caste by marrying a stenographer of indifferent morals, the General Staff demanded and secured the dismissal of the Field Marshal. A great psychologist with intuitive genius, Hitler has known how to be autocratic; but he has never been unaware of the nicety of the balance of power. This awareness inspired the Berchtesgaden technique. Hitler has quarreled with individual generals and dismissed or intimidated them, but he has never overridden the great General Staff on a fundamental issue which in the opinion of the majority of generals would have endangered either the preparation or the prosecution of the war.

His Berchtesgaden technique is elemental. When the German Reich faces a decision upon fundamentals, Hitler withdraws to the mountaintop. Dictatorship never gets rid of the partisan struggles of parliamentary procedure—it merely drives the wrangling from the press and public rostrum to the smoke-filled clubs and hotel rooms. Hitler rises above these bitter, if unpublicized, quarrels, wrapping himself in the godlike mantle of the mists of his mountain peak. His spies and informers report the progress of alignments whether the struggle is in the political or in the military field. When the "mind" of the General Staff becomes clear, Hitler descends from the mountaintop. He issues categoric orders. He tells the generals what they must do and it is generally precisely what they have decided they ought to do. This is how it has been possible for the Nazis and the generals to work together with such efficiency and precision. Much was made abroad of the apprehensions of the General Staff when Hitler ordered the reoccupation of the demilitarized Rhineland. The generals knew that if France, supported by Great Britain, opposed that move by force, Germany was not prepared for war. The year, it must be remembered, was 1936. The General Staff consequently issued secret orders to the German army not to give battle but to withdraw in that event. But these orders were approved by Hitler just as the majority of the General Staff were in complete agreement with the Fuehrer that the gamble of entering the Rhineland should be undertaken.

Five years later when the German army stood before the suburbs of Moscow, equally sensational reports of a struggle between Hitler and his generals were broadcast. What was the situation in Russia in the winter of 1941? The Germans had failed to keep the timetable schedule, and militarily it was necessary to go on the defensive before exposed armies were caught in subzero weather. This naturally was the advice of the General Staff. Politically and strategically, however, a new factor obtruded. The moment for the entry of Japan into the war was at hand, though the Germans had not reached the Volga. To insure action by the Japanese— a people who make their own decisions—it was desirable to renew the attacks against Leningrad and Moscow. This political consideration outweighed all others in the grand strategy, and any General Staff which failed to agree would have been stupid in the extreme. Naturally the generals smarted under the inevitable reverses and casualties which followed. But Hitler boldly, and somewhat generously, assumed the full responsibility when he invoked his "intuition." Much was made by some observers of the fact that certain generals were relieved of their commands when in truth the General Staff was glad to be relieved before the German nation of the responsibility for the failure.

Hitler and the generals have worked together because the vast differences which separate them—differences of birth, breeding, and character—matter less than the common goal which unites them. Hitler may talk in terms of German racial superiority and the generals in terms of German military superiority. Set in motion, the two have rolled steadily forward—a mighty juggernaut—toward the conquest of the world. The generals have been able to use Hitler as no military clique ever used a chancellor. When they can no longer use him or when he becomes a liability to their program the generals will not hesitate five minutes to be done with him. In the moment when they envisage the military defeat of Germany the generals will hand Hitler over to the United Nations or hand him a revolver. They know that Hitler is capable of killing himself provided the audience is large enough or the moment sufficiently dramatic.

From June 30, 1934, consequently, the world has faced the same mentality, the same program, and the same aims which took Imperial Germany to war in 1914. Hitler served to unite civilian Germany politically, to mobilize the whole of its resources in peacetime, and finally to inspire in the masses a passionate and almost religious belief in the tragic, if ludicrous, theory of their own racial superiority. Of Hitler's vision of German destiny the generals had few doubts. They had known and used him when he was a nobody. Corporal Hitler was demobilized in 1920 and within the year the Reichswehr hired him as an "educational officer." He made speeches to the troops which were so "nationalistic" as to be treasonable to the Weimar Republic and treasonable in the eyes of all but the German militarists. His nationalism consisted of the explanation that German militarism had not lost the war. The brave army had been stabbed in the back by the socialist "vermin" who now ruled the Weimar Republic. The army should remain beyond the control and contaminating touch of Republican leaders. The generals hired him also as a spy. He gave them regular reports on political activities which they felt to be "subversive"—that is, critical of the army and the army class—and on movements which they felt might lend themselves to the "rehabilitation of the Fatherland." General Ritter von Epp and Captain

Ernst Roehm gave Hitler money and arms to organize the
S.A. They gave him part of the funds with which he founded
the *Voelkischer Beobachter*. When Hitler's newspaper went
too far in preaching army revolt against the Republic, the
Republic's War Office ordered the suppression of the *Voelkischer Beobachter*. General von Lossow, Commander of the
Seventh Division, in Bavaria, refused to carry out the order.
Later when Hitler was tried for the Beer Hall *Putsch* in
1923, the military party came to his aid. Wilhelm Frick,
director of the political section of the Munich police, testi-
fied: "We held our protecting hand over Herr Hitler because
we saw in him the germ of Germany's regeneration." When
Hitler had served only six months of his five-year sentence
for the unsuccessful *Putsch,* the military influenced the judi-
ciary. The Bavarian Minister of Justice—a sworn, if disloyal, servant of the Weimar Republic—had the effrontery to
remark: "We must support the National Socialists because
they are flesh of our flesh." Thus Hitler was freed.

If the generals knew Hitler, the industrial families with
whom the generals intermarried knew him too. The nationalistic and war-minded elements among the industrialists—
the armaments interests—were represented by Alfred Hugenberg. Hugenberg worked for Krupp and dispensed the political funds of big industry. He was chairman of the German
National party, the proprietor of a news agency and a chain
of newspapers; and he controlled the principal motion-pic-
ture company of Germany. Hitler went on Hugenberg's
pay roll a few years after the Beer Hall *Putsch*. Joined by
Schacht, they campaigned against German ratification of the
Young Plan, by which reparations were to have been scaled
down. The industrialists, like the military, knew Hitler.
They had known him in what we Americans call the "pre-
convention days."

The June 30 purge brought into the open a conspiracy of
fifteen years' duration. Power was now in the hands of the
generals, the Krupp munitions makers, and the one politi-

cian whose single consistent and honestly held program had been revenge for Versailles and a final German effort at world conquest. Strasser's revolution had been betrayed, Roehm had been shot, Hugenberg had been dropped, and many another was to suffer from the treacherous opportunism of Hitler; but the program marched on. It was the program laid down in *Mein Kampf.*

For Hitler and the generals were agreed that Germany could win the next world war. If the democracies had learned nothing from 1914–1918, the Germans had. Sea power and the British blockade had destroyed the Kaiser almost in the moment of his triumph. But sea power was being transformed by new methods of land transport and by the airplane. Hitler, no less than the German generals, was profoundly influenced by the writings of Sir Halford J. Mackinder, the great British geographer. The propositions laid down in *Democratic Ideals and Reality,* which Mackinder published in the first weeks of 1919, were perverted by the Germans. They were utilized by Major General Haushofer, whose Institute of Geopolitics was established at Munich in 1924 as a blind for the General Staff, which Berlin under the Versailles Treaty had been forbidden to reestablish. Mackinder had warned the United States, Great Britain, and France to create a strong League of Nations based upon the recognition that if Germany were permitted to fight another war she would probably prove invincible.

Mackinder believed that another German effort at conquest was inevitable in an unorganized world. He argued that sea power, which had once preserved the democracies, now depended upon the productivity of the land base. The great productive land base was the world-island of Europe, Asia, and Africa. He held that if a single predatory power were ever to establish control over this area the Americas would then become a lesser island, inferior in population, resources, and every other element of strength. Within the world-island there lay a heartland, which he described as a contiguous region embracing a quarter of Europe and a half of Asia. Germany needed merely to extend her control through Russia and she held this heartland. Thereafter her conquest of the world would become easy. Sea power could not reach and harm the heartland base which Germany would organize, thanks to modern methods of transportation, as she began at her leisure to outbuild the naval powers of the world. Mackinder argued that the last war was precipitated by the revolt of the Slavs against German domination and he held that Germany would have conquered the world if, instead of dispersing her strength by the invasion of France in 1914, she had first knocked out Russia and secured the heartland.

This application of geography to global strategy was studiously pondered by the German generals, but it was seized upon by Hitler as a sort of divine revelation. The tendency of the British, French, and Americans to confuse their prejudice against Communism with the fact of Russia's geographic position seemed fortuitous to Hitler. He said repeatedly to the German generals from the day of the purge onward—as Blomberg himself twice told the author—that the new German army would fight but one war, the war against Russia. In his contempt for the democracies Hitler believed until the British and French declarations of war that they would be duped by his crusade against Communism. He believed that they and the United States would be conquered without a struggle.

Many observers had seen even before the purge what Hitler was driving at. Edgar Ansel Mowrer had written *Germany Puts the Clock Back;* Hamilton Fish Armstrong had prepared his remarkably penetrating *Europe Between Wars?;* Leland Stowe had published *Nazi Germany Means War.* Stowe's title summed up succinctly, already in 1933, what we urgently needed to know about modern Germany.

Almost ten years later there were Americans who remained incredulous. Certainly in 1934 those of us who wrote that the June 30 purge made war inevitable were frowned on. Someone coined the phrase "warmongering correspondents."

I remember writing my brother from Berlin: "Unless preventive war is undertaken in time by the British and French, you and I are going to cut our clothes to the soldier's pattern." He wrote back with that patient tolerance which a younger brother often feels for an older one. He had done premedical studies at the University of Munich in 1929. As a student in Bavaria, he had made the acquaintance of many Nazis and knew the mind of the young German. "I told you," he wrote, "almost five years ago that nothing but the invasion of Germany would stop the Nazi movement and I told you that its sole purpose was to wage war."

What had happened in Germany was clear even to a young medical student because he had lived among the Germans and come to know them. My brother in 1929 had listened to German youths explain apologetically just how they would conquer the world in a few years and why it would be better for America to surrender without a struggle. After the June 30 purge it became clear to all Germans who believed in democracy and sincerely repudiated war as an instrument of national policy that, whatever they might think, Germany was marching to war. Every school child in Germany was already being compelled to sing each day:

> Storm, storm, storm!
> Sound the bells from tower to tower;
> Call the men, the young, the old;
> Call the sleepers from their rooms;
> Call the girls down the stairs;
> Call the mothers from their cradles.
> The air shall roar and yell;
> Raving, raving thunder of revenge!
> Call the dead from the vaults!
> **Germany awake!**

Even the children knew that Germany prepared to go to war.

"This purge is wonderful," said the Communist news vender with whom I talked regularly.

"Why?" I asked in some bewilderment.

"Because now nothing can prevent war. Hitler and the new militarism can be destroyed only by war."

American businessmen, or rather those of them who spoke German and understood something of Germany, got the same thing on every hand. I remember an American industrialist who had opened a branch factory in Germany. It was in full production and showing profits which already justified his investment.

"Funny thing," said my American friend. "The man I made director of our company here in Germany came to me the other night with tears in his eyes. 'You have made me director of your plant,' he said. 'I can never thank you enough. I came up as a mechanic. Here in Germany I never could have become a director and it was the dream of my life. You have forgotten class distinction and in making me your Herr Direktor you have treated me as if I were your own son. Now I come to you as a son to his father. I come to warn you. There is to be war again between your country and mine. I warn you that, though I hate the thought of this war, I am a good German. What my Fatherland asks I will do. I am loyal to you as a son to his father. But when the war comes my loyalty is not to you but to my Fatherland.' "

My American friend shook his head sadly. "My director said another thing," he added. "He said, 'The war will come years before it is declared against you. The war—it has already begun.' "

Appeasement was born, of course, in this moment. It so happened that this friend faced the future unblinkingly and prepared to cut his losses and get out of Germany. Many American and British businessmen were less courageous, however. Clinging to their investments in Germany, they put dollars first and country second. It was simply that their investments in Germany were concrete—damned concrete, when you had to amortize them and face your stockholders. The war, on the other hand, was not concrete—it seemed only a possibility in the mind of pessimists. How did you know, anyway, that war was inevitable? People who said that war was inevitable were warmongers. So, without meaning to be disloyal, hundreds of businessmen minimized and then denied the danger to America or Britain or France. Getting on the defensive with your conscience is like telling a lie —one step backward leads to another. And so many an American and Briton persuaded himself that the Nazis were grand fellows. If the Germans were confiscating $1,000,-000,000 in Jewish property, why, to hell with the Jews anyway. And if the Germans wanted to knock over a lot of silly, wrangling European countries and unite that continent, why shouldn't they?

Some executives did not want to believe that Germany was as bad as the picture painted by correspondents, especially if they had just built a hundred-million-dollar factory in Germany. I used to talk with the president of a large American corporation whose views never changed in six years after 1934. Even in 1940, when Germany was already fighting against an isolated Britain and wanted to negotiate peace in order to gain time against America, he used to say to me, "Let's stop the bloody show. Washington is the referee. Let's tell London, 'Drop your guns and make peace—we aren't going to help you.'" This man did not care what happened to Britain and he would not face the problem of what might happen to America if we made the German victory complete. He cared for his hundred-million-dollar investment in Germany and he wanted "peace at any price."

In the same way, the most spectacular of the Wall Street speculators could not see why any American should worry about German war aims or plans. Two weeks before the invasion of the Lowlands and France, this operator said to me, "Wait until you see the tanks and the airplanes the Germans are going to throw into France! These Germans are all right. Why should you dislike them? All that nonsense about the Gestapo and persecution? The Germans have always been damn nice to me. I don't have any trouble with them. You don't fall for this warmongering propaganda that they would try to invade America, do you?"

As a correspondent I did not have to wait until 1939 for the announcement of Hitler's war. It began almost immediately with the 1934 purge. On July 25, 1934—less than a month after the June 30 purge—Chancellor Engelbert Dollfuss was murdered in Vienna. The incident was dramatic, almost Graustarkian. At noon our telephone to Vienna went dead. Elliott and I could not reach the *Herald Tribune* correspondent there. An hour later I was on my way to Vienna and the next morning I stood in the Ballhaus, where the Congress of Vienna made peace in 1815 after the Napoleonic wars. In one of the rooms of that old palace the Nazis had shot Chancellor Dollfuss. I stood with the Chancellor's valet, Hedvicek, a giant, inarticulate peasant, who had witnessed the slaying of his master. With tears in his big eyes Hedvicek told me the story.

"They broke into the chancellery at one o'clock. Chancellor Dollfuss quit the room where he was in conference with members of the cabinet. I ran to his aid and lifted him bodily into an anteroom as the Nazis began to beat on the door. I knew a way out. I took the Chancellor by the hand through the rooms of President Miklas toward the archives wing, which would have led to the street."

Nine men rushed in; their leader raised his pistol at close range and fired twice. Struck in the throat and under his right arm, Dollfuss raised a hand in slow bewilderment to his face, looked at the men in the room, and fell backward, crying, "Help! Help!" His head hit the floor with a crack.

Hedvicek went down on his knees and touched the blood-soaked rug where the Chancellor fell.

"I thought the Chancellor was dead. He did not die for

nearly three hours. They carried him into the salon and placed him on the sofa there. He bled to death. I pleaded that they get a doctor; but they left him on the sofa and, while they pinned me to the wall, I saw him bleed to death, the color going out of his face slowly."

The success of June 30 had gone to the head of the war party in Germany. There was a mountain of iron ore in Austria and there were forests. The German war machine needed this iron ore and this timber. In characteristically forthright fashion, the Germans had gone after what they wanted. Dollfuss stood in their way; they shot him. The war, which was to carry German troops and planes across virtually every frontier in the world, had already begun. When Italy mobilized and Britain and France guaranteed the independence of Austria, the Germans halted. They were not yet ready for world war. They could bide their time. Austria could wait. Except that the Germans failed, the Austrian *Putsch* was typical of all their subsequent attacks.

Germany was arming and the Reich was already ringing to the tramp of marching boots. The days when I had heard the Nazi orators scream "Do you want shoes? Do you want bread?" seemed centuries ago. The German masses were now ready for Goering's harsh injunction—"cannon, not butter." The German leaders were at work over the whole of Europe.

Three months after the murder of Dollfuss, King Alexander of Yugoslavia was assassinated in France, where he had gone to discuss a preventive alliance against Germany. German and Italian gold jingled in the pockets of the assassins. When they buried Alexander, I was in Belgrade. I can never forget an interview with Goering in the German legation there. In the midst of our talk he tiptoed to an anteroom, quietly opened the door a fraction of an inch. Peering through, I saw an array of Yugoslav officers.

"Ha! Ha! Ha!" whispered Goering. "Behold! Twelve

Yugoslav generals. Twelve loyal allies of France who do business with me today." The German chuckled with immense satisfaction.

German leaders were at work; German factories roared. And, most ominous of all, German youth were singing. Their voices thundered a song I was to hear them raise later in Austria, when they tried there again, and in Spain, Czechoslovakia, France, and even Italy. They sang:

> Heute wir haben Europa,
> Morgen die ganze Welt!
> (Today we have Europe,
> Tomorrow the whole world!)

The purge had made the militarists supreme once again and it led inevitably and inexorably to the dark night of August 31 and September 1, 1939—the night when the Nazis marched into Poland and precipitated world war. The most apposite and revealing comment on what had happened to Germany was given by Kaiser Wilhelm II, exactly two weeks before the attack on Poland. The Kaiser was saying farewell to John Wheeler-Bennett, the distinguished British historian, who had been the German's guest at Doorn.

"This is farewell forever," said the Kaiser.

"Why?" asked my friend.

"Because the war will separate us and I will die long before its end."

"But is the war inevitable?" asked Wheeler-Bennett.

"Yes," replied the Kaiser. "The generals have got Hitler just as they got me. He can never stop the German military machine."

III

NAZI GERMANY MAKES WAR PAY

THE impending collapse of Nazi Germany was predicted with glib regularity through the six-year period (1933–1939) of German preparation for war. Actual dates for this felicitous disaster were fixed and refixed perennially. Bankers, professors, and others who estimate national wealth in terms of gold alone shook their heads knowingly as the Nazis accepted the Marxist notion that wealth consists of the productivity of labor. To them the German efforts to disguise inflation were transparent and it seemed plain that the German state, like a spendthrift individual, lived beyond its means and faced an inexorable day of reckoning. This mood of "You just wait and see," compounded in equal portions of wishful thinking and outraged orthodoxy, was responsible, even more than Hitler's Charlie Chaplin mustache, for the fact that German power was underestimated by its victims.

American, British, and French businessmen were encouraged in this optimism by Germans who drew, for their benefit, a distinction between so-called "radical" and "conservative" elements within the Third Reich. It took considerable naïveté on the part of the listener and a certain eloquence on the part of the German apologist to convince a democratic banker or businessman that a dope fiend, murderer, and warmonger was "conservative," but Marshal Goering was so described. The eloquence on behalf of the German "conservatives" was supplied by one of the least conservative men in the world—Herr Doktor Hjalmar Horace Greeley Schacht. As Germany's leading banker and Hitler's financial wizard Dr. Schacht had a positive genius for telling visiting bankers and businessmen precisely what they wanted to hear. This estimable rascal affected old-fashioned high, starched, linen collars; he had a knobby forehead over bulbous cheeks and his watery eyes bulged formidably. Dr. Schacht looked like a caricature of himself and the exaggerated gestures with which he accompanied his outbursts of ersatz emotion came straight from the East Lynn school of "melodrammer." I never heard him wring the hearts of Montague Norman and other international moneylenders who met monthly at Basel, Switzerland, because we journalists were rarely allowed beyond the dreary lobby of the Bank for International Settlements. I have been present, however, when Dr. Schacht, in benefit performances for visiting bankers, wept crocodile tears on some of the best parlor rugs in Berlin.

"It's frightful what the radical elements of the National Socialist party are doing to my country," Dr. Schacht would begin, half whisper, half moan. "They have made inflation inevitable. They have undertaken a program of armaments and a program of public works simultaneously. The printing presses are rolling, treasury notes are being issued, and every kind of short-term paper is out for discount. You and I, as sound businessmen, know what that means."

Having invoked the infallibility of his attentive group of "sound businessmen," Dr. Schacht would place a hand over his heart, hoist his collar on his Adam's apple, and turn anguished eyes toward a far corner of the room.

"The time will come when this paper must be paid off," he would continue. "But you and I know that arms are not productive. Consequently the national wealth of the country will prove insufficient. The radical Nazi elements are making inflation and the ultimate collapse of the Fatherland inevitable."

The lying rogue! The policy Dr. Schacht denounced was his own—carefully worked out with Hitler, the generals, and the munition makers. It was the purpose of these men—and their whole purpose after June 30, 1934—to demonstrate that arms can be made productive. Surrounded by democratic and pacifist neighbors, reluctant to defend themselves, much less to attack Germany, Hitler and the generals and the munition makers gambled the whole wealth of the German people upon their own plan for a war of conquest. *Any* rearmament program conducted by such men in the face of such foes could have had scarcely any other meaning. But when the German program became total, absorbing annually more than 70 per cent of the national income year after year through six years of peaceful preparation, it became clear, first, that this nation had invested its future as well as its wealth in war and, second, that the planned economy of this totalitarian state was working to a timetable and a blueprint. Upon the completion of this program Germany would be bankrupt in everything but arms and trained man power. In that moment Hitler and the generals would face two alternatives. Either they would conquer their neighbors and make them foot the bill for the preparation of the military might of the Third Reich or they would stand by idly as Germany went into economic collapse and revolution.

Of course arms are not productive under our democratic system or in any sane, organized world community. A tractor is productive because with a tractor man cultivates the soil and increases its yield. Cannon and tanks are purely destructive weapons. Consequently the masses in the democratic countries shook their heads in bewilderment when Goering announced the national policy of "cannon, not butter." It was sad to see a whole people adopt a program of tanks, guns, and airplanes. We said that the Germans were turning the clock back, that they were returning to the Stone Age mentality. Too few of us realized that the Germans meant to make these destructive weapons productive by Stone Age standards. For the German rearmament program Schacht invented many new financial tricks, but in the main he resorted to the issue of the kind of treasury notes with which the Kaiser had financed Germany's last war effort.

When the tank manufacturer needed capital with which to negotiate the purchase of raw materials Schacht gave him treasury notes. The German government promised to pay upon their due presentation. Now when a tractor is manufactured under such a scheme of credit inflation the ultimate payment is made possible by the increased national wealth which comes from the use of that tractor. The transaction is sound. But when treasury notes are issued for the construction of tanks and cannon which create no real wealth, how is payment on them to be met? Hitler and Schacht, the generals and the munition makers, had the answer. With tanks, guns, and airplanes the Germans garnered more wheat than they ever harvested with tractors. Before Germany ever invaded Poland her instruments of destruction had already produced for Germany a bonanza yield in Austrian iron ore, timber, and foodstuffs; in Czech lignite, hops, and factories (including the Skoda works) ; in Spanish iron, copper, and fats. The very shadow of these instruments of destruction had yielded Germany the produce of the Balkans on her own terms. The treasury notes and the other short-term paper were presented for payment. The Germans presented them to one conquered people after another. For Hitler and his generals had planned well. Unmolested through six years, they had painstakingly prepared a colossal, world-wide program of larceny and loot.

The feverish activities of this six-year period are worth studying in perspective. Such a study confounds those who have tried to understand Nazi Germany in terms of ideologies, persuading themselves, as did Mr. Neville Chamberlain, that Nazi Germany stood as a counter and alternative to Communism, or those who persist even in wartime in drawing a distinction between Germany and Nazi Germany. I use the qualifying phrase, Nazi Germany, only to indicate a distinction in time, for in outlook and program Nazi Germany is the Germany of Frederick and Bismarck and Wilhelm; Weimar Germany was only a strange interlude which created some illusions abroad but very little satisfaction among those Germans who think of themselves as destined to rule. German individuals are endowed with the praiseworthy qualities which we cherish in other lands, and Burke was wholly sound when he reminded the world that it cannot indict a whole nation. And yet we cannot blink the existence and behavior of the German *state*. And we cannot ascribe to the German *state* those praiseworthy qualities which we find in the German individual.

It is clear to the whole world now that Germany in the period 1933–1939 was preparing for war. A study of that preparation shows that Germany, in the Nazi period, did nothing else. Much was made in some quarters of the "Nazi system" and of "Nazi economic theories." Some foreigners even talked of the "economic miracle." An American ambassador said in 1937 that there was "much in the Nazi system which we could profitably study." Pressing him, I found that he was echoing the Nazi boast that Hitler alone had defeated the problem of unemployment, while rich, democratic America had twelve million unemployed (the figure was a gross overestimate) who had pounded the pavements in desperation. The German boast and the German jibe at us were equally irrelevant. Great Britain has had no unemployment since Dunkirk and the United States ultimately will feel the want of man power which comes with total war. The Nazis pulled no rabbit out of the economic hat. They merely took Germany "to war" in 1933. They originated no policy which is not undertaken by any other country in time of war. Excesses of German character and Nazi methods make the Nazi economy very different from our war effort. It will be plainly seen, however, that they began to face in 1933 the problems which we were to face eight years later in 1941. These problems were of their making. They were forced upon us, and as a result there is not the remotest likelihood that the sacrifices we make voluntarily in this war effort will turn America into a totalitarian state. It was a German character—and the German answer to the question of ultimate sovereignty—which made it possible for Hitler and the generals to saddle a war economy and totalitarian dictatorship on the German people in a period when there was not even a threat of war.

The Nazis acted swiftly once President Hindenburg had handed Hitler the chancellorship. While the German generals and their highly trained Reichswehr watched approvingly, the Nazis began the regimentation of labor. Nazi gangsters seized the headquarters of the trade unions and rifled their treasuries or insurance and other funds—a tidy bit of loot in itself. Most important of all, they outlawed the strike. The workers were forced to join the Labor Front. Thanks to these expeditious measures, the generals, the Junkers, and the industrialists were guaranteed cheap labor, no agitation, and no strikes. Backed by the bayonets of the army and the rubber truncheons of the Gestapo, the Labor Front passed far-reaching rules and regulations. The German worker found, for instance, that he could not change occupations or even go to another employer for a job. The worker had a clearly defined role. He was to work, stay put, and keep his mouth shut. The Nazis called this "giving new dignity to labor." There were some compensations. Labor Front orators explained that if the worker's standard of living grew no better he could at least thank the Fuehrer for the fact that there was no more unemployment. Bands played music at factory meetings. The Strength through Joy organization took workers to the seashore and on cruises off the English, the Norwegian, the Baltic, and the Spanish coasts. A new "comradeship" was held before the eyes of the worker. Courts of Social Honor—controlled by Nazi war leaders—offered the prosecution of employers as a sop to the notion of the new "dignity." In one instance the daughter of a factory owner was haled into court on the charge of having called her father's employees "filthy workmen" in a moment of exasperation. The court fined her the equivalent of $1250 for this burst of temper.

The regimentation of labor began in a moment when the

Gestapo was hounding down Communists and Socialists. Thousands were shot or beaten to death in German concentration camps. The mass of German workers found it healthy to work, stay put, and keep their mouths shut. The bayonet and the rubber truncheon are strangely persuasive. Others rather liked the regimentation, the Strength through Joy, and the brass bands. The system had already jelled before the workers realized the true nature and purpose of the Labor Front. Wallace R. Deuel, in *People Under Hitler,* points out that the average official rate of pay for all skilled German workers in 1932 was 20.4 cents an hour, according to the Reich Statistical Office. Four and one-half years later it was 19.5 cents an hour. Average pay for unskilled workers fell during this same period—or, rather, was forced down by the Nazis—from 16.1 cents to 13 cents an hour. The cost of living rose, however, despite inflation controls. In addition the German worker, with his new sense of "dignity," had the privilege of making "voluntary" contributions to the Nazis— a privilege which the worker could utilize voluntarily unless he wanted to lose his job and risk imprisonment. Deuel estimates that "voluntary" contributions to the Winter Relief Fund and the Labor Front average 5 per cent of the gross earnings of the man in the street, who also pays 5 per cent to unemployment insurance, 5 per cent to health insurance and pension contributions, 3.5 per cent to poll tax. Thus the worker pays 18.5 per cent of his gross earnings back to the party, according to the statistics of the Nazis themselves.

Such a reduction of the standard of living would be deplored in America, but in Germany the regime felt that it was not only necessary but desirable since it prepared the masses for wartime self-denial. Rationing was made nationwide and compulsory in peacetime. Long before Germany was ready to invade Poland in 1939, her citizens had been schooled and trained against the British blockade. The ration-card system and the extortion of "voluntary" contributions distressed the skilled worker, but his position was

immeasurably better than that of the unskilled laborer. Unskilled workmen were organized in battalions and used as
slave labor. A hundred thousand of them at a time were
marched off to lay out airdromes or build the West Wall—
the vast fortification system which Hitler hastily constructed
in face of the Maginot line.

The task of making labor like its bread and circuses was
in the competent hands of Dr. Robert Ley, the Labor Front
Minister. This gentleman mixed a brutal contempt for truth
with a persuasive sentimentality that became tearful when
he indulged his appetite for alcohol—which was frequently.
I shall never forget the tour of German factories which Dr.
Ley personally conducted for the Duke of Windsor. After a
year's surcease from his duties as a monarch, the Duke of
Windsor was in bad training for a conducted tour. After inspecting ten factories in a day Windsor would confide to us
journalists that he was exhausted, but Ley would clap his
hands and suggest an eleventh. As some one thousand
workers would stand at rigid, if curious, attention, Dr. Ley
would address the Duke of Windsor in a voice pitched to
embrace the whole factory force. Dr. Ley belonged to the
lapel-clutching school of oratory and he was a spitter. Grasp-
ing Windsor firmly by the lapel and rocking all of us with
whisky fumes, Dr. Ley would orate. The little Duke, struggling unsuccessfully to free himself from the chubby clutch
of his cicerone, would turn brick red, draw a pocket handkerchief, and hide—as well as wipe—his face.

Some months later I attended a luncheon in Paris at which
the Duke was a guest. He was asked for his impression of
labor conditions in Germany. The Duke said that he had
been thrilled by certain housing projects and he felt that the
Nazis were doing more for labor in this field than any other
government. Edgar Ansel Mowrer, of the Chicago *Daily
News*, asked the Duke which housing projects had been
shown. The Duke was quite specific. He had visited five
and named them off. Mowrer pointed out that, of the five,

four had been built by the Weimar Republic, while the fifth had been projected under Chancellor Bruening and completed by the Nazis. The Duke was taken aback and, after questioning Mowrer rather searchingly, thanked him with obvious sincerity. Plainly the Duke of Windsor suspected Dr. Ley of an imposition on his royal credulity.

Once labor was regimented, the German leaders were ready for the great production effort—the internal industrial boom. Krupp and the like had already been rearming Germany secretly and they were prepared to rush forward with the creation of a vast machine-tool industry and the construction of new plants. Motoring through the German countryside on week ends, we marveled to see ground broken in every dimpling valley of the Third Reich, workers' cottages and barracks going up as steel girders rose for the factory itself. No time was lost. There was small doubt about the program being nationwide and fully integrated. As new plants and workers' dwellings rose for the aircraft industry, a hundred thousand young workers would sit down simultaneously for schooling as machinists and mechanics. Their apprentice work would be completed when the factory plants were ready.

"By staggering government expenditures, financed in the first instance by borrowing," writes Deuel, "the Nazis raised the value of total national production, including both industry and the handicrafts, from 38 billion marks in 1932 to 77 billion marks in 1937, an increase of 39 billion marks, or 102.6 percent." Man power? Almost 9,500,000 more persons were gainfully employed when the war was launched in 1939 than had been at work in the depth of the depression in 1932. The average number of hours worked per week increased from 41.46 to 47.04 during this same period. Up by the boot straps? The national income was increased from 35,000,000,-000 marks in 1932 to 76,000,000,000 marks in 1938.

As the armaments boom got under way the delight of the German industrialists was wonderful to behold. I can remember the expansive enthusiasm of the Stinnes family, powerful in coal and heavy industry, when they had an American banker in tow. One of the Stinnes sons even clapped his hands like a child. "It is too good to be true," he said. "You cannot imagine what a wonderful creature the German worker has turned out to be now that Hitler has stopped all this nonsense about agitation and strikes." Stinnes prophesied accurately that the earnings of labor would be frozen but inaccurately that there would be no limit to industrial profits. What a happy dinner table it was as they laughed at the "disciplining" of labor. The American banker was visibly impressed. A few years later the manner of the Stinnes sons had altered radically and, I regret to report, for the worse. As we sat in the Esplanade Hotel there was a shifty, unhappy look in the Stinnes eyes. There was no clapping left in the Stinnes hands. Like thousands of industrialists, the Stinnes brothers had found out that the armaments boom was a process of robbing Peter to pay Paul. With consternation, even a sense of aggrieved injustice, they had learned that the Herr Hitler who at one time or another had betrayed every other class in Germany was capable of betraying the industrialists too.

For in good time Hitler and his war machine cracked down on the capitalists. The armaments boom was booming, but dividends were limited. Six per cent was the ceiling. Of course, you could get an 8 per cent dividend in certain exceptional instances if you trafficked with that new major industry of Nazi Germany—Corruption, Inc.—but the "take" of the Nazi party grafters just about equaled the additional 2 per cent. Moreover, the state told a man what to manufacture and how. Had Hitler saved capitalism from Communism? The answer of the industrialists was given in the anecdote about Communism taking your cow but turning back part of the milk, while Nazism left you the cow—and the right to feed and milk it—but claimed all the milk for the state.

Hitler and his party took the milk all right. Your meager profits were a privilege, they said. You had the privilege of serving the state with them. You could buy government bonds, for instance, and you could put them into further plant expansion. If a mere suggestion was too subtle, you fell foul of the party machine and somebody muscled in on the management and ownership of your plant. The technique was smooth in the extreme. After all, raw materials were rationed. If you were slow to catch a hint, somebody held up your raw-materials supply. When your factory became idle, there was a scandal and the state intervened to put control and management of your enterprise into "more competent hands." We foreign observers in Germany listened with some sense of irony and detachment to the rising wail of businessmen who had been so pleased when the regime "regulated" labor. Capital suddenly felt sorry for itself. Earnings on investments soured. In 1939 the Reichsbank discount rate averaged 3.5 per cent as against 5.21 per cent for 1932. In the same period the yield on 4.5 per cent mortgage bonds was chiseled down from 8.38 per cent to 4.54 per cent. It is regrettable that the Germans have so little sense of humor. What a speech Herr Doktor Ley could have made on the "dignity" of the capitalists, for the capitalist no less than the union worker had to learn what the Nazis meant by the "new comradeship." ·

It became necessary to regulate exports and imports if the war machine was to have raw materials and if Germany was to maintain a balance of payments. A rigid control operated against imports. No individual, firm, or corporation could find foreign exchange for purchases abroad unless these purchases were approved. The government concentrated in its own hands all gold and *valuta*. Nothing was brought into Germany which was not required for the war machine. From 1934 the government ruthlessly forced the bankruptcy of nonessential enterprises which depended upon imports from abroad. Hitler and the generals needed iron ore, rubber, petroleum, tungsten, and the like—for war. They saw to it that the wealth of the German people went abroad for such articles and no others. The severity of Nazi controls was remarkable and Hitler and Schacht could boast that imports rose from 4,667,000,000 marks in 1932 to 6,051,000,000 in 1938. Over the same period, moreover, the Germans maintained their exports at roughly 5,000,000,000 marks, despite the organization of a world-wide boycott and Nazi preoccupation with armaments. Both the import and the export policies were war measures from 1933 onward and showed as clearly as anything else, to anyone who wanted to see clearly, that Nazi Germany meant war.

Nazi imports and exports were maintained by tricks now famous. Schacht used clearing agreements with the neighbor countries. He would build up a balance so large that the neighbor, waking up a year or two later, realized suddenly that trade with Germany bulked too large to sacrifice. Unable to cut its losses, the neighbor continued on German terms. Schacht also invented the Aski mark, by which he gave an arbitrary value to the German currency regardless of international exchange rates whenever inducements were needed. Out of these two devices he fashioned the famous barter system which made Balkan and South American countries dependent upon Germany even when it became clear to them that there was no profit, and much loss, in such trade. The German policy was full of innovations which successfully took in the innocent and the greedy. For a few years the Germans would buy a large percentage of the total crop in several commodities from a Balkan or South American country. The producers of these crops had a vested interest, consequently, in good relations with Germany. The Germans would use this element to bring political changes in the policy of the Balkan or South American country. When Germany would threaten to cancel all purchases from Greece or Chile because the governments of Athens or Santiago declined to play a pro-Nazi game, the producers in those two countries who had become dependent upon Germany to buy their crops outright faced bankruptcy. Consequently they would move heaven and earth to have their governments adopt a pro-Axis policy. The world at large believed, almost until the invasion of Poland, that Schacht's export-import policy was born of necessity and undertaken in desperation. I remember an exception. In the last months before the London Economic Conference of 1933 Herbert M. Feiss of the American State Department had already seen through Germany's war strategy. Both of us had studied German activities in the Balkans, and Feiss concluded that Schacht was using clearing agreements and the like as political instruments of German imperialism. Here, as in everything else, the German effort was an integrated part of the war plan from 1934 onward.

Describing themselves as the "master race" which would conquer and rule the world, the Germans neglected no aspect of their all-embracive program. They needed man power if they were to be top dog. They undertook political and military projects to strengthen the Reich by some ten million German-speaking folk who lived as a nation in Austria or as minorities in other independent European states. Meanwhile they organized German minority elements in North and South America and Africa. At home they planned and carried through with incredible success a program to increase the birth rate. With fierce Nazi efficiency they put an end to the 700,000 abortions which had interrupted every year a full third of all pregnancies in Germany. The result showed immediately in the birth rate. In their thoroughness they improved the quality as well as the quantity of the breed, sterilizing 375,000 Germans as unfit because they suffered anything from epilepsy to acute alcoholism or even hereditary deafness. And always and everywhere the Gestapo and the propaganda office were working to create what the Germans call "like-mindedness." They were not content with the obvious concentration camps or dismissals from work. They had devilishly subtle tricks. A full four years before the war I was able to write from Berlin that the Reich was already providing gas masks for the German people. Unlike the British or French, they did not issue the masks directly. A Gestapo agent explained the advantage of this. "The worker in the factory and the *Hausfrau* in the home," he explained, "must prove their political reliability in order to be certain of having a mask in a moment when masks are needed." He chuckled heartily. "Can't you see what a deterrent that is to any German who feels tempted to talk or act against the regime?"

During all this period of total preparation the best was none too good for the German soldier. The German nation pulled its belt very tight under a rationing scheme which transformed the German diet to foodstuffs which would be available throughout a British blockade. But the German soldier had meat and butter in plenty. How hard and how happily the army worked! I can remember the enthusiasm of officers who would talk by the hour of the quality and speed and endurance of the new army. The Germans strove for individual initiative by abandoning the old-fashioned notions both of training and of maneuvers. Every unit from a squad to a division was trained by the new tactic of "mission," whereby each was given a task to perform. How these tasks were performed was left to the unit, which had to show initiative and speed. I never went to Germany in the last years before the war without seeing units at work all over the country. Motorcycle scouts would be given a point on the map sixty miles away; in attempting to reach it, they would come to bridges marked "Blown," fields marked "Under enemy artillery fire," and they were compelled to cross unbridged streams and make wide detours under realistically trying conditions.

As a result they learned how to get there. They learned speed. In one maneuver a German division went from bivouac into line of battle in forty-nine minutes. I asked an

American military attaché how long it took an American division to move from bivouac to line of battle. He calculated the time required for headquarters to prepare and issue orders to tank units, supporting air force, field kitchens, the quartermaster, and all the other wheels of that creaking, ponderous machine which is a combat division. He estimated that the American Expeditionary Forces of 1918 required about eleven hours for what a division of Germany's new army was learning to do in forty-nine minutes. I suggested to my American friend that the German division must have rehearsed its operation in order to impress and confound us with its speed. We took some comfort from this speculation, but the truth, as we both knew, was this: the German army was rehearsing daily all the varied tasks of combat. Their purpose was not to impress us in maneuvers but to confound us later in the field.

Nothing was too good for the German air force. This was the pet creation of Marshal Goering. This man was a murderer and a former dope fiend, a brute who took positive pleasure, once the fighting had begun, in the traditional German weapon of "frightfulness," bombing and machine-gunning thousands of women and children from one end of Europe to the other. Goering was also a great airman and a great administrator. During the first World War, Goering had taken over the "Flying Circus" after the death of Baron Richthofen. Gallant officer though he was, Richthofen had almost never given fight unless he had superiority. Goering tore into the Allied air forces with a recklessness which decimated and practically destroyed Richthofen's famous squadron. Charged with the creation of the new German air force, he had a blank check on German funds. Goering's granite Air Ministry became the most impressive, if most ugly, building in Berlin. His young airmen aped the Marshal's recklessness and Goering was prodigal in the loss of their lives during the long years of training.

Much has been made of the idea that the Germans, incap-

able of innovating, adapt and perfect the inventions of their
enemies. The Germans took the tank from the British and
the dive bomber from the Americans. Ernst Udet, a former
member of Richthofen's and Goering's squadron, a barn-
stormer who liked nothing better than to drink with American correspondents, was the man who tested and selected
types for the German air force. In thinking of the German
air force one is likely to think of Udet with Goering because
these two swashbucklers curried and petted and pampered
the young pilots, who lived like lords in veritable clubhouses
with deep leather chairs, choice cuts of meat, butter, and
champagne. Actually, other and more obscure men perfected
the tactics which enabled the German army to crush Poland
in a matter of weeks and to reduce France from her pinnacle
as the greatest military nation in the world to the state of a
mob, howling in an abyss, deserted by generals and politicians
alike. Chief of Air Staff since 1939, General Jerschonnek
created the combined arms cooperation of aircraft, tanks, and
motorized troops. Jerschonnek is the kind of professional
officer who fashioned the elite troops of the German army,
ended the static trench warfare, and put the mobility of
lightning into *Blitzkrieg.* Entering the German army in
1915, when he was a stripling of sixteen, Jerschonnek soon
found his way into the air corps and developed the new conception of war which characterizes the forceful forty-year-old
generals of the Third Reich—the Jerschonneks and the Rom-
mels.

There are a hundred like them. They created the new
army, and they were the soul of Germany—Nazi Germany,
Kaiser Wilhelm's Germany, Bismarck's Germany, Frederick's Germany. These forty-year-olds have never regretted
the first World War. Over a few whiskies and sodas or a half
dozen bottles of Rhine wine, they will beat the table with
their fists and whine that they were cheated of the victory.
It never seems to occur to any of them that Germany, in attempting world conquest, gambled and lost. Straight-backed,

stiff-shouldered, with frozen jaws and narrow eyes, they do not resemble in appearance the stumblebum pugs of the prize ring; but they, too, are men who whine that they were robbed of the decision. These forty-year-olds were line officers in the trenches of France. They are too intelligent to blame the Socialists, accused in German propaganda of the "stab in the back," or to blame the British blockade though they invariably describe it as "inhuman and unfair." They blame the Kaiser for going to war several years too soon and they blame the General Staff for lack of imagination and inelasticity in tactics. Let me quote the most intelligent and humane type—a Catholic who has posed for years as an internationalist.

"Ah, we should have won the war if the General Staff had only listened to us front-line troops. I was a captain of machine-gunners and I made suggestion after suggestion as to new tactics by which we would have certainly won. But our superiors would not act on them."

Putting down his whisky glass, this German clenched his fist around an imaginary machine gun. A hard and cruel smile brightened his face as he narrowed his eyes over imaginary sights and shook as if from the recoil.

"Gott in Himmel!" he cried. "But we piled them high. We front-line soldiers knew how to win. We wanted to break up trench warfare. We wanted a tactic of infiltration. We said, 'Pull our troops out of the front during the enemy barrage and hold the position with a selected few. Then rush forward with a carefully trained elite, organized and equipped for speed—mechanized.' By this tactic we could have knifed into British, French, and American positions, disrupting and slaughtering our enemies with no unnecessary loss to our own troops, who would have been withheld from enemy artillery fire until we were ready to drive clean through the enemy position."

These are the men and ideas behind *blitz* war. They worked and gloated and cheered as the factories hummed,

the aircraft zoomed in practice dives, and eighty million
"like-minded" Germans began to goose-step, not from habit
alone, but from the joy and pride they expected to take in
their future victories. Nothing had been neglected that human ingenuity could foresee.

One inherent German weakness remained—the shortage of
raw materials required for world-wide war. This would not
handicap Germany if Hitler, operating on the strategy outlined in *Mein Kampf*, could divide his enemies and take
France and Russia singly. But could Germany be sure that
the British and Americans would be lulled to sleep? No.
Something had to be done against the potential threat of
British and American sea power. In 1936 the Germans faced
the problem squarely. In that, the third year of Nazism,
Hitler decreed the Four-year Plan. Marshal Goering undertook to rationalize all the various German efforts at autarchy.
German deposits of iron, copper, lead, and zinc were in-
tensively exploited, as were aluminum and magnesium;
plastic, glass, and other substitutes were worked out. The
program embraced foodstuffs, rubber and rubber substitutes,
and every kind of petroleum. Goering's success is a monument to German ingenuity. Year after year refugee "experts"
have predicted shortages in fuel oil and the like; year after
year German aircraft have kept to the skies and German
tanks have rolled across new frontiers.

Finally, in 1939, Hitler was ready to throw the switch and
start up the great war machine. Once again Germany had
staked all on the proposition "rule or ruin." The national
wealth had been mortgaged irretrievably. Germany itself
could never foot the bill for 100,000,000,000 marks of armaments. But Hitler and the generals never intended that Germany should foot the bill. They believed that tanks, guns,
and airplanes are productive. Those instruments had already
yielded Austrian iron ore and Czech lignite. The very threat
of them brought in Hungarian wheat and Rumanian oil.
Now the Germans were ready for the big push. Behind the

German nation lay six years of mass production, military training, and ration cards. Before them lay the riches of the bourgeois capitalistic world, held in the uncertain hands of statesmen and peoples who, to the master race, seemed decadent and blind. The success of the Germans surprised their own wildest hopes. Within a year of their attack on Poland and within a few weeks of their having rolled into the Lowlands and France, the Germans had collected enough loot to pay the bill for their six-year war program.

No other people in the whole panorama of history has ever found such plunder. In Poland alone the Germans seized Polish state property to the value of $2,400,000,000. Norway, Holland, and France provided greater riches. If these seizures seem intangible, gold bullion is real. From the conquered countries the Nazis have taken publicly owned gold to the amount of $1,500,000,000. This is the estimate of "Thomas Reveille," or Rifat Tirana, whose book *The Spoil of Europe* provides the most trustworthy, if conservative, figures of German loot.

The Nazis collect at the point of the bayonet and they are forthright in determining a nation's capacity to pay. Tirana shows that in each instance the Nazis calculated that they could loot from a given country each year the total appropriations provided for in the last budget voted before the Nazi invasion. In short, the Germans collect from a conquered country the maximum amount the nation thought it could raise to govern and arm itself and to fight for its existence. These charges are called the "cost of occupation," but in France the actual cost of the occupying army has been far below the total of the sums extorted. The Germans have been collecting annually from the conquered countries of Europe 10,480,000,000 marks. Of this sum only two to three billion marks go to the maintenance of the occupying forces. The net balance of between seven and eight billions is used by the Germans to "buy" coal and iron mines, steel mills, and shipyards.

Sentimentalists in America and Britain who cried against the "iniquities" of Versailles and held that the French were too harsh when they occupied the Ruhr neglected to study the provisions of the Treaty of Brest-Litovsk, which the Germans imposed on the Russians. It is to be hoped that at this late date they will not neglect to contrast the Franco-German Armistice of 1940 with the reparations clauses of Versailles. During the seven-year period in which the Dawes and Young plans were in effect, the Germans were called upon to pay 10,000,000,000 marks. They paid less than half of that sum and virtually every German payment came out of the yield of loans which the democracies pumped into Germany. Ears still ring with the German wails. From 1924 to 1931 the Germans paid to France—whose lands had been devastated by German occupation—a total of only 4,000,000,000 marks in reparations. For the first two years of the occupation of France the Germans have collected from the French the sum of 4,000,000,000 marks every six months. The Germans have extorted semiannually from France alone as much as they were forced to pay to the Allies in more than six years.

The cost of the German arms program in preparation for this war, announced by Hitler as 90,000,000,000, is usually estimated at 100,000,000,000 marks. The Germans collected that much from their victims in the first year of war! Thus Hitler and the generals built the greatest war machine in history on the cuff, and a year before Pearl Harbor they were already out of the red. They faced America with a neat profit on their investment. In German hands tanks, guns, and airplanes become productive. In German hands they are the instruments of loot.

The Nazis have proved that the Prussians have not changed. In modern history they alone glorify war and *make war pay!*

IV

MACHIAVELLI'S MIMIC

MUSSOLINI was feeling melancholy about the state of the world on that sunny afternoon in the spring of 1937 and I, as a journalist, groped clumsily to find out why. Six weeks before this interview he had summoned me to tell him my firsthand impressions of Spain. Offering my honest opinion that General Franco enjoyed the support of less than 5 per cent of the Spanish population, I had urged Mussolini to withdraw, warning him that Italian troops were neither properly organized nor trained for that war.

"Your Excellency is courting in Spain a disaster which will destroy the prestige gained by Italian arms in Ethiopia and, worse than that, continued intervention will drive Italy irretrievably into the German camp," I said.

We conversed in French and Mussolini, frowning, said shyly, "Peut-être . . . peut-être."

Immediately after this interview Mussolini went to Libya to receive the "Sword of Islam" and I accompanied him on what turned out to be a ludicrous inspection of Potemkin villages. In Libya I was awakened at dawn one morning and rushed by automobile to the Governor's palace at Tripoli. Mussolini, unshaven and fierce as a desert lion, paced up and down the palace garden. Shaking a sheaf of telegrams in my face, he told me the story of the rout of the Italians at Guadalajara.

"You were right," he said.

"Will Your Excellency withdraw from Spain now?" I asked.

"No. Now, never," he said.

I considered myself dismissed and felt that I had enjoyed the last of my interviews with the Duce. Returning to Rome, I was surprised, however, to receive an invitation to the Palazza Venezia.

Talking with the dictator again, I was at a loss to understand a melancholy which drove him to the cheap tricks of bombast and posturing which ordinarily I had seen only in his public appearances. To inflate his own feeling of self-importance Mussolini began to pop his eyes and to thrust his jaw out. He even mounted the six-inch rostrum in the alcove window of that long and impressively bare room which served as an office near the balcony from which on momentous occasions he addressed the Italian nation. Thus the politician looked down on the journalist, who, standing respectfully at attention, grew increasingly uncomfortable as grandiloquence gave neither meaning nor value to a repetitious monologue. Then Mussolini motioned me to a chair with a quick gesture, sat down himself on the edge of his desk, and began to talk simply without a trace of boisterous swagger.

"I am going to make the most important change in the foreign policy of Italy in the history of United Italy," he said.

"Next fall I am going to invite Hitler to come into Austria and make Austria German. Hitler is determined at any cost to incorporate Austria into the Third Reich. Continued efforts to defend Austrian independence by an economic policy are useless. It means throwing good money after bad. A military guarantee of that country's independence by Italy would play into the hands of England and France, countries whose peoples are essentially anti-Fascist and whose weakling leaders would abandon Italy at an issue of arms with Germany. Sta bene! I shall come to terms with Hitler. Meanwhile as a counter to German expansion I shall organize the Balkans. In a few weeks an Italo-Jugoslav trade treaty will be announced and thereafter cordial relations will develop between me and the Serbs. The other Balkans will look to Italy for leadership once Austria is German."

"That is certainly an important change in Italian policy," I said. "The history of modern Italy has been only the record of continuous resistance to Germanic expansion toward the Adriatic. In 1934—only three years ago—when the Nazis murdered Dollfuss you mobilized the Italian army. You said that if Hitler marched into Austria you would fight. Were you bluffing then, Excellency?" I demanded.

Seated on the desk, Mussolini's feet were a long way from the floor. He let himself down and walked toward me, and then returned slowly to the desk. Out went his jaw again. Then he smiled; shrugged his shoulders; and threw his hands out, palms up.

"Of course I was not bluffing. In 1934 I could have beaten Hitler's army."

Mussolini was right. In 1934 the German armaments boom had only begun. The Germans had not even organized headquarters staffs for their expanding army corps. In 1934 Italy had reached the apex of her military strength and relatively was one of the military powers of Europe.

"Then I could have beaten the Germans. Today I cannot," said Mussolini.

The Italian narrowed his eyes.

"Listen," he said. "The time is coming in a few years—three or four—when it will not be a question of Italy against Germany. Then Germany will be completely militarized. Germany will be so strong that no combination of powers in the world can stand against her. Look at your contemptible democracies. You stand in blind impotence before the most important historical development in centuries—the militarization of modern Germany. Neither Great Britain, France, nor America has a serious armaments program. The Germans are outbuilding our combined production. Not one of you has a foreign policy. Instead of a policy you have a hope—especially you Anglo-Saxons with your inevitably pious, puritanical hope—that the Nazis and the Fascists will become embroiled. Bah! My dear fellow, I won't do it for you."

"Excellency, you do paint a gloomy picture," I said. "Suppose Germany is so strong three years from now that no aggregation of powers in the world can stand against her? What then for the future of Italy?"

The big little man sprang from the desk. He shook his clenched fist in my face. Out went his chest and he fairly strutted.

"Ah, in that moment," he said, "Italy will be the ally of Germany."

This explains *rationally* the subsequent Axis alliance and Italy's ultimate entry into the war. Dictator of a docile people, denied the restraining safeguards of a parliament and opposition press, Mussolini played power politics with a cool, detached, and resourceful daring not seen since the days of Bismarck in Germany and Cavour in Italy. The Italian people gave him a free hand in this reckless game. He had inflated the importance of Italy; he had unwopped the wop. Nothing succeeds like success and Mussolini as a modern Machiavelli had enjoyed more than his share. Retrieving Italy from one perilous position after another, he had given his country a position and influence far beyond that which her economic and military strength, or even her geographic position, had justified. Working hand in glove with his son-in-law and foreign minister, Count Galeazzo Ciano, Mussolini had proved himself the most audacious poker player in modern history.

In 1937 Mussolini was not the blustering, humorless, megalomaniac he had been pictured abroad. He was vain to a fault, of course. He loved to pound the table, to let himself go in sudden moods of anger, and to indulge quick, half-cocked whims. Is there a politician with Italian blood in his veins who does not? Even New York's Mayor La Guardia likes to chase a fire engine. But underneath, Mussolini was a cold fish. He read Machiavelli, and in private conversation he quoted his master until he was never sure whether the well-turned aphorism was his own or Machiavelli's.

When Mussolini made a speech it was made to the Italian people or to the other players in the game of power politics. It may have sounded mad to Americans, yawning over the New York *Times,* but it was well timed for Europe. Like any orator, Mussolini responded to the crowd and enjoyed the very dramatics which his oratory evoked. But the brain remained coldly calculating. He was as detached as the actress who used to stand at the stage exit waving to friends in the wings while she entoned closing lines to tear hearts in the audience.

Picture Mussolini astride a tank, some monument of ancient Rome against the backdrop of umbrella pines, a square of bristling bayonets at his feet. I stood with Ciano beside Mussolini's tank, on such an occasion. That is the first time I understood the man.

"Tempered as we are by the Fascist climate, we will adorn the points of our bayonets with the oak and laurel of victory!" the dictator shouted.

"Duce, Duce, Duce!" the crowd roared for a full minute.

In that minute Mussolini whispered to Ciano, "Is that hot enough for them, or shall I make it hotter?"

Up came the clenched fist and the scowling face, as Mussolini, calling his people "voluptuaries of danger," went on with a warlike speech which dismayed America but created in Europe precisely the effect desired by Mussolini and Ciano. For in those years Mussolini was the cool and analytical dictator who upon his first meeting with Hitler, at Venice in 1934, turned to Ciano to say, "Hitler is a man with whom I can work, if necessary, but with whom I can never have a meeting of minds." His was the intellectual snobbism of a rational statesman shocked by a German who heard voices and consulted the stars. Mussolini's scornful manner was part of the showman's tricks and was reserved, like showmanship generally, for public occasions.

How profoundly Hitler, a sort of German Father Divine,

shocked the innate reasonableness of mind which the Italians have inherited from the Renaissance! Ciano, especially, found it difficult on occasions to disguise his dislike of Hitler and all things German. Skeptical, even cynical, the Italians feel contemptuous of a people which has so much "soul." German sentimentality, like the music of Wagner, makes an Italian face go very wry indeed. There is deep mistrust between these two peoples. And it grows out of the Italian sense of intellectual superiority. Why? You can see this in the very marble-and-onyx maps of the Roman Empire's expansion with which the Fascists have adorned the old Roman walls along the newly constructed Imperial Way. On the map you can see the empire at the height of its power under Trajan, early in the second century of the Christian Era. The Roman people, whose mission it was, said Vergil, "to crown Peace with Law, to spare the humble, and to tame in war the proud," had extended their way of life not only through Asia Minor and the East but also westward through the present frontiers of France, Spain, and England. On the map all those regions are white, for they knew the Pax Romana and the civilizing force that was Rome. Only the lands of the German and the Russian are black on the map. To Romans through all history they have been the lands of barbarism—the lands whence periodically the Hun has descended.

If the Italians mistrusted the Germans as a people, they respected them as soldiers. Indeed they feared them, for Italy lay directly south of Germany. Italy's land of sunshine has been the envy of Germans since before Goethe's time, and the Teuton's song speaks longingly of the land where the lemon blooms. Not Mussolini alone, but every Italian, has known since the rise of Hitler that the 300,000 German-speaking folk who inhabit the Italian Tyrol could serve as a pretext for German invasion—a second Sudetenland. It was elemental, therefore, that Italy could not oppose her policies to those of Hitler once Germany became the first military power of the world. It was a question not of liking or disliking the Germans but of political realism.

Mussolini and Ciano evolved what they thought was a very clever course. They made an Axis alliance with Hitler immediately Germany became the dominant power of the continent. Aggression by Britain or France was not feared. Aggression by Germany had to be reckoned as a possibility always. Mussolini thought that the Axis alliance would save him from invasion by Germany, provide an opportunity to blackmail Britain and France, and give him consequently a key position in the balance of power. Mussolini could always argue, in bargaining with Britain and France, that the Axis alliance made it possible for Italy to restrain Germany. Under the consultative clauses Germany could not go to war without informing Italy. Mussolini worked out an escape clause for himself. After all, the Triple Alliance, which had bound Italy to Germany and Austria-Hungary before the war of 1914–1918, stipulated, in a secret clause, that Italy expressly reserved to herself the right to stand aside from any war which would bring her into conflict with Great Britain. Mindful of this stipulation in the Triple Alliance, Mussolini inserted in the Axis alliance a provision that the Axis partners were not to go to war for three years. Knowing that the crisis over Poland would come long before the expiration of the three-year period, Mussolini was content. With such an escalator clause it seemed to him that he could have his cake and eat it too. If war came, he reasoned, Italy would declare her nonbelligerency. Neither Germany nor the Anglo-French Entente was likely to attack him, certainly not in the initial phases of the conflict before one side or the other seemed likely to win. Thus Mussolini felt that he had maneuvered Italy into the happiest of positions. He felt that the country should be able to fly to the aid of the victor. Mussolini little dreamed that, like Faust, he had signed his name in blood.

The first shock came in the summer of 1939, only a few weeks before Hitler invaded Poland. The Germans told the astonished Italians that they were going to make war against Poland. I had the whole story from Ciano at the time, and a more disillusioned young man I never saw. Ciano took me from his formal showroom office, where he received ambassadors in the high-ceilinged dank Chigi Palace, to a simple workroom. Around this bare workshop there were only the dossiers, the dispatch boxes, the private telephone to Mussolini, and a portable radio near the window which opened on the Corso Umberto. In that safe place Ciano kept three small books, one bound in red and two in blue. Opening the second of the blue volumes, he read me from his diary the dramatic story of his conversations in Salzburg.

The decision to make war on Poland was announced to Ciano by Joachim von Ribbentrop, the Nazi foreign minister. Getting nowhere in his effort to restrain this former champagne salesman, Ciano telephoned Mussolini and then demanded to see Hitler. On the mountaintop at Berchtesgaden, with all the beauty of the Alps spread around them, Hitler told Ciano coolly and with no trace of hysteria that Poland had to be taught a lesson, that he meant, in short, to make war. Taking his guest for a walk, Hitler spoke bitterly of the persecution of Germans by Poles. To a realist like Ciano, it seemed incredible that Hitler had come to believe his own propaganda. "My God," said Ciano to me, "this man believed his own atrocity stories." When they returned for tea, Ciano marshaled the arguments against war, attempted to dissuade him, and said that Italy could not follow Germany into any such adventure. Hitler rose from the tea table and almost plaintively uttered the single interrogation, "Warum?"

"Why?" repeated Ciano. "Why, because the British and the French will fight."

And then the storm broke. The voice of the Fuehrer shrieked. It did not suit his plans to believe that Britain and France would fight. He would not hear it and he would not believe it. Ciano tried to argue. The German turned on him, screaming and spluttering in his paroxysm. "You ass! You son of an ass!" he said.

Worshiping his father, an admiral who was one of Italy's naval heroes, Ciano has never forgiven the Germans and has never trusted them since. Ultimately the Germans will murder him. Ciano knew from then on how dangerous the game had become—for Italy and for himself. He began to work desperately a full month before the Germans struck at Danzig to build a bridge back to London and Paris. When the British said publicly some months later that Ambassador Attolico, Ciano's appointee in Berlin, had labored whole-heartedly to preserve the peace, the tribute was sincere. Ciano had never wanted the Axis alliance which Mussolini had insisted upon; now that the war had come, Ciano was afraid of the German Frankenstein. He worked day and night (though the Germans denounced him to Mussolini) in an effort to make Italy neutral·rather than nonbelligerent. Ciano might have succeeded, but in the moment of crisis Mussolini failed his son-in-law and his country.

Power corrupts. Mussolini was no exception to the rule laid down by President Masaryk of Czechoslovakia: "The dictators always look good until the last five minutes." This was the tragedy of Mussolini when the Nazis invaded Poland. In the eighteenth year of Fascism Mussolini had lived too long. In the spring of 1939—three months before the invasion of Poland—Mussolini suffered a stroke that for several days caused a partial paralysis of the face. He was confined to bed, with the greatest secrecy, near Milan for five weeks. Later he rested in a private house near his birthplace at Forli. Near Forli he was visited by a Swiss eye specialist because the left eye was affected. This stroke came at a moment of decision which was crucially important for the future of Fascist Italy. It came, moreover, at a moment when for the first time Mussolini had become aware both of the ravages of age and of the loneliness of great power. His loneliness was a horror to him. His brother Arnaldo, the editor, had been his only friend and Arnaldo had died. Margherita Sarfatti was the only woman Mussolini had ever trusted, but warmhearted Margherita got old and ugly and she was a Jewess. Mussolini turned to his daughter Edda, the Countess Ciano, and she, with no interest in anything beyond the frivolities of life, failed him utterly. Busy proving that one can be a dipsomaniac and a nymphomaniac at the same time, Edda was no companion to a tired man disillusioned of power now that the game had become too dangerous for a country with Italy's limited supply of blue chips.

Politically the situation of Italy had become equally bitter and disappointing to the dictator. After seventeen years Fascism had run down. It was all very well to rob Peter to pay Paul, but now both Peter and Paul stood with empty pockets. The Italians wanted bread, not circuses. It was all very well for the Fascist propaganda machine to talk about "living like lions"; the Italians were tired. Ethiopia and Spain had been exhausting performances. Instead of having trained up a "people of steel," Mussolini found that the Italians had not really changed. Instead of having created a hard-bitten elite, Mussolini found that his most trusted ministers only wanted more graft and a letup in the tension. The obvious failure of Fascism as a system was an impelling motive in Mussolini's signature of the Axis alliance. Mussolini hoped to revitalize Fascism, Ettore Múti, Secretary General of the Fascist party told me, by coupling it to the younger and more vibrant Nazi revolution. But being coupled to Nazism had failed to put steam back into the Fascist system. These are the personal and political disappointments that Mussolini mulled over as he lay in bed in the last months before Europe went out to fight that war which Mussolini himself had always glorified.

Lonely, frightened, and sick, Mussolini—once the daring pupil of Machiavelli, Bismarck, and Cavour—reverted to type. He became Mussolini the peasant, the son of the blacksmith and innkeeper who had been arrested as an anarchist. He became the boy at whose innards unvaulted ambition gnawed, the boy who fled into Switzerland to escape military service during the Libyan War against which he inveighed in 1911, crying "Down with war! Down with imperialism! Down with bloody adventures in Africa!" He became once again the struggling young editor who first demanded Italian neutrality in the first World War and then agitated for intervention against Germany after the French found his price and sent him 50,000 francs with the promise of 10,000 francs a month for his newspaper.

Told by his doctors that he must rest and avoid the strain of public appearances, Mussolini sought refuge in eroticism. In each of my five interviews with the dictator he has told an off-color story. He had the Italian peasant's love of smut for smut's sake. The German Ambassador in Rome, Hans Georg von Mackensen, son of the Field Marshal, learned that he could ingratiate himself by providing young girls for the aging Italian's whims. Many a Fascist minister told me how Mussolini in the midst of the discussion of serious business would cackle and say, "I have a girl every day." A doctor who occasionally attended Mussolini whispered to me, "He ought to have his prostate out." Even the man in the street in Rome knew about Mussolini's affair with two sisters. They knew all over Italy when Mussolini fell in love with a woman half his age and built her an imposing three-story home on one of the hills of Rome. This girl was the daughter of a physician, descended from a long line of doctors and apothecaries, against one of whose ancestors a Pope once railed out bitterly, charging the whole family with dishonesty and charlatanism which made them little better than panders. At first Mussolini came to see this girl in her father's home. The poor physician! With the dictator's motorcycle escort and ubiquitous police, the patients could not reach the doctor's office-home and the dubious distinction of the Duce's patronage almost wrecked the good man's practice. It was then that

Mussolini built the three-story villa, and he installed an escalator.

More than the peasant's love of smut came out in Mussolini. The superstitions which he had ridiculed suddenly came to haunt him. Almost all Italians believe in the *jettatore*. They fear certain individuals who are believed to carry the "evil eye." Any contact with these individuals is likely to bring disaster. King Alfonso of Spain was a hapless man, thirteen attempts having been made on his life before he lost his throne and sought refuge in Italy. The Italians believed Alfonso bore the evil eye. I have seen Roman princes torn between vanity at being asked to play bridge with the ex-King and fear of the *jettatore*. Poor Alfonso once confided to me that he knew how the Italians felt about him. To touch steel or the horn of an animal is potent magic to ward off the evil eye. "My God," said Alfonso. "I was sitting unnoticed in a cinema when a newsreel picture of me was shown. There was a din of rattling key rings. Every man in the theater reached frantically for steel." Mussolini began to reach for steel and to knock on wood. The dictator began to suspect every cabinet minister, every general, and every admiral whose enterprises failed. Unhappily for a superstitious man, the failures became legion. Indecision marked every effort of Mussolini to make new appointments. He searched back into the records of all his lieutenants and trembled in sheer fright lest he entrust some vital mission to a man cursed with the evil eye. This once disdainful and blasphemous dictator, now as hallucinated as an illiterate peasant, was no longer the master of vices which ate the character out of the man.

Aware of Mussolini's stroke and his resultant fears and apprehensions, Hitler and his agents dealt shrewdly with him. They flattered him, saying that the two revolutions were the same but that National Socialism had been fathered by Fascism and nurtured by the parent system in the early days of its struggle. If Hitler won his war, they said, this century would be known through all history as the "Century of Mussolini." They told him such things, and the aging dictator, fearful for the future of Fascism, relished the sound of them. Except for his stroke, I think Mussolini's cunning, peasant shrewdness might have saved him. Because he was not very well, Mussolini had to give up public appearances and private conversations. He lost touch with his own public opinion and he saw almost no advisers or counselors except the Germans. Bocchini, the head of Italy's secret police, was a levelheaded and fairly temperate man. But in the last year of his life—the crucial period when war began—Bocchini's efforts to apply the brakes only infuriated his chief. And then Bocchini died and with his death there was no one who could calm the apprehensions of the frightened dictator.

Paranoia peered round the doorways of Mussolini's palace. After acting the role with cynical derision for nearly twenty years, in order to shout down his opposition or frighten his lieutenants, the actor had become the man. When he faced the moment to decide for peace or war, Mussolini had become as horrible a megalomaniac as Nero or Caligula. There was nothing Augustinian about this modern Caesar. Mussolini's scornful truculence had been an effective political weapon in the days when it was only a technique. Towering rage is all right when you are play-acting; it is not too costly when you know your own tricks and how to laugh at them yourself. Mussolini once told a story of how he browbeat a group of Italian politicians and stilled their criticism of his political poker playing. There was a session of that anachronism the Italian Senate in the period during the war in Spain when Mussolini was trying to drive Anthony Eden, the British Foreign Secretary, from office. A cluster of Italian Senators stood in the doorway discussing the dangers of this reckless policy. They were afraid of war with Britain and France. Mussolini strode in, surprising them in the midst of their whispering.

"Ah!" he said. "So you are criticizing my policies!"

"No, Duce," lied one of the Senators. "We were merely suggesting that you are too harsh with Chamberlain and Eden. You humiliate them publicly."

"Bah!" said Mussolini. "I have the measure of Chamberlain and Eden. They aren't men to be afraid of. Why, if they were Italians I would put them in the Senate with you."

Amusing as an illustration of the man's effrontery, this story is nevertheless tragic. It exemplifies the first of the two fundamental errors which were in the end to destroy both Mussolini and Italy. For in final analysis Mussolini blundered into the war, first, because he underestimated the resources and strength of the British people and, second, because he put party, or Fascism, before country, or Italy.

For years Mussolini had confused British pacifism with British decadence. It was wishful thinking. The British Empire was rich; Italy was poor. If the empire was crumbling, Italy would seize her share and find in the ruin of Britain her own place in the sun. Mussolini had never been to Great Britain, and the kind of Englishmen who came to Italy, far from being representative, were only too frequently types who might have persuaded Mussolini or anyone else that Britain was decadent—pale-faced, long-fingered youths in flannel slacks who looked like Shelley and behaved as viciously as Byron. "And what should they know of England, who only England know?" demanded Kipling when he sang of the empire builders who sowed the seven seas with English bones. And what should Mussolini know of the English when it was only the Wodehouse idle whom he saw? In 1935 when he was preparing war in Ethiopia, Mussolini gave me his judgment. "When one country knows what it wants and is willing to go to war to get it," he said, "and another country is pacifist to the core—casts eleven and a half million votes in a peace ballot—then the country that is willing to fight will get what it wants from the country that will not fight, and will get it without having to go to war at all." This is nothing but blackmail and it has always been Mussolini's policy toward

Britain and the other democracies. The gangster levied tribute by threatening violence to peace-loving citizens interested in business as usual. I was once credited with a remark which I wish I had made. Someone else said, "There stands Mussolini in shining blackmail."

Far from leading Mussolini to see the errors of his ways, the British governments of Baldwin and Chamberlain confirmed him in his judgment of the democracies. If the easy conquest of Ethiopia had left him in doubt, the attitude of Britain and France in Austria, Spain, and Czechoslovakia would have confirmed his low opinion of the democratic peoples and of their statesmen.

The second fundamental error lay in the totalitarian, or absolutist, nature of Fascism itself, a system whose weakness lies in the fact that it can never show itself to be weak. Mussolini created this Frankenstein and it was perhaps inevitable that in the end he would be devoured by his own creature. As a nationalist, aping Bismarck's *Realpolitik* and perverting Cavour's liberalism, Mussolini had enjoyed in foreign affairs remarkable successes. But unlike Cavour, whose broad liberalism made him free to work for Europe as well as for Italy—free even to resign office—Mussolini could not quit his own Frankenstein. Under his system the Italians who were not Fascists had been disenfranchised, and even within the Fascist party itself no one was allowed to think or to ponder policy except Mussolini and the sixty-odd members of the Fascist Grand Council. Fascism had destroyed the parliament and the press. No machinery existed in Italy for the normal interplay of opposition ideas. A mere handful of men had to see eye to eye on questions of major policy and had to impose upon the nation what the nation was to think. With no safety device for a party machine which always worked under full steam, any profound disagreement on fundamentals within the Fascist Grand Council terrified the rank-and-file party workers. These ward-heeler politicians lived by what is known as the "party line." They were told what to think and what to compel the Italian masses to think on everything from a new issue of state bonds to the latest sordid affair of Edda Ciano. Men who got the "party line" wrong were removed from their jobs or imprisoned.

It was no secret in Italy in the period when Germany was ready to go to war that the Fascist hierarchy was divided. The pro-German element was headed by Farinacci, a Jew-baiting, Roosevelt-hating machine politician who shook the stub of his right arm in the face of everyone from Ciano to the Pope. Farinacci lost his right hand in Ethiopia—not fighting, but hunting small game with grenades. A rabbit jumped up at his feet and he fumbled a hand bomb after having released the pin. On the other hand, Ciano's increasing respect for the British and French, like his detestation of the Germans, was well known. Dino Grandi, former Ambassador to Great Britain, had started his Fascist career as a bloody-handed gangster; but now he had his nails manicured regularly, and the excesses of the Nazis were known to cause him positive nausea. The ablest, if most brutal, Fascist of them all, Italo Balbo, the Governor of Libya, spoke fluent French, believed in British sea power, and was dead set against Italy's Axis alliance and her entry into war. Then there was Count Volpi, a successful financier and business-man with international connections. In the Palazzo Venezia there is a full-length picture of Count Volpi standing arrogantly with his hands thrust into his pants pockets. Mussolini used to say, "I like that picture of my old Finance Minister—that's the only time we ever caught him with his hands in his own pockets." There was some doubt about Volpi's financial honesty but none about his attitude toward the Germans. Quarter Jew, he had a French mistress; he was madly in love with her, and he wanted to legitimatize their bastard son.

This deadlock among the Fascist leaders shook the morale of the rank and file of the Fascist party. They were confused and bewildered by Mussolini's policy of vacillating between his alliance with Hitler and his fear of the British and French. The little men became querulous. They asked questions. Why didn't Mussolini impose his will upon this divided Fascist Grand Council? It was dangerous to wait around. Balbo, especially, was an energetic and courageous man. Certainly Ciano had always been 100 per cent loyal to Mussolini. But was it not possible that Ciano and Grandi would swing to Balbo and build a new regime based on the army, which was believed to be anti-German? That would mean the end of Fascism and it would mean that the party workers, if they were lucky enough to save their lives, could no longer be leeches on the public; they would have to go to work. They could see no reason for this vacillation. Reading nothing but their own censored press, knowing nothing of the British, the French, and the Americans, they were convinced of German victory. They were equally convinced that in the event of a democratic victory Fascism in Italy would be destroyed.

The German agents of Himmler's Gestapo and Goebbel's propaganda offices were quick to exploit the fears of these Fascists. German efforts consequently overcame the dislike of Germans which the Fascist party workers shared with all Italians. It was not difficult, when these individuals were frightened for their own hides, to make them put party before country. The Germans contrived to make them put Germany before their party as well as before their country. The essence of the party line lay always in the mumbo-jumbo motto "Mussolini ha sempre ragione" ("Mussolini is always right"). The Germans attacked at this key arch, persuading the mass of party workers, and especially the police, that perhaps Mussolini was not infallible and that he would surely blunder if he endangered the survival of the Fascist party by remaining neutral. German-printed literature and German gold served as arguments and as inducements to the "war horse" bullies of the Fascist rank and file. The Germans organized hoodlum bands out of the more violent

Fascist ward, heelers, and their activities in the streets at night threatened a showdown between the mob and the state and turned the heat on Mussolini himself.

I had some personal acquaintance with these estimable cutthroats. At midnight on the rainy evening when Mr. Churchill took over from Mr. Chamberlain, they suddenly plastered the walls of Rome with posters which ridiculed the British and French and predicted their early and complete conquest by the Germans. I pulled up in an automobile before one of the hotels to drop Virginia Cowles after a dinner party. Miss Cowles, before going to the American Embassy in London, was the charming and clever correspondent of the North American Newspaper Alliance, but I ought to sue that organization for damages because she had a positive genius either for getting me into trouble or for being with me when I got her into trouble. We were accompanied by two members of the British Embassy staff. We stood at the hotel doorway reading one of the posters and remarking that the Italian in which it was written seemed awkward and marred by the German habit of saving the verb until the end of the sentence. Without warning, fifty men rushed around the corner as a policeman, calling them on, screamed, "Inglesi! Inglesi!" We knew, as these Italians pummeled us, that the Germans could want nothing so much as an incident involving two attachés of the British Embassy. Each of us felt compelled, therefore, to fight a defensive fight—a sort of "strategic evacuation." I rolled with the blows and kept pretty well covered except that, with five or six men coming from all sides at once, I got hit pretty badly in the back of the head and neck. Virginia Cowles was as cool and crisp as her elegantly tailored clothes, and the icy tones of her outraged voice could be heard over the melee. It was she who screamed for us to fight our way into the hotel because its narrow doorway would cut down the somewhat disadvantageous odds of fifty to three.

This little affray was significant for only two reasons. The man with whom we ultimately made terms spoke Italian so badly that our diplomatic parley went better when we spoke German with him. The blond heaviness of his face and the fact that he wore a short leather coat created a presumption that this Fascist ringleader was a member in good standing of Dr. Himmler's *Geheime Staatspolizei*. After all, the German Gestapo wears that kind of leather coat and speaks Italian less elegantly than the propaganda agents of Dr. Goebbels. In the second place, the fact that an Italian policeman whose duty it was to protect the citizenry whistled this group of hoodlums onto us created a presumption, in my mind at least, that the police force, too, was beginning to know the touch of German gold.

German-organized disorders of this sort turned the heat on the dictator who had signed with Hitler. Alone, sick, and frightened, Mussolini disliked the temper of Italy as much as he disliked the necessity of vacillating between the Germans on the one hand and the British and the French on the other. Had he remained the cool poker player who successfully manipulated the Ethiopian War and the invasion of Spain, he might have maintained Italy's neutrality. But he underestimated the British, and that tempted him to gamble; and, having created a regime of violence, he found himself handcuffed to his own Fascist Frankenstein. He was sick with worry. He wanted a decision. As the Cockney said, "It ain't the 'anging I 'ates; it's the swinging to and fro." Hitler had told Mussolini a few months before the invasion of the Lowlands and France how those offensive operations would go. It is no wonder that when Hitler's most optimistic predictions were borne out on the field of battle Mussolini's last doubts vanished.

Clutching at the coattails of the triumphant Nazis, Mussolini and the Fascist rank and file alike felt at last that they were safe. Mussolini told a friend of mine, "We must go to war immediately. Fascism has triumphed. Democracy is dead. France will collapse in a matter of days and Britain's capitulation will follow swiftly. If we are to share in the spoils we must strike before Hitler brings the hostilities to a close." And so on June 10, 1940, in one of the least impressive speeches of his long career, Mussolini formally declared war on Great Britain and France.

From the point of view of the destiny of Italy this act was a criminal blunder. The country was in no way prepared for war. Vital types of armament and equipment were lacking for the army. No reserves of fuel had been stored for either the air force or the navy. No raw materials had been stocked for Italy's war industries. Finally the Italian people, profoundly distrustful of their traditional foe, Germany, wanted strict neutrality, and they were shocked at the enormity of the attack against prostrate France. The nation was not prepared economically, militarily, or morally for the sternest of all national tests—the great clash of two systems in which, as Mussolini himself had said, "we or they survive."

As the Duce ended his peroration and the crowd emptied from the great piazza, knowing at last that they were at war, a fitting judgment was passed on Mussolini's career by David Williamson of the American Embassy. Quoting Thomas Jefferson on Napoleon, Williamson said, with a sardonic grin, "Had he reflected that such is the moral construction of the world that no national crime passes unpunished in the long run, he would not now be in the cage of St. Helena."

V

LIVING LIKE TIRED LIONS

Mussolini's declaration of war on June 10, 1940, provided a dramatic denouement to nineteen years of flamboyant Fascism. His blunder, based on the assumption that Great Britain as well as France was beaten, disclosed to the Italian people the true nature of his regime. The whole nation lost its illusions and its will to fight when the Fascist system was weighed in the scales against the French in the Alps, the British in Libya, and finally the Greeks across the Adriatic. When the will to fight went out of them the Italians lost their national independence too, for in the end the Germans marched in and effectively occupied the peninsula. It was startling to behold the unanimity with which Italians of every class and point of view suffered dire disillusionment. We observers in Italy who had seen the inherent unworkability of the system all along were asked by our Italian friends, "Why didn't you tell us about Fascism?" I remarked that one friend after another used identical phrases in describing his disgust. And not the simple Italians alone. One cabinet minister, one of Italy's highest-ranking generals, and one important Fascist editor said in substance exactly the same thing.

"This is unbearable," they all said. "Look what Fascism and this madman have done to us. They have wiped out every decent page in Italian history and sullied everything we stood for as a people. They made us—Italians—plunge a knife into the back of prostrate France and then turn and attack the unoffending Greeks. And for what? To play jackal to the one nation in Europe, the German, which despises us, precisely because we are the cradle of civilization—a nation which thinks of us as a serf people and prepares for us a serf future under the *Herrenvolk*.

"We should have known what we were doing. We should have known what the end would be when we handed over everything a people ought to value into the hands of this cheap, common criminal, Mussolini. He murdered Matteotti in cold blood because Matteotti, as the Socialist leader in the parliament, had the courage to oppose him and to warn the Italian people. We should have known what the end would be."

My best Italian friend was Prince Camillo Caetani, the last male of a thousand-year-old family which bested the Borgias, gave the Catholic Church one of its really great Popes, and supplied Italy with rather more than one family's share of statesmen and heroes. On his last night in Rome, before going off to join his regiment in Greece, Prince Caetani came to my house for a cocktail.

"Hating Fascism and your German ally, how can you go off to fight in Greece?" I asked.

"Oh, you wouldn't understand," he said. "It's a purely personal matter with me. I have come to hate Fascism, yes. These Fascists have made me ashamed of every drop of Italian blood in my veins. But I have got to go to Greece. I have got to prove to myself that under fire I will behave like a Caetani. I have got to prove that, though an Italian, I can act like a man."

Camillo of the laughing eyes and quick wit did act like a man. He showed the lionlike courage of the uncle who beat an Austrian army in 1917. But his Fascist soldiers let him bleed to death in no man's land. Not a one had the courage to crawl out and drag in the wounded *tennete*. I know. I read his colonel's report in the Italian War Office.

Now while the Italians are not a great warlike people, they are not cowards either. I was with their armies in Ethiopia. There they fought bravely and well. I saw their troops in

Spain. There, despite Guadalajara, which could have happened to any army, they fought bravely and well. After all, it was the invading Italian army which won the decision in Spain. But in the Alps, in the Libyan desert, and in the mountains of Albania the Italians did not fight well. After nineteen years of living a lie, their eyes were opened to the true nature of Fascism. They became like cowards. Something killed the little spark that makes a man a man. I suppose the spark got damped out under "the wave of the future." The Italians as a people had no quarrel with the French, the British, or the Greeks. And they knew it. At the whim of a dictator they were compelled to bear arms as allies of the detested Germans.

The morale began to go to pieces as soon as the Italians found fight in their foes. Invading France, they met unprecedentedly adverse weather conditions and then the French, almost as if to regain their self-respect after the collapse of the Maginot line, fought with stubborn heroism against the Italians. Mussolini sent two Fascist cabinet ministers to orate to the troops. This was when I detected the first deterioration of morale—only ten days after Mussolini's declaration of war. The regular army colonel who presided at the open-air address to the troops made a very brief introduction. "Soldati," he said, "we have here two Fascist cabinet ministers. They have flown this morning from Rome and they will go back to Rome tonight. They are the men who declare the wars. You and I, soldiers, are the men who fight them." These Fascist politicians undoubtedly would have ruined the career of that colonel. They did not have a chance. The colonel died three days later in action.

This simple incident, high in the French Alps, snowballed. In a few months Italian prisoners, to the tune of 100,000, were going over to the British. Uniformed peasants who had suffered frostbite in Greece were waving the stumps of amputated arms and swearing to kill Mussolini. One wounded Italian, when asked by the Countess Ciano if he recognized her, rose on his elbow and spat in her face. And not the simple foot soldiers alone. Marshal Badoglio retired to his villa under a police guard. Marshal Graziani went to a villa in Capri, where he, too, was under surveillance.

The armed forces of Italy were destroyed not by their foes but by Fascism. As a system, Fascism made it impossible for the army, the navy, and the air corps to function as armed services. They had become mere appendages to the Fascist party and political instruments. In Italy the party ruled the army, whereas in Germany the reverse had been true. For seven years Hitler and his generals had worked together for military efficiency and military efficiency alone. The Nazi party had become only an instrument in that work, not an end in itself. The only decisive collision between the army and the party had come in 1934 and a few weeks after the June 30 purge the 2,500,000 S.A. members had been dissolved, put in the uniform of the army, and made answerable to the generals. In Italy regular army units were always brigaded with the Blackshirt party militia, an independent force with its own general staff. Until the eve of Italy's entry into the war the militiamen received twice the pay of the regular army troopers. A Blackshirt general was a political boss who could appeal to the party and cause the removal of any regular army general who had crossed him. If a Blackshirt general, through incompetence, broke liaison, left a flank hanging in the air, or moved the whole command into ambush, the regular army career general could not relieve him of his command. Instead he found it expedient to recommend him for the highest medals. The Blackshirt general who took a column into ambush in Ethiopia through criminal negligence—and I knew him personally—should either have been reduced to the ranks or shot. Instead he was given the highest award. The Blackshirt generals who were responsible for Guadalajara in Spain were all decorated and promoted. In the Ethiopian War, General Pirzi-Biroli, one of the ablest of the professional soldiers, reprimanded Blackshirt officers for their incompetence. After the war Pirzi-Biroli was retired—his career wrecked at an early age.

This is an impossible situation with which to confront any army. And yet under Fascism it cannot be changed. The militia are necessary because otherwise a united army, independent of politics and loyal to the King, would make Mussolini and his patronage machine answerable to public opinion. With the army loyal to him and with no Fascist fighting force to oppose him, the King could dismiss Mussolini and either call for elections or appoint a minister to succeed him. Staying in power is more important to the Fascists than building an efficient army. Mussolini built up his Blackshirt militia; Hitler dissolved his Brown Shirt militia. As a result Italy remained a party state and Germany became a military state.

Mussolini not only kept the Blackshirts; he saw to it that the highest posts in the army, fleet, and air corps went to officers who were politically amenable. That explains why the work of the Italian General Staffs was crudely incompetent. In the months before Italy's entry into the war, the staffs had been shuffled and packed with officers who would not oppose Mussolini's Axis policy on military considerations and who had no other qualification for their tasks.

What Fascism had done to the Royal Italian Navy was even more tragic from the point of view of the many gallant professional naval officers who hung their heads in shame. For years the navy had been run on political considerations and the personal whims of Mussolini rather than upon the recommendations of professional officers. In order to bargain diplomatically in the poker game of power politics, Mussolini had constructed 122 submarines when his officers cried for fewer ships and more money for submarine personnel. In a fleet review for Hitler which I watched several years before the war, ninety-odd submarines were on parade; but a submarine commander told me later that eighteen of them were under the command of yeomen and that the admiralty had held its breath for fear that these petty officers, with no training in navigation, would wreck them all. An Italian admiral once said to me, "We can get a new battleship out of Mussolini, but we can't get the paint to keep the old ones in condition."

Half the gun crews of the Italian navy had never fired the guns themselves. British peacetime target practice had required the relining of the gun tubes about once a year. Italian battleships and cruisers had gone as long as six years without the necessity of relining the tubes while Italian naval officers had burned their hearts out in anticipation of the failure of their men in actual combat. But, worse than this, Mussolini insisted, once combat came, in directing naval battles as well as naval strategy, from his office in the Palazzo Venezia. One admiral spoke very frankly and bitterly to me of this.

"In the first weeks we had a chance to smash the British navy a crippling blow," he said. "The navy itself wanted to move the submarine and destroyer force into the harbor of Alexandria. We would have taken heavy losses, of course, but we could have sunk British capital ships and cruisers. We could have moved toward parity since we would soon have been able to put six capital ships of our own into the Mediterranean.

"Mussolini flatly refused. He was confident of quick victory. He wanted the fleet intact for bargaining with Hitler at the temporary peace before the war was carried first to Russia and then to America. The navy protested in vain. Now it is too late for that type of action. Now we are short of fuel oil. Now we have orders not to give fight to the British fleet because of the fuel shortage and for fear of political repercussions should we lose our capital ships and the British be able to shell our coastlines."

The position of these officers was doubly tragic since a few months later the backbone of their fleet was pinned down and broken at Taranto. British torpedo planes dealt swift destruction there. "Short of fuel, we did not have steam up because of the direct orders of Mussolini," said the commanding admiral.

The reverse of the picture was given me a year later by the victor of Taranto, Admiral Lister, Fifth Sea Lord, in charge of Britain's naval aviation, a handsome and still youthful man.

"When did you begin to study this operation against Taranto?" I asked Admiral Lister.

"About two years before the war began," he said.

The abler type of Italian officer looked up to his British opposite number and wanted British, not German, victory. I shall never forget one Italian naval officer.

"I give you the navy of King George and the ultimate victory of Britain and decency," he said, lifting his whisky and soda. Ten days later—his heart torn between shame and duty —he died on the shell-smashed bridge of his destroyer after having torpedoed a British cruiser.

If Fascism crippled the army and navy, what did it do to the Italian air force? This corps, after all, was the creature of the Fascist party, designed by Mussolini to be the irresistible striking force of the new Roman Empire. From the day twenty years ago when an Italian general invented the theory of totalitarian bombing power, Fascism nurtured the fliers as its very own and made them the spoiled darlings of the new militarized Italy. There are few Italian pilots without a row of medals across their chests and certainly no bar in Italy that has not heard them boast of their exploits in Ethiopia, Albania, and Spain. Even an American air enthusiast, like Major Al Williams, listening to them, was persuaded that they were willing to dive down the funnels of British warships and, more important, that they had planes that could do just that. How did they measure up as an air force when the going got hard? Their failure was greater than that of the army or the navy. And it was more significant because it served to reveal to Italians the inherent, essential, inescapable weakness of the Fascist system, which cannot show itself weak or recognize and admit inferiority.

"Mussolini is always right." That is the motto of the Fascist party. To point out a weakness or a mistake of train- ing in the Italian air corps was to point out that Mussolini was wrong. Similarly, to bring charges against grafters was to break party solidarity. Consequently the youngsters who composed the mass of the Italian air corps went into the war thinking that they were the best in the world. The high-ranking ministers and officers knew better, or should have known better, but they were reaping the rewards in the graft and patronage that are the due of Fascists who know how to keep their mouths shut. They weakened the air force, but they never let Mussolini or the party down by putting their loyalty to the air force first.

As for the poor devils of badly trained pilots whose inferior planes were shot down over France, England, Egypt, and Greece, Fascist ideologists merely retort that they do not matter: Mussolini's totalitarian Italy is rich in cannon fodder. Let the bones bleach, and if mothers pine for lost sons give them posthumous medals! They are only sentimental mothers in the eyes of the hard-boiled Fascists who sit at desks in Rome.

What was the record? As the arm that was to prove sea power outmoded, the Italian air force, despite perfectly placed bases and a narrow sea, failed to sink a single capital ship or to close the Mediterranean to a single British convoy. As the eyes of the army, the Italian air force could not even inform Graziani that the whole of Wavell's little army was being moved forward to launch an offensive. As a bombing force, it could neither smash up Greek communications, despite the inadequate air defense of that pitiable little country, nor attack England. The Italian air units which co-operated for several weeks with the Germans against England were withdrawn from the Channel ignominiously. The planes were not good enough for daylight raids and the pilots were not trained for night flying. Finally, when Italy lost in the first twelve months of war some 2000 of its total of 3500 planes the Italian aviation industry was in no position to replace them.

The failure of the air corps and the aviation industry was due essentially to their being shot through with Fascist politics and corruption, against which no one could protest. Marshal Balbo once told me himself that he argued with Mussolini for the purchase of Wright Whirlwind motors because of the inferiority of Italian engines. He was banished to Libya because of his blunt criticisms and ultimately he was shot down by his own antiaircraft fire, the gun crew being badly trained and excited. Another air minister who recognized air-force weaknesses was dismissed in the year before Italy went to war. In addition, pilot training and staff planning were bad. Against 250 hours of basic training of American cadets the Italian had only 100 hours in the air before receiving a commission. Italian emphasis—and this is true of the Germans too—has been for group work rather than for individual enterprise, and both partners of the Axis treasured a plane more than a pilot. When an American pilot cracks up, his commanding officer says, "Bad luck —better landing next time." When an Italian or German smashes that many thousands of dollars' worth of equipment, there is hell to pay. The result? Listen to an Italian pilot I have known for years. "When we are bombing Malta," he said, "I am no good if British fighters break up our formation. Only our squadron leader has been trained in navigation. If I lose him in a general breakup, I might as well be shot down because none of us in the other planes knows how to find his way home. We have visions of giving out of gas in the middle of the Mediterranean. Do you think the bomber goes on with his bombing mission or the fighter concentrates on British fighters? Hell, no. Each of us is fighting or bombing with three-quarters of his mind on the squadron and how to get home." Finally, the Italian air force reached the apex of efficient expansion at the time of the civil war in Spain, where it was relatively superior; and the staff, forgetting that conditions in Spain were not typical, rested on its laurels. The staff was like a football coach who brings his team to the peak early in the season before the hard games.

The awakening of the Italian pilots was rude. They drank a bitter brew of disillusionment. Their own propaganda had persuaded them not only that they had better planes and training but also that British youth was decadent. I talked with a fighting pilot home from Libya. "These bloody Englishmen are wonderful," he said, "and their planes beyond compare. The first time a Hurricane hit my squadron he shot down four fighters before we knew he was on us. It was like a real hurricane." Another pilot, home from bombing England, moaned, "My God, we didn't have any training in night flying." Once the darlings of the Fascist regime, these pilots now hate Fascism. "They let us down and they lied to us" rises in a chorus of wails.

It was an air-corps officer who started the best gag about a country whose only victory was the signature of the armistice with France, an armistice made possible not by Italian but by German arms.

"What is the difference between Italy in this war and in the last?" he asked.

"In 1914 we prepared, then we fought, finally we made the armistice. In 1940 we made the armistice, then we fought, and now we must prepare."

Wavell's victory in Libya, where 20,000 British soldiers routed an army of 200,000 Italians, cut the heart out of Italian professional officers. Mussolini's interference with Marshal Graziani, one of the best colonial generals in the world, made that commander reluctant either to pursue the offensive or to prepare a proper defensive position. Graziani demanded tanks and more air support for an offensive. Mussolini talked with Hitler about the tanks and the Fuehrer agreed to provide them but only on the condition that they carried German crews. Graziani opposed this condition. As for aircraft, Mussolini dissipated them. And then Wavell struck with blinding rapidity and a reckless disregard for the conventional or outmoded rules of warfare. Wavell adapted the technique used by the Germans in the Lowlands and France, running his mechanized columns clean through the enemy and counting for safety upon the confusion and destruction of communications. It was a brilliant operation, notable because it proved the excellence of British staff work and demonstrated once again, even in the desert, that offense is the best defense and that great generalship consists of pressing and exploiting an advantage. Poor Graziani. His well-merited reputation was destroyed overnight. He alone among the Italians had anticipated and feared British offensive action.

Libya wounded the pride of the professional officers, but Greece—"the invasion in reverse"—struck a blow felt by the whole Italian people. Italians repeated bitterly the anecdote of the French wit in the Alps who put up a sign reading, "Greeks, stop here. This is the French frontier." The inside story of this campaign is funnier than P. G. Wodehouse and more melodramatic than E. Phillips Oppenheim. Mussolini bribed key Greek generals to betray their country. They went to Premier Metaxas and he proved himself the wiliest Greek of modern times. "Pocket the money, be true to your country, and keep me informed," Metaxas told each general. They did exactly that; and Mussolini, expecting to conquer Greece after only forty-eight hours of token resistance, found that his fifth-column arrangements had gone wrong. Three weeks before Mussolini's "unexpected ultimatum" and his "precipitate" invasion, I was able to cable the day and hour of his attack on Greece. I learned later that Edward C. Reed, the American chargé d'affaires, had informed Washington at the same time. We two Americans, with different news sources, had been correctly informed and yet Mussolini was able to deceive his own General Staff. The chief of staff, Marshal Badoglio—because he opposed the attack on Greece —was sent away from the War Office on the fateful week end with assurances that nothing would be done. And then, counting on the fifth column of bribed Greeks, Mussolini ordered invasion with inadequate strength and preparation since Badoglio, believing that the invasion plan had been canceled, dropped any effort to reenforce the army in Albania. Thus Badoglio, like Graziani, fell a victim to the Fascist system, which subordinated even the leadership of the armed forces to the whims of the dictator. Badoglio justified himself later in the following statement to his most intimate friend, who repeated it to me from notes.

"Militarily it was impossible to invade with the dispositions we had made," Badoglio said. "We had only seven divisions in Albania. Two of them were necessary to hold the Albanian population from going into revolt. Two others were in reserve. That left us three divisions with which to undertake an offensive. Against us, the Greeks disposed of fifteen divisions. We might have been able to undertake an offensive had those figures been reversed.

"The Greeks had good staff work and good luck. They got their divisions into position, carrying out concentrations which were facilitated by the fact that we could not make *blitz* war in such mountains or under such weather conditions. Knowing that we meant to drive for Salonika, they massed their forces in the region of the Kostanza frontier. When impossible weather conditions bogged us down in Epirus, our position was strategically untenable. The air force failed to prevent Greek concentrations. The navy failed to land below Corfu. It was not a military operation. It was a political adventure. No officer in the Italian or any other army would have approved such a military offensive."

Despite this explanation Badoglio, as chief of staff, came out badly. Mussolini outmaneuvered him. After the initial fiasco Badoglio told the King that he meant to resign in protest. The honor and prestige of the army had been sullied by the same Fascists whom Badoglio, before the March on Rome twenty years previously, had characterized as "riff-raff" to be swept from the streets with a single army regiment. The King dissuaded Badoglio from resigning and sent him to Mussolini to make his peace. The dictator, whose spies had informed him by telephone of the royal audience, rose when Badoglio entered his office. "Your Excellency's resignation has been accepted and is effective immediately," said Mussolini curtly.

The bewildered old general was thus made the butt of the misadventure. Even his fellow officers criticized him. He should have contrived to keep himself informed of Mussolini's machinations and he should have either prevented the invasion or resigned before it was undertaken; but once the Italians had attacked the Greeks and were being beaten Badoglio should not have resigned, they said. Thus Mussolini, insinuating that Badoglio had approved the operation, made him responsible before the public for its failure and put him in the position of deserting under fire. More, however, than Badoglio's long and distinguished career was wrecked in the mountain passes of Albania and Greece. More than badly clothed and badly armed peasants lie in the shallow graves of the frozen soil of Epirus. Italian Fascism died there too.

Italian morale snapped so suddenly that the nation seemed ripe either for revolt or for separate peace with Great Britain. Consequently Hitler took over. The Germans struck against their ally during the Christmas holidays of 1940. Having already infiltrated their agents into every key position in the land, the Germans decided to consolidate their control. Without warning, 122 major train services in Italy were suspended. This rolling stock was earmarked for the task of hauling German troops and German equipment into Italy. Two *panzer* divisions were moved into Italy, ostensibly and ultimately for service in Libya. Three more were later concentrated in Sicily. Tens of thousands of German soldiers moved into the peninsula proper on one pretext or another —some to guard military objectives, such as factories, others merely to "convalesce" in the sunny Italian countryside. Within ten days the Germans had placed 1400 airplanes on Italian bases, with more coming daily. For the protection and servicing of these airplanes alone, ground crews and land forces of not less than 20,000 men were established at various airdromes. Italians in scattered regions of the country woke up to find that their allies had taken them by the arm. The Germans were very friendly. They only took what they needed and when there were difficulties they acted through Rome. The owners of palatial homes answered the knock to learn that the German staffs for these various occupying forces wanted to requisition their villas or palaces. Two families I knew tried to resist the excessively polite inquiries of the Germans but received prompt orders from Rome to vacate their premises. The Italians woke up to find that their nightmare had come true. The German domination of Italy, finally ended in 1870, weighed on Italy again.

Infiltration had begun long before the Germans moved in their troops to awaken the Italians with a jolt. The way was prepared once Hitler had persuaded Mussolini of the advantage in principle of merging Fascism and Nazism. The Nazis made this merger effective by pressing home every opportunity. What could be more reasonable than the German suggestion that the two allies should coordinate their efforts in every field? What could be more thoughtful than the German suggestion that coordinators should enjoy honorary rank in the Fascist militia? Observers began to see thick-necked blonds in the uniforms of Blackshirt generals and ministers. In every ministry from foreign affairs to transportation, German officials were given offices and began to share responsibility for decisions with the Italian minister. But despite their excessive politeness and their Italian uniforms, the Germans knew what they wanted.

When Count Ciano showed that he had a mind of his own the Germans effectively removed him from the Foreign Office. They suggested to Mussolini that Italian morale could be improved if the younger cabinet ministers served with troops at the front. Ciano, accordingly, became a major of aviation in command of a bombing squadron. In his absence the Germans had a free hand in the Foreign Office. Ciano was called back only when they wanted him to sign a protocol with the Rumanians or Hungarians or some other satellite group. In like fashion an Italian complaint that Germany was draining too much food from the country merely afforded Dr. Clodius, the German economics director, an opportunity to arrange that Germans should take direct charge of rationing in Italy. When Italian industries began to feel the pinch of British sea power, the Germans supplied them with certain raw materials; but they used this service as a pretext to take over the industries themselves. Consequently the Germans began to control the factories as well as the political offices. German technicians took over the managerial posts in the key factories. They arranged, moreover, to buy stock in many of the factories, profiting by a wholly arbitrary exchange value for the mark and the lira.

Less than twelve months after Italy went to war, the Germans directly or indirectly controlled 50 per cent of Italian heavy industry and Clodius negotiated an economic accord whereby the whole fiction of a clearing account between the two countries was dropped. As a result Italian economy was no longer independent in any sense. Thanks to the black-shirted Germans in the Ministries of Labor and Corporations, the Nazis soon controlled the very labor of Italy. In a six-month period I watched the Germans take out of Italy ´117,000 industrial and 200,000 agricultural workers. They put Tony and Pepe in boxcars and shipped them off to work in German fields and factories. I used to try to imagine one of these workers demurring.

"I don't think I'd like to go to Germany," said my imaginary individualist. "You see, I have talked it over with my wife. My wife thinks I ought to stay at home,, especially in this moment. She isn't very well and the children need a man at home."

Actually the workers talked in no such fashion. I talked with scores of Italians who were going off to Germany. But they wouldn't say much. As a rule Italians will always talk, but any workman who talked like my imaginary Italian would have fallen foul of the authorities. And not the Italian authorities, either. "Labor problems," like morale generally, were already being dealt with by the German Gestapo itself. In short, there was almost no phase of Italian life any longer which did not reflect the close coordination which bound the two allies in what Mussolini called the "pact of steel."

Take olive oil and *pasta,* or spaghetti, which, together with tomatoes, are the basic items of the diet of the Italian poor. Within a few months of the German occupation of Italy, even these staples—the foundations of Italian life— were controlled. The German rationing system allowed the Italian peasant as much olive oil and *pasta* in one month as he used to have in one week. The old standard of living had held the Italian masses at little more than subsistence level. The new ration brought malnutrition to the masses. I fear that by now thousands of Italians have the honor to starve for the greater glory of *Groesser Deutschland.* The Germans wanted the olive oil for lubrication of bombsights and other war needs. The tomato disappeared entirely. More tomatoes were being grown in Italy than ever before. But no Italian could buy a tomato from one end of the peninsula to the other. The Germans took the whole crop to Germany. Tomatoes contain vitamins. They were needed for the master race.

In providing the Italians with the advantages of Nazi efficiency, the Germans were very much aware of what they imagined to be their superiority. They were very correct, just as in occupied France. The only difficulties came from individual German officers. A few, when drunk, said sneering and abusive things. In several instances, individuals, unaccustomed as yet, perhaps, to the responsibilities as well as the privileges of a master race, were involved in rape. There was some trouble about this in Sicily, where the Sicilian men were slow to learn the prerogatives of the *Herrenvolk*. Many Italians, of course, were unfair to the Germans. The presence of German aircraft brought British bombers. As so often happens, especially when military objectives are under attack and the bombing is accurate, more civilians were killed by antiaircraft shells than by bombs. The mayor of one Italian village told me that this problem created incredible difficulties for him because his townspeople wanted to throw the German gun crews into the sea. The Italians were unreasonable about another matter—really quite petty. It angered them to watch the Germans eat. The "Huns" violated the ration rules in restaurants and it infuriated even a good Fascist to watch them gorge.

Having destroyed the independence of his country, Mussolini, as the puppet of these detested Germans, waits in the bombproof cellar of the Villa Torlonia, or the well-guarded Palazzo Venezia, for the assassin's gun, which is already loaded. He has today the personal loyalty of scarcely more than a few hundred Italians. The millions who applauded him yesterday are through with him today. He must dread the end which is now inevitable, whether America or Germany wins this war. There have already been three attempts on his life and, while no one could question his physical courage, he knows fear. Once a diplomat of my acquaintance told Mussolini about watching Stalin during a public review in the Red Square. My colleague explained how Stalin repeatedly wiped perspiration from his hands with a handkerchief. "Ah, so Stalin, too, knows what it is to sweat with fear" was the Italian dictator's comment. The Germans know that Mussolini is in danger and their agents in Italy discuss this aspect of the Axis alliance with bold frankness. The Germans say that Mussolini is Hitler's personal friend. With a shrug of the shoulders the Germans add that Mussolini alone stands between the Italian people and the master race—a sort of Protector. The German agents then express a touching solicitude for the welfare of the Duce. It is this fear of German reprisals against the Italian people which in part stays the hands of many would-be assassins. But there are other reasons why the Italians bide their time. Cynical and skeptical, they do not know yet who is going to win this war. And, disillusioned as they are by twenty years of Fascism, they do not know where to turn for another leader.

The royal family is as bankrupt politically as Mussolini. Until the German occupation I never heard any Italian speak of the House of Savoy except with reverent affection. After the Germans took over I heard bitter hatred on every side. A Roman prince who had been a member of the royal household said, "The King is worse than Mussolini. The King is ga-ga. He is a cynical, selfish, dirty old man. He cares nothing for Italy or the Italian people but only for his own throne. He has never intervened for the nation against Mussolini. He said to me once, 'I go with Mussolini because, whether he is right or not, he is lucky.' What a way for a monarch to talk. What a way for a monarch to serve his people. All the King has wanted was to spare himself trouble. He is a coin collector. By such a notion of his duties Victor Emmanuel has destroyed his nation and his House in the third generation of United Italy. Mussolini was born a hoodlum. The King was born a king and of him much was expected." This prince spoke for millions—less articulate but equally bitter.

The Crown Prince Umberto has lost his popularity too. Servants as well as the nobility speak for the first time of his being effeminate. Officers who had revered him suddenly describe him as a dupe. "The silly playboy!" exclaimed an Italian major who had served on his staff. "He let the Fascists show him maneuvers when the only thing the troops had been trained in for a year was that precise maneuver. We officers would have wrecked our careers if we had protested. But Umberto was the Crown Prince and he should have known how badly the army was trained."

Military personalities like Badoglio and Graziani, around whom the people might rally, are equally tarnished. Italians point out the palatial modern show place that the regime has built for Badoglio. "There is the Marshal who once offered the King to clean out the Fascists with a regiment of troops," they say. "He has sold out. Would he stand against the invasion of Greece? No. He approved it and then resigned after it failed." Of Graziani the people speak no more. He was a great general, but he failed. "Once beaten generals fell on their swords," say the modern Romans, with more heat than fair-mindedness. "Now they go, like Graziani, to rest amid the beauty of Capri." That, too, is unfair because Graziani is a sick man, suffering perhaps from cancer of the throat.

In their bitterness the Italians even rail out against the Roman Church. They say that the present Pope is pro-German because of his long residence at Munich and that he has condoned Fascism and accepted a German victory as inevitable. This is palpably false and unfair, but it is significant of the present mood of the people. When the Pope's encyclicals have inveighed against totalitarianism, Italians have objected that the Church ought to stay out of politics. Now they say that it should have enlightened them on the true nature of Fascism. Frightened by the threat of British bombing, even though the presence of the Vatican protects them, the Romans have made a brutal joke.

"When the history of the Church is written," they say, "the present Pope will not rank high among the pontiffs. But we have to admit that so far he has been a very good antiaircraft defense."

In this mood the Italian people, as distinct from the

Fascist firebrands, were ripe for revolt had there been a leadership capable of creating the illusion of hope. Recognizing this fact, the Germans made effective propaganda. It is not the least of Goebbels's accomplishments that he embittered Italians against America. The Nazi propaganda machine spread mistrust and hate. America was described as 40 per cent Jewish; "Rosenfeldt" as an unscrupulous dictator with ambitions for world conquest; and the American people as soulless Protestant moneygrubbers, too cowardly to fight but opposed to the Axis out of a feeling of inferiority in the face of the countries that produced Dante and Goethe, Wagner and Verdi. These arguments were effective because they were based on the face-saving idea that the Italians would already be enjoying peace and victory except for the Americans, who, though unwilling to fight themselves, helped England "in order to prolong the war and enrich themselves at the expense of an exhausted Europe." Thus the Germans capitalized the Italian longing for peace at any price. If the war went on, the Germans argued, it was because of these insufferable Americans. It was time to give these moneygrubbers a lesson. After all, Americans only know how to fight with dollars, said the Germans.

I summed up the purpose of these German propaganda efforts in a cable, dispatched in March, 1941, which said: "Italy, in short, is German and its public must be prepared for Hitler's declaration of war [against America], as Axis spokesmen sometimes say in Rome, if America begins to make aid to Britain decisive by convoying armaments directly to British ports."

Once the Italians believe that Germany can be defeated, the country will be ready, in my opinion, for revolution. The Italians were too shrewd to believe that Britain alone could stand against Germany. They are too shrewd to believe that America, so long as she remains on the defensive, will be able to win against the tripartite powers. Successful military operations by the Americans and the British will inflame the imagination of Italians. Once the Germans are being beaten, the Italians will raise daggers against them with incredible fury. Sicily has always waited enthusiastically for landing forces and the peninsula, too, will welcome Anglo-American expeditionary forces—if in previous landings elsewhere on the continent we have already proved our ability to win. For only when the Germans are in retreat will the Italians fight for us. There are memories of Garibaldi deep in the Italian soul, but this nation has been debauched by twenty years of Fascism. The Italian people is in no heroic mood and is not likely to regain its soul until it has expiated Fascism in the blood of revolution. Meanwhile too few Italians dream of us as liberators or hope that their peninsula can serve us as a bridge. Their cities tremble and their people panic under the weight of our bombs, but the Germans are more feared than the Americans and the British because the Fascists have made much of the ruthlessness and the proximity of Mussolini's Axis ally. Debauched, cynical and wholly unheroic, the Italians believe that we would be well advised to invade Germany through France or the Balkans.

VI

A SLIGHT CASE OF MURDER

GERMANY had reoccupied the Rhineland and completed
three years of rearmament by the summer of 1936; and Italy,
emerging successfully from the Ethiopian war, had bolstered
Fascism at home and increased the country's prestige abroad.
The two dictators—increasingly confident as they felt out the
weaknesses of the British and French—saw an irresistible
opportunity in the internal situation of Spain. That country, situated on the Atlantic, the Mediterranean, and in
Africa, was in the fifth year of its democratic experiment.
King Alfonso had been exiled on April 14, 1931, after a swift
and bloodless revolution which had established the Spanish
Republic. Governed by liberals of the sort who tried to appeal to the better nature of dynamite, the Republic had
been slow to initiate the reforms necessary to modernize that
backward land. Preferring gradual correctives to the disruptive methods of revolution, the Republic had neither
disenfranchised nor dispossessed the reactionary elements,
which worked in undisguised hostility to the new democratic
system. Indeed, these reactionaries, who were proud to obstruct all progress, had come to power under the electoral
system. The Republican parties formed a coalition consequently of all Marxist, radical, and liberal parties, and this
Popular Front, as it was called, won the elections in February, 1936. Out of this election a Popular Front government
was formed by the middle-of-the-road liberal elements and
this government was described by the reactionary opposition
as red, though it included neither Socialists nor Communists.

The reactionary elements, by so characterizing the gov-

ernment, persuaded the professional army officers that social unrest with resultant disorder could be avoided by the
creation of military dictatorship. For the landlords planned
nothing less than a bloody seizure of power. Count Ro-
manones, who had been Alfonso's most wily counselor, spoke
frankly to Claude G. Bowers, the American Ambassador.
"The rebellion? We planned it the day we lost the election,"
he said. Having laid their plans, the reactionaries decided,
in the first place, to get in touch with the German and Italian
governments and, in the second place, to create incidents
and spread terrorism which was answered in kind, not by
the Popular Front government, but by the more radical
elements outside of the government. The right murdered a
popular leftist leader and the left retorted in swift reprisal.
They struck down Calvo Sotelo, the ablest politician among
the rightist plotters. This murder was used to set off the
military *coup d'état*. There was a military rising in Morocco
on July 16 and it became nationwide on July 18, 1936.

In May of 1939—three years later—Hermann Goering and
Galeazzo Ciano revealed that German and Italian specialists,
many of them disguised as tourists, went to Spain to aid this
revolt from its outset. The Nazis and the Fascists had prepared to assist the rebels long before the proclamation of
revolt was raised in Morocco. Having denied their com-
plicity through the whole of the "civil war," the Germans
and Italians boasted, once the war was won, that their intervention had been decisive. The official Italian *Informa-
zione, Diplomatica* proudly announced that "Italy replied to
the first call of Franco on July 27, 1936: first casualties date
from that time." In his own newspaper, *Popolo d'Italia,*
Mussolini wrote: "We have intervened from the first to the
last."

In the first weeks of the fighting, numerous Italian airplanes flew Foreign Legion and Moorish troops from Africa
to the Spanish mainland. As early as July 31 twenty Italian
army planes flew to Africa to reenforce the transport planes

already operating from Morocco. Two were forced down in French North Africa. The Fascists had not bothered to disguise the military markings of the airplanes and the pilots were found to be carrying military passports. Later, according to the Italians, Mussolini's regular army pilots made 86,420 air raids on Republican Spain and, in some 5318 bombardments, dropped 11,584 tons of explosives. Though the Italians and Germans treated the totals of their effectives as military secrets, I estimated that at one time Italy had not less than 140,000 soldiers in Spain, while the Germans maintained a fixed establishment there of 10,000 technicians and 10,000 troops. These are my own estimates, however, and were not cited by Goering or Ciano.

The Germans and Italians said, and persuaded millions in the democracies to believe, that they intervened in Spain only after the Russians were there and in order merely to save Spain from Communism. It is well established now that no Russian arms reached Republican Spain before October 20, 1936, and that no Russian troops or "volunteers" were ever sent. Several Russian generals did serve in advisory capacities with the Republican militia, and many months after the rebellion scores of G.P.U. agents were sent to Spain in an abortive effort to propagandize the militia and seize control of the government. The Spanish government held a large gold reserve, possibly the third, certainly the fourth, largest in the world. This gold was used for the purchase of arms and airplanes in France, Belgium, Austria, or wherever else they could be found for sale. It became possible to buy arms in the Soviet Union in October—the fourth month of the rebellion—and the Spanish government paid in gold for all shipments received.

I can vouch personally for the validity of this record because I was at the various fronts with the German and Italian tank and artillery units serving the Franco cause, when we saw the first Russian tanks and airplanes arrive in late October and November. I remember talking in the third week of October with the German pilots who flew to Cartagena to attack the first shipments of arms from Russia. They had expressed astonishment that antiaircraft guns had been unloaded and set up immediately so that they were met with a heavy curtain of flack. They were facilitated throughout the raid, however, by a German pocket battleship which lay off the harbor and signaled the objectives. These young blonds from Goering's *Luftwaffe* chuckled because the Republicans had not been able to black out an international lighthouse which, together with searchlights from the pocket battleship, facilitated easy runs over the target. A year later, when I had gone from the rebel side to Barcelona, I heard an amusing story from a Republican.

"A Russian ship put into Valencia in September," he said. "There were shipping cases on the deck marked as oleomargarine and marmalade. I clapped my hands with joy. 'At last we are getting machine guns,' I thought. We ripped open the cases. Sin virguenza! They really had sent us oleomargarine and marmalade."

The rebels never had a chance to win in Spain. Victory was won by the Germans and Italians, who twice rescued Franco from imminent disaster, and by the United States, Great Britain, and France, who denied arms to the Republicans—especially in the moment when they were in a position to take the offensive and sweep even the Germans and Italians into the sea. The rebels planned a *coup d'état*. Their preparations had been minute. The various garrisons rose as planned, except for Valencia, Frasco, and Barcelona, and the mass of army officers acted together with negligible exceptions. By the very act of the rebellion Spain was theirs. The government had neither troops nor arms. The rebels declared that there was no longer a government and they proclaimed their own victory. Only one thing was wrong with this classic seizure of power. The *coup d'état*, like some vaccinations, had failed to take. Deep in the body politic of Spain there ran a healthy self-respect and a passionate pride in the Republic. Not very efficient, and dilatory certainly, in its program of reform, the Republic had given the people of Spain, nevertheless, the feeling that it was their Spain —a new Spain of schoolhouses and food for all, and public sanitation and freedom from police spies. When the reactionaries delivered their well-planned and well-timed blow the Republic was struck to the ground.

There was chaos from one end of Spain to the other. But the simple man and woman, the peasant and the worker, the newly rising middle class, the professors, the intellectuals, rose as a mass, leaderless and chaotic, but angry and heroic. They did not know how to restore the Republic, but they knew how to strike down its assassins. They went out into the streets with pistols and knives and scythes and wrenches and paving stones. They fought as the true conservatives and loyalists of Spain. But they took the law into their own hands. They had made their Republic without bloodshed and ruled with moderation, not vindictive nor revolutionary, but willing to retire on full pension any army officer who was reluctant to swear allegiance to the Republic. And now that Spain ran with blood, they knew the men who were the enemies of the Republic. They sought them out. Many of them were priests as well as landlords and generals. They shot the priests too. It was many months before these excesses, especially by the Spanish anarchists, could be controlled by a government which regained the reins slowly. But meanwhile the Republic had been saved. It had been saved by the masses, who struck down its assassins in the first two weeks of a *coup d'état* which failed to take. The rebels had been beaten then and there.

During the first month after the failure, small rebel columns, utilizing the arms they had seized in various barracks, made progress in the rural regions and raised the standard of rebellion over the sparsely settled mountains and deserts. But in Spain generally and in the cities especially the Spanish people were mobilizing. In their vast numbers they were organizing to crush the rebel bands—gun against gun, bayonet against bayonet, since the Spanish army had few modern weapons which could give the rebel soldiery decisive advantage against the Republican masses. It was the invasion of Spain by the Moors, ferried across the straits from Africa by the Italians and Germans, which saved the rebel traitors from the firing squad. Rushed over from Morocco in Italian planes and aided in the field by German planes and arms, these professional mercenaries were superior to such units as the Republicans could fashion out of undrilled men, hastily armed and sent into the field.

Marching with these Moors, I watched them flank, dislodge, and annihilate ten times their numbers in battle after battle. Individual heroism among untrained soldiers is not enough against professionals supported by aircraft. The Republicans used to fight stubbornly until they could no longer stand under the fragmentation bombs and the artillery fire of the German and Italian "specialists"; then the Moors would charge and dislodge them from the relative security of their trench systems. With no professional officers and no training in the simple tactic of changing front, the beaten Republicans would mill into some village, rushing madly for the illusionary protection of stone houses. Then the German and Italian bombers would go for them. Droning backward and forward at six thousand or even three thousand feet, with neither antiaircraft fire nor interceptor planes to worry them, the great black bombers would unload their high explosives in leisurely fashion. I used to watch the big bombs turning over and falling slowly. When they crashed, hundreds of Republicans died under the blasted masonry—men who might have lived if they had been trained to maneuver in the open and if professional officers had held them in the trenches instead of letting them rush to the stone houses.

Having lost the *coup d'état* only to be saved by the Moors and the Italo-German air force, the rebels next lost the "civil war" by their badly conceived and costly assault on Madrid. I stood at the outskirts of Madrid with the Moors and watched General Franco destroy himself and his cause in a futile frontal attack against that proud city. With their backs to the walls of their capital, the Republicans needed no officers and no tactical knowledge. There was no question of their changing front or being maneuvered into the open. The individual stood where he was until he died. For Franco hesitated before the attack long enough for the Republicans to organize their defenses and to take precautions against the fifth column. This phrase was born in that moment. Franco approached Madrid with four fighting columns, but, as General Mola had said, he counted for victory upon the operations of a "fifth column" composed of Franco sympathizers within Madrid. Franco delayed in order to consult with his German and Italian advisers. He asked the classic copybook rules. General Faupel, the special German Ambassador, who was also in charge, incidentally, of Nazi relations with Latin America, responded like an old-fashioned Prussian. There were machine-gun nests in Madrid? Very well then; bring up artillery, bombers, and tanks to clean them out.

Franco might have resorted to the painstaking and slow flanking approach by which the British general who later became the Duke of Wellington had taken Madrid. Or he might have repeated the swift audacity of General Varela's frontal attack on Toledo, sweeping into the city before its defense could be organized. Franco did neither. He listened to Faupel and he waited two days for the guns and the bombers and the tanks. In that interim the Republicans kept the road to Madrid open, pouring in arms and supplies. Equally important, some 1900 volunteers of the International Brigade streamed into Madrid, to be followed ultimately by another 1550. These men were volunteers—anti-Fascist Germans and Italians, backed by tough Frenchmen who joked about blondes as they served the machine guns.

The moral effect of the arrival of the volunteers far exceeded their numerical importance. The Republicans, mauled and butchered by Moorish mercenaries and foreign air corps, suddenly felt that the Republic was no longer alone. They believed that the conscience of the democracies of the world had been stirred. They expected arms to follow from Britain, France, America, the Soviet Union. They believed that to die now was not to die in vain. They held Madrid.

How they held Madrid I was to see with my own eyes. I crawled down to the Frenchman's Bridge, hoping to be the first correspondent with Franco's army to cross the Manzanares River into the city. The fire was too heavy and I lost my nerve. But through field glasses I watched the Moors clean out the six- and seven-story tenements just across that narrow and bloody little river. A detail of fifty Moors would surround a building, silence the ground-floor defenders, and rush in. Then they would clear the second story with submachine guns and hand grenades. These Moors were calm and tight-lipped, expert workmen. They would clear each building floor by floor. There was one difficulty. By the time the Moors had reached the top floor there were no Moors left. The khaki-painted new motorized artillery of the Germans, backed by a hundred-odd Heinkels and Savoia-Marchettis, would clear out another area of Madrid, methodically, block by block, with the flames and pillars of smoke shutting the city itself from our view. And then the Moors would charge in to mop up. They would find that the buildings just beyond the devastated area bristled with machine guns. The Moors would clean these buildings floor by floor and the Moors would die floor by floor.

The unyielding and unending Republican resistance took the starch out of Franco's troops. In their long triumphant procession from Badajoz through Talavera de la Reina to Toledo, San Martín-de-Val de Iglesias and Navalcarnero, and thence to Madrid itself, the Republicans had never stood against them successfully. Now the Republicans stood like a wall. I understood what happens to the psychology of such an army. A youngster fights a boxing match against a boy he thinks is easy. He sees an opening, gets set, and hits flush on the chin with everything he has got. The boy shakes it off, grins, and wades in for more. In that split second the youngster is beaten. He is beaten, not three rounds later when he is knocked out, but in the split second when he hit with his best blow and found that it was not enough. That is what happened to General Franco's army. The pushover would not push over and the steam went out of Franco's punch. In war it is extremely difficult to change the psychology of troops from offensive to defensive operations. Franco's men could not understand the need for their own entrenchment. They lay in open shallow ditches, expecting always to crash into Madrid the next day or the day after. *Mañana por mañana.*

Somehow the Republicans got planes from the French and the Russians. They massed everything they had. On one day they achieved the impossible. They put 127 planes in the air at once—almost a third of the calculated preponderance which Berlin and Rome maintained. It was bad bombing, but it knocked me off my feet twice and it killed Franco's soldiery—that and the steady, hammering fire of all the artillery on the Republican side, massed in Madrid and served by gunners who scarcely knew one piece from another. Lying in scooped-out ditches, Franco's Moors died by the thousands. I talked with Colonel Castejon, the commander of the fourth of General Franco's columns. He lay wounded, his hip shattered. "We who made this revolt are now beaten," he said. He explained that the reports in Franco's headquarters estimated that of the 60,000 Moors engaged not less than 50,000 were casualties. The Falangistas were unfit for front-line duty—cowards who played politics and killed behind the lines—and the Carlists, the bravest soldiers in Spain, were already destroyed. Franco had no army left. Imitating the Fuehrer and the Duce, Franco had assumed the title of Caudillo. But he was a *caudillo* without an army and without a country.

I talked with Captain Roland von Strunk, Hitler's special agent in Spain. Strunk had just left headquarters after a conference with Franco and General Varela, ablest of the rebel field commanders since Mola had failed at the Escorial.

"Franco is finished," said Strunk. "He cannot stand against red counterattacks now or later. I am going to Salamanca to telephone the Fuehrer and ask for the immediate disptach of German infantry. Franco must have twenty thousand German soldiers."

What Franco's headquarters knew the Spaniards behind his lines knew. Uprisings against the Franco occupation took place in Cáceres and Benito and in half a dozen sections of Andalusia. There was even an attack on Talavera de la Reina, which brought me out of my bed one morning when a shell blast blew in the windowpanes of my room. Unable to put down these risings, Franco importuned the German and Italian air corps. I remember the disgust of an Italian army pilot I had known in Ethiopia. He dined with me after having razed Benito to the ground.

"First we dropped leaflets which said, 'Red atheists, prepare for death.' Then we circled back and dropped high explosive and incendiaries. I don't mind bombing troops. I don't like murdering old men and women and children in villages."

Like most Italians, my friend had come to loathe the whole rebel side. Even Germans like Strunk, a spy and a killer, said that he was outraged by the methods of the rebels. But the Italian and the German agreed that Franco could be saved only by the prompt arrival of foreign troops. While the Republicans dreamed of gathering strength to prepare an offensive, Mussolini sent Franco a mass army of 100,000 Italians. Hitler declined to send the 20,000 Germans for whom Franco had asked through Strunk. He already had that number in Spain, half soldiery, half specialists. Instead of doubling that strength he promised aid in matériel. German and Italian money was given to the penniless Franco so that he was able to bring over 70,000 additional Moors—about 40,000 of them recruited from French Morocco, where there was a famine and where certain French officials were Fascist sympathizers. Once again the foreigners imposed upon the Spanish nation new victories on behalf of a group of conspirators who had failed even to rally an army of Spaniards to their cause.

This Franco, who was never able to raise a Spanish army, aroused the most lyrical enthusiasm among certain foreigners. The Paris newspaper *Candide* wrote: "Franco is not tall; he is a little heavy; his body is timid. Ah! His glance is unforgettable, like that of all rare beings. A troubled and trembling glance, full of sweetness; the man is delicious and mysterious. He is a miracle of tenderness and energy. . . . The ravishing thing about Franco is his purity." The American apologists who were sincerely enthusiastic stressed the Catholicism of Franco. He was a great Christian, they said. The British described him in the image of the cultivated Tory. Even so distinguished a British editor as Mr. J. L. Garvin said that Franco was a "great gentleman." To this Mr. John Gunther replied that Franco "has broken his oath twice; first to the King, when he took service with the Republic; then to the Republic, when he rose against it."

Personally I found Franco shrewd but disconcertingly unimpressive. I talked with him first when he was still slender and later after he had gone to fat. A small man, he is muscular; but his hand is soft as a woman's, and in both instances I found it damp with perspiration. Excessively shy as he fences to understand a caller, his voice is shrill and pitched on a high note which is slightly disturbing since he speaks quietly, almost in a whisper. Although effusively flattering, he gave me no frank answer to any question I put to him; I could see that he perfectly understood the implication of even the most subtle query. A less straightforward man I never met.

Discussing Franco with his fellow officers, I got something more than the picture of an energetic soldier who fought with distinction against the Riffs, studied in Paris under Marshal Pétain, and became the youngest general in the Spanish army. Speaking with the frankness which comes with a generous resort to brandy after a day of battle, these officers described an inveterate careerist. To them Franco was not only a sly Gallego, with the reticences and indirections of the people of that predominantly Jewish province; he was also a puritan. Championing the popular reactionary aspirations—renovation of the Spanish army, regeneration of the Spanish people, restoration of the Spanish empire—this ambitious little man was also concerned with less-inspiring generalities. Throughout the whole of his career Franco bore witness before his superiors to the gambling debts or marital infidelities of a score of comrades in arms. It was perhaps only a coincidence that many of these men stood in the way of Franco's steady progress toward what Mr. Kipling called advancement and pay. Among the officers who commanded his columns in the field, Franco was neither popular nor trusted.

I talked many times with the late King Alfonso about Franco. While the Spanish War continued, Alfonso said, "I wish well to Franco, for I am only a simple soldier in the ranks." Later when Alfonso, before his fatal heart attack, was arranging to renounce his throne and provide the succession of Don Juan, a prepossessing young man of character and ability, Alfonso was more outspoken. "I picked out Franco when he was a nobody," said the King, who liked the American and used it naturally. "He has deceived and double-crossed me at every turn. In him you see what we Spaniards mean when we are suspicious of the type which comes from Galicia."

When I try in my own mind to make an estimate of Franco's character, I am reminded of a casuistical phrase used by the London *Times*. In describing Dr. Antonio Salazar, the Fascist dictator of Portugal, the *Times* admitted that he was a dictator, but argued that he was a "Christian dictator." I suppose the people who grew lyrical about Franco in the democracies made the same sort of distinction and qualification. For them Franco is a "great gentleman" and a "great Catholic." For me he is the man and the type who are responsible for the 1,500,000 Spanish dead, for Badajoz and the other butcheries, for Guernica and all the other blackened ruins. He is responsible for the 300,000 Spanish reds being slowly done to death in the Franco prisons three years after the war, and for the negotiations with Hitler and Pétain to enable him to swell their numbers with more than 100,000 Spanish reds from the French concentration camps. The notion of a Fascist dictator who is also a Christian dictator is as illogical to an American as the notion that there is truth with a little t and Truth with a capital T.

Franco's apologists in Britain, France, and America—except the hired Nazi and Fascist agents—knew very little about Spain. They knew Spaniards who traveled abroad and who, by that very fact, were scarcely representative. Few of them knew Spanish reactionaries in Spain. The magazine *Life*, scarcely a "red" publication, wrote of the "ruling class" and the "best elements" that they "were probably the world's worst bosses—irresponsible, arrogant, vain, ignorant, shiftless, and incompetent." They were the royalists, the landowners, the generals, and the Catholic hierarchy, as distinct from the Catholic masses or, for that matter, from the Catholic middle classes of Catalonia and Vasconia. They represented the 1 per cent which owned 51 per cent of the land. They represented the 21,000 officers, of whom 700 were generals and against whom the Republic had acted so "harshly" when it retired from among their number 7000 known enemies of the Republic—relieving them from active commands but retiring them on full pensions. They represented the 40,000 priests and the religious orders which, in a country second only to Portugal in illiteracy, owned mines, industries, shipping, public utilities, banks, transportation systems, and vast agricultural enterprises. I talked with them by the hundreds—not in New York or London or Paris but in Spain. If I could sum up their social philosophy it was simple in the extreme. They were outnumbered by the masses: they feared the program to educate the masses and they proposed to thin down their numbers.

"We have got to kill and kill and kill, you understand," said one of Franco's chief press officers, over and over again. He was Captain Don Gonzalo Aguilera, Count of Alva de Yeltes. A great landowner and sportsman, Aguilera had served as the Spanish military attaché in Berlin and he perfectly mirrored the mentality of the militarists who tried to bring Spain into the first World War on the side of Germany.

"You know what's wrong with Spain?" Aguilera used to demand of me. "Modern plumbing! In healthier times—I mean healthier times spiritually, you understand—plague and pestilence could be counted on to thin down the Spanish masses. Held them down to manageable proportions, you understand. Now with modern sewage disposal and the like they multiply too fast. The masses are no better than animals, you understand, and you can't expect them not to become infected with the virus of bolshevism. After all, rats and lice carry the plague. Do you understand now what we mean by the regeneration of Spain?"

Aguilera suffered that harshness of throat so noticeable among Spaniards. I don't know whether it comes from the aspirates in their language or from the quality of the tobacco they smoke. Aguilera would wet his throat with another tumbler of Spanish brandy and proceed to the approving nods and comments of the leading officers of Franco's army.

"It's our program, you understand, to exterminate one-third of the male population of Spain. That will purge the country and we will be rid of the proletariat. It's sound economically too. Never have any more unemployment in Spain, you understand. We'll make other changes too. For instance, we'll be done with this nonsense of equality for women. I breed horses and livestock, you understand. I know all about women. There'll be no more nonsense about subjecting gentlemen to court action. If a man's wife is unfaithful to him, why, he'll shoot her like a dog. It's disgusting, the idea of a court interfering between a man and his wife.

"The people in Britain and America are going communist the way the French have gone. There's that man Baldwin in England. Doesn't even know he is a red, but the reds control him. And, of course, that man Roosevelt is a howling red. But it goes back farther than that. It begins with the Encyclopedists in France—the American and the French revolutions. The Age of Reason indeed! The Rights of Man! The masses aren't fit to reason and to think. Rights? Does a pig have rights? Then you pick up with the liberal Manchester school in England. They are the criminals who made international capitalism. You people had better clean up your own houses. If you don't, we Spaniards are going to join the Germans and Italians in conquering you all. The Germans have already promised to help us regain our American colonies, which you and your shameful Protestant liberal imperialism stole from us. Do you understand?"

Aguilera was one of the bravest men I have ever seen. He was actually happiest under fire and, when I wanted to get to the front, he connived with me on trips of our own, after the propaganda bureau had vetoed them. When I came to know the field commanders from having been through one battle after another with them, I went up on my own. Aguilera began to feel that I was seeing altogether too much of the Franco methods firsthand and he began to doubt my "political reliability." Franco's propaganda bureau let in no correspondents unless it felt certain that they were Fascists. They let me in because the Italians during the Ethiopian War had decorated me with the *Croce di Guerra*. Aguilera suspected that I was no Fascist. He and a German Gestapo agent woke me one morning at 2:00 A.M., when I had just tumbled into bed after returning from the front lines.

"Look here," said Aguilera in his hoarse voice. "You are not to go to the front any more except on escorted tours. We've arranged your case. The next time you're unescorted at the front, we'll shoot you. We'll say that you were a casualty to enemy action. Do you understand?"

I quote Aguilera at length because his social and political ideas were typical. I heard his own ideas voiced by scores and hundreds of others on the Franco side. Except in this broad outlook—the destruction of the proletariat and an ultimate war against the democracies—they were split with their own divisions and cleavages. There were the Alfonso royalists and the Carlist royalists. There were the landowners and the Catholic hierarchy, glorying equally in the mentality of the sixteenth century. And there were the Falangistas, Spanish Nazis who hated the landlords and the Church. Of them all, this last group was the most successful. When the revolt came the membership of the Falangistas numbered less than 50,000. Within six months their enrollment stood at 500,000. While the army officers, the Carlists, and the Moors were fighting, the Falangistas were busily organizing behind the Franco lines. For they became the pets of the German Gestapo. Recruited from small shopkeepers and the like, the little disappointed men of each community, they were the equivalent of the followers of Father Coughlin in America. To their side flocked all the anarchists and killers trapped on the Franco side.

The German Gestapo instructed the Falangistas in the technique of terrorism. In order to preserve themselves for the ultimate political control of Spain the Falangistas stayed away from the front. It is doubtful whether they killed 100 Republicans in battle. They alone shot down not less than 500,000 behind the lines. They contrived to keep away from the front not only by playing politics with Franco, in the period when he was a relatively obscure general anxious to become Caudillo, but also by the simple expedient of proving untrustworthy on occasions of emergency when they were compelled to go into the trenches. Colonel Yague, commander of one of Franco's four columns, had become a Falangista for political reasons. And yet I sat in his headquarters one night and heard him telephone Franco for the fourth time, demanding reenforcements if he was to hold his position against an impending Republican counterattack. Franco said he would send up Falangistas. Yague cursed for a full minute. "Are you trying to destroy my column?" Colonel Yague demanded. "The Falangistas will deliberately withdraw from the line and their example is likely to panic my command." Ultimately the Falangistas demonstrated the political wisdom of running away in order to fight another day.

José Sainz, the leader of the Falange for the District of Toledo, I knew well. He showed me a neatly kept notebook. "I jot them down," he said. "I have personally executed 127 red prisoners." Sainz patted the heavy German Luger pistol on his hip. He had been at work then for only four months.

For two months I kept a room at Talavera de la Reina which served as a base camp for trips to the front. I slept there on an average of two nights a week. I never passed a night there without being awakened at dawn by the volleys of the firing squads in the yard of the *Cuartel*. There seemed no end to the killing. They were shooting as many at the end of the second month as in my first days in Talavera. They averaged perhaps thirty a day. I watched the men they took into the *Cuartel*. They were simple peasants and workers, Spanish Milquetoasts. It was sufficient to have carried a trade-union card, to have been a Freemason, to have voted for the Republic. If you were picked up or denounced for any one of these charges you were given a summary, two-minute hearing and capital punishment was formally pronounced. Any man who had held any office under the Republic was, of course, shot out of hand. And there were mopping-up operations along the roads. You would find four old peasant women heaped in a ditch; thirty and forty militiamen at a time, their hands roped behind them, shot down at the crossroads. I remember a bundle in a town square. Two youthful members of the Republican assault guards had been tied back to back with wire, covered with gasoline and burned alive.

I can never forget the first time I saw the mass execution of prisoners. I stood in the main street of Santa Olalla as seven trucks brought in the militiamen. They were unloaded and herded together. They had that listless, exhausted, beaten look of troops who can no longer stand against the steady pounding of the German bombs. Most of them had a soiled towel or a shirt in their hands—the white flags with which they had signaled their surrender. Two Franco officers passed out cigarettes among them and several Republicans laughed boyishly and self-consciously as they smoked their first cigarette in weeks. Suddenly an officer took me by the arm and said, "It's time to get out of here." At the edge of this cluster of prisoners, six hundred-odd men, Moorish troopers were setting up two machine guns. The prisoners saw them as I saw them. The men seemed to tremble in one convulsion, as those in front, speechless with fright, rocked back on their heels, the color draining from their faces, their eyes opening with terror. I ran into the ruins of a wrecked café. There a Moorish soldier had found a battered player piano. It had roll music and his feet worked the pedals frantically. He cackled and shrieked with delight and the piano tinkled out a popular American theme song from Hollywood, "San Francisco," as the two guns suddenly roared in staccato, firing short lazy bursts of ten or twelve rounds at a time, punctuated by the silences. Then, or later, I have never understood why the prisoners stood and took it. I always thought they might rush the machine guns or do something—anything. I suppose all volition is beaten out of them by the time they surrender. They must have become like the Germans who commit suicide without first trying to kill Hitler.

Franco's fixed policy of shooting militiamen brought protests. An Italian general made an issue of the fact that 20,000 Republicans who had surrendered to Italian troops were subsequently executed by Franco. Strunk told me that he had twice intervened with Franco on the ground that the reds had fought bravely and merited treatment as prisoners of war and also on the ground that it was stiffening Republican resistance. "Why, this sort of thing can't be right, Captain Strunk," said Franco. "You are not the sort of German to get the facts wrong." Bitter at Franco's patronizing manner, Strunk explained to me that there had been a careful division of labor. Civilians behind the lines were executed by the Falangistas. Prisoners of war were executed by Franco's soldiery and on his express orders.

Such stories of these atrocities as leaked out were categorically denied abroad by the propaganda bureau and its apologists. The executions in the Badajoz bull ring were first reported in America by Jay Allen, in the Chicago *Tribune*. He had been the first correspondent to interview Franco and he had generally proved himself the best informed journalist in Spain. His story was denied and he was villified by paid speakers from one end of the United States to the other. A typical trick was to deny that Allen had been in Badajoz at the time it was taken. Allen's dispatch said categorically that he had arrived later, that he was not able to send any eyewitness story but that he was quoting Franco sources. Colonel Yague, who commanded the Franco forces at Badajoz, laughed at these denials.

"Of course we shot them," he said to me. "What do you expect? Was I supposed to take 4000 reds with me as my column advanced, racing against time? Was I expected to turn them loose in my rear and let them make Badajoz red again?"

The men who commanded them never denied that the Moors killed the wounded in the Republican hospital at Toledo. They boasted of how grenades were thrown in among two hundred screaming and helpless men. They never denied to me that they had promised the Moors white women when they reached Madrid. I sat with these officers in bivouac and heard them debate the expediency of such a promise. Some contended that a white woman was Spanish even if red. This practice was not denied by El Mizian, the only Moroccan officer in the Spanish army. I stood at the crossroads outside Navalcarnero with this Moorish major when two Spanish girls, not out of their teens, were brought before him. One had worked in a textile factory in Barcelona and they found a trade-union card in her leather jacket. The other came from Valencia and said she had no politics. After questioning them for military information, El Mizian had them taken into a small schoolhouse where some forty Moorish soldiers were resting. As they reached the doorway an ululating cry rose from the Moors within. I stood horrified in helpless anger. El Mizian smirked when I remonstrated with him. "Oh, they'll not live more than four hours," he said. I suppose Franco felt that women had to be given the Moors. They were unpaid. Franco had no funds and I personally witnessed the payment of Moorish soldiers on one occasion in German marks from the inflation period. Similarly, they had been reissued a curious uniform—an overall battle dress which had the Sacred Heart of Jesus stitched on the left breast.

The Franco Spaniards talked knowingly of death, fondling the word as if it were a woman, repellent yet seductive. Knowing that the program called for the murder of a third of the male population, such men gave a weird unreality to this land where effects were already heightened by El Greco colors and where the smell of rotting corpses, sweetly sickening like a bad walnut, was always in our nostrils. I tried filling my nose with brandy, but it could not shut out that odor. Many killed without malice or anger. They would hand a cigarette to a Republican militiaman and wait until he had smoked it to the end. Others killed in a frenzy. It was not Spanish character alone. I remember an Irishman of a well-known family, a volunteer lieutenant in Franco's army. The late Webb Miller and I gave him a lift back from the front in our car. The Irishman boasted of having personally machine-gunned fifty-odd red prisoners taken by his company the day before. Our chauffeur ran over a dog in the road. The Irishman became hysterical and wept like a child. "Think of a man who will run over a dog," he said, and, until Miller and I reassured him, our chauffeur feared for his life. Our driver knew, and we knew, that Captain Aguilera had shot his chauffeur for running him off the road. "He was a red all the time," explained Aguilera. The ruthlessness of the Franco rebels must have stemmed from the Inquisition. They killed their prisoners methodically and without pity— because those men were wrong. They were on the wrong side. Bigotry and fanaticism make murder easy.

On the other side there were murders too. But they were done by individuals and groups that got out of hand. When the government regained control these murderers were punished. At no time did the Republic undertake mass executions. There was a very real distinction between "red atrocities" and the Franco "executions" committed with organized discipline as part of a fixed program to purge Spain of reds. This is the thing which impressed me most on the Republican side. There man had self-respect. They were fighting for "their" Republic, and even the anarchists—the most unstable element in the country—astonished me by talking constantly of the need for discipline. They admitted that in the first weeks of the rebellion they had murdered the well-to-do indiscriminately in whole villages. But they were ashamed of this. "We had to stop this if we were to have the kind of Republic we want," they would say. I heard this on every hand from the illiterate who proudly showed me books and said that part of militia training consisted in teaching every Spaniard to read and write. I heard this from the anarchists who had always argued that man was good but that he had been perverted by government, so that the solution was the destruction of all organization so that man could start once again.

Now these men saw the necessity for organization and for discipline. Their nihilistic idealism had been transformed by the struggle to build an army and establish the authority of a government. This was the great accomplishment of the leaders of the Republic. They were equally successful in combating the Communist agents who were rushed into Spain in the fourth month of the war. They let in the G.P.U. because Russia was selling arms when the Republic could get them nowhere else. But the Communists tried to get control of the government. They were blocked. Then the Communists began to organize their own secret police. It was in this moment that the first of some 2000 American volunteers reached Spain to serve in the International Brigade. G.P.U. agents collected the American passports of these boys—very valuable for Communist agents and spies. The Republican government was outraged. Slowly it froze out the Communists. Finally when the government was being transferred to Barcelona the Communist agents rushed there, hoping to gain control of the police organizations in the confusion of changing capitals. Then the government used force against the G.P.U., smashing their organization in swift police action on the outskirts of Barcelona. Juan Negrín, the Spanish Premier, was then able to persuade Joseph Stalin to withdraw his agents and abandon his attempt to control the Republic.

When I went to the Republican side in the spring of 1938, the major offensive had failed for want of arms. The government had been driven from Madrid to Valencia and from Valencia to Barcelona. So long as the United States continued to embargo arms shipments the Republic had only one chance to survive. It had trained an army, but it could not organize an offensive and rout the Italo-German forces without arms. Its one chance lay in holding on until Germany attacked Great Britain and France, thus forcing the great democracies to recognize that Spain fought their war too. This the leaders of the Republic were determined to do. But they asked their consciences, and they asked observers like me, if this policy—sound strategically—was too cruel to impose on the Spanish masses, who were dying and starving so bravely. Since I had been on the Franco side, they wanted to know whether Franco might spare the masses concentration camps and firing squads. The leaders thought, not of themselves, but of the people.

I had known Alvarez del Vayo when he was the correspondent of the *Manchester Guardian,* when he became an Ambassador, and finally when he was first named Foreign Minister. I took him from France soap, cigarettes, and marmalade. He and his lovely wife were delighted when Richard Mowrer, of the Chicago *Daily News,* and I delivered them. They took the soap and the marmalade to the hospitals; they gave the cigarettes to the troops. "But you are a chain smoker," I protested. Del Vayo shook his head. "I haven't smoked a cigarette in eleven months," he said. "When the troops can't get them, I have no right to smoke." Into my mind there flashed a contrast. I remembered during the Ethiopian War when Italians were asked to boycott British and French goods in retaliation against sanctions. "I don't worry," said Mussolini's daughter, Edda Ciano. "The pilots on the Italian air line bring me my lipstick from Paris."

The contrast between Franco and Juan Negrín was equally sharp. A professor of biology, with a profound culture, firmly rooted in the humanities, the Republican Premier was a man of modesty and lively humor. Winston Churchill was slow to comprehend the nature of the Spanish War. Finally he went to Spain to see for himself. Taking the measure of the Republican Premier, Churchill said that Negrín was the ablest statesman in Europe. He was that, and more. After he was already in exile I asked Negrín why his government had been less effective in cleaning out the fifth column.

"That was my most difficult problem," said Negrín. "You would see a man day after day and be absolutely sure that he was working for the enemy. But you could do nothing about it."

"Why couldn't you do anything about it?" I asked.

"Because you cannot suspend the courts system and the rules of evidence. If you fight to preserve a Republic you destroy the Republic if you resort to Fascist methods. You cannot have your cake and eat it too."

"But surely in the crisis of war you suspended normal court procedure," I suggested.

"Oh, yes, we had to create special courts," said Negrín. "But we couldn't arrest a man on suspicion; we couldn't break with the rules of evidence. You can't risk arresting an innocent man because you are positive in your own mind that he is guilty. You prosecute a war, yes; but you also live with your conscience."

These were the Spaniards—the imitators of our system and our methods—to whom we denied arms and foodstuffs in violation of international law. While we slowly shut them out from all access to the means of their defense, we permitted Germany and Italy to violate the nonintervention agreement by sending Franco arms and men. Is it any wonder that Mussolini scoffed at the democracies after the victory of Franco?

Claiming that Italy had made that victory, Mussolini said in a public speech: "Foreign anti-Fascism is truly incurably, stupendously ignorant of Italian ways—all of which does not disturb us in the least. After all, it is better not to be too well known, for surprise will then have its full effect. Our enemies are too stupid to be dangerous."

In Great Britain, Clement Attlee, the leader of the opposition, rose to protest the Franco victory which the Chamberlain government had made possible and which it proposed to make secure by the immediate recognition of the Franco government.

Major Attlee said: "The government's sham of nonintervention was really designed to prevent the Spanish government from exercising its rights under international law. The British government connived at the starving of women and children, the bombing of open towns, and the slaying of men, women, and children. Now it is scrambling with indecent haste to try to make friends with Franco. This is not in the interests of democracy or of the safety of the British Empire. The government is thinking all the time of the interests of British capitalists. What does it mean to the government if Gibraltar is in danger if we get Río Tinto dividends? . . . There was a time when this country was universally known as the friend of liberty and the freedom of peoples and as the enemy of tyrants. It is now being regarded more and more as a nation that will acquiesce in any form of tyranny and always stand in favor of the dictatorships."

Major Attlee did not mean that the British policy of non-intervention had been designed to protect British interests in the Río Tinto copper mines. He meant that Chamberlain's haste in recognizing Franco was inspired by that consideration. The destruction of the Spanish Republic came not from the machinations of international capitalism but from the incomprehension of the British, French, and American peoples and the incompetence of their governments. It is true that the Spanish War disclosed an extraordinary and perhaps unprecedented phenomenon of international capitalism, the emergence of class feeling over monetary self-interest. Spain had the third or fourth largest gold reserve in the world and yet she found that the international arms manufacturers, oil companies, and the like declined to sell to her in the very moment when they were willing to extend credits to Franco. It would be a service to the American public if someone ventilated the activities of certain New York corporations and law firms. But the story of the betrayal of Spain is the story still of the failure of democracy before the superior propaganda methods and statecraft of Hitler and Mussolini. Brains won in Spain and our enemies had them.

The Germans and Italians succeeded in dividing American

opinion and in making this nation forget to observe developments in Spain from the coldly realistic point of view of our own national interest—the interest of a nation which lies in a hemisphere which is half Spanish-speaking. The American government left the initiatives to Great Britain and France. Acting with the most praiseworthy motives, these two democracies announced the policy of nonintervention. They proposed to localize the struggle in Spain by calling on Berlin, Rome, and Moscow, as well, to abstain from intervention. Léon Blum assembled a diplomatic parley on August 8, 1936 —three weeks after the inception of the rebellion. We anticipated the decision. On August 7, in a statement by William Phillips, the acting Secretary of State, we declared that we would "scrupulously refrain from any interference whatsoever in the unfortunate Spanish situation."

The statement read by Mr. Phillips admitted that our embargo legislation "has no application in the present situation" —since it was contrary to international law to deny the purchase of arms to a legally constituted government acting to put down rebellion or civil war. Nevertheless we did deny the Republic that right. We brought suasion to bear immediately on American exporters and subsequently, January 8, 1937, the White House and State Department persuaded Congress to enact a formal embargo. Naturally the Germans and Italians made a travesty of the nonintervention policy. When Mr. Roosevelt was urged—in face of the fact of Italo-German intervention—to raise the embargo, he pleaded the division of American opinion. The Germans by then had made a travesty of that too. Great Britain, France, and America—in order to spare themselves trouble—had invented a diplomatic solution which denied the Spanish Republic its rights. No one of the great democracies championed democracy in Spain. Hitler and Mussolini risked world war to champion and achieve the victory of Fascism there.

American policy had been doomed to failure from the first because it had been based on a fundamental fallacy. For some generations the State Department has tacitly accepted a vaguely defined theorem that we would follow, or at least not obstruct, British policy on the continent of Europe and, as a corollary, we have assumed that the British would respect our initiatives in Latin American affairs. There was nothing wrong with this policy except that it was outmoded. It depended upon Britain's effective manipulation of the balance of power in Europe. But by 1936 Great Britain, unless supported by the United States, could no longer assert the authority which she had maintained for nearly a century. Historically Britain had lost that eminence after the exhausting efforts of 1914–1918. From Versailles onward the balance of world power had shifted from London to Washington. Even in European continental politics Britain was no longer the supreme arbiter. By 1936 Germany was outarming the Anglo-French combination almost two to one. Great Britain could reestablish her control of continental affairs only at the risk of war. This she was loath to do. Germany and Italy could be defeated in Spain and the Monroe Doctrine protected from Fascism in South America only by the effective intervention of American diplomacy. This was difficult so long as America remained isolationist, with the Congress intimidated by a minority faction of the American Catholics. Did President Roosevelt and Mr. Hull see the Spanish issue clearly, or did they lack the courage to inform and lead American opinion? History will tell us—unless history is written by Dr. Goebbels.

Since their victory the Franco Spaniards have worked against us in every country of Latin America. Our ships have been sunk as fast as we could build them because Spanish embassies and consulates—formally charged with the affairs of Germany, Italy, and Japan—have sent voluminous espionage reports in diplomatic code. More than a hundred Franco diplomats went into Germany for special schooling in German espionage before they were sent into Latin America. They helped the Germans turn countries like Argentina against us. They spread German propaganda against the United States among the Catholic clergy and the reactionary business elements of the Americas to the south. They instructed in sabotage. They organized the espionage and the fifth columns for the Unholy Alliance of Germany, Italy, and Japan.

When I was last in Spain, six months before Pearl Harbor, the Spaniards made no secret of their plans. Serrano Suñer, the Foreign Minister, spoke to Mr. Alexander Weddell, the American Ambassador, with a truculence which showed his confidence in our ultimate defeat. Since Mr. Weddell has now been replaced by Mr. Carlton J. H. Hayes, and the Foreign Minister removed, it is no indiscretion to repeat that Serrano Suñer informed him that he "believed in, desired, and worked for German victory." His statement is amplified daily in the Spanish press which appears under the direction of certain of the 2000 German agents resident in Madrid.

When General Franco dismissed Serrano Suñer as foreign minister and secretary of the Falange party in September, 1942, his action in no way changed the basic foreign policy of Spain. Franco has the unhappy example of Mussolini before him. He does not intend to strike a blow for Hitler unless and until he is persuaded that it can be the final blow. Spain is too vulnerable before the British blockade. Three years of Franco's regime have done as much to destroy the nation's economy as three years of Franco's war. There is actual starvation in Spain. Accordingly Franco welcomes such relief as America and Great Britain are willing to extend him. In dropping his own brother-in-law, Franco has exploited Serrano Suñer's unpopularity and the nationwide realization of how badly Spain has been ruled by the Falange. The move was essentially a reflection of the internal unrest and instability of the Franco regime. The Caudillo had already long ago persuaded the Fuehrer that neutral Spain could serve the cause of Germany better than belligerent Spain. And then the American troops landed in North Africa.

VII

PEACE IN OUR TIME

THE night is somber under sullen thunderclouds as Prague waits, intense and breathless, for the German bombers. Our hotel suite has been blacked out and velvet curtains, ransacked from God knows where, hang over the doors to the balcony. These faded curtains are somehow theatrical and they make the room seem more unreal and oppressive—a room in a bad dream where the walls close in on you relentlessly. Too nervous to sit still, I go repeatedly to the balcony over Wenceslaus Square to listen to the patter of feet in the streets far below as men, made purposeful by mobilization, hasten toward the Wilson-Masaryk railway station. Why do they walk in silence? If only they were less quiet, less hurried. Then I wander back into the windowless bathroom, where we have put a bootleg electric light into the socket. Folding towels into the lavatory to make a firm base for the typewriter, I sit sideways on the toilet seat and begin to write my dispatch.

The restlessness disappears with the clatter of the keys and I chuckle approvingly at acoustics which would have satisfied the most exacting bathroom tenor. The words flow into sentences and paragraphs—a long dispatch—4000 words of copy for fifty-odd newspapers half a world away, written for readers who yawn over them with breakfast coffee, for complacently comfortable Americans with the spectator complex —Americans to whom the crucifixion of another nation is remote and impersonal like a flood in Yünnan or an earthquake in Chile. Thinking about such readers—if a nation values anything more than freedom . . . if a nation forgets that peace is universal and indivisible—I find that I must go back to the balcony.

I beat my way there over and over again, but twice I have stumbled already on the gas mask and the steel helmet. Finally I kick them under the bed in surprisingly savage temper. On the balcony my will power fails me. In spite of myself I search the murky skies and listen, tightfisted in my concentration, for the first distant drone of the planes. There are one thousand bombers earmarked for a job on our town, according to the German agents who have already cleared out. There won't be any warning. They'll just arrive and unload. This is the real McCoy. It's on us now and it's our job to stick and take it and then to write about it. We've had it before on one story or another but never the way this is going to be.

I make my old joke to H. R. Knickerbocker. "Are we ready for the Red Indians?" He and I mean "Can we take it when the torture begins?" This is the real thing this time and Knickerbocker grins. Finally my disptach is ended. I don't like it and pencil through it to smooth the hastily constructed paragraphs. It's ready now for America—maybe my last dispatch for America. Knickerbocker chuckles, "You can't go home with it."

The dispatch began: "Unafraid before the military might of Greater Germany and ready if need be to defend its independence with arms, Prague, the capital city, is blacked out. It has already been emptied of military reserves under forty years of age, and many a home, with the husband and father gone, waits tremulously for the air-raid siren.

"Across the frontier in Nazi Germany is Hitler, the man who can send the airplanes. The peace, not merely of this little democracy but of all Europe, rests in the hands of that dictator. Czechoslovakia has done all that it could. Hitler asked that this little country should cede to him the area which is inhabited by German-speaking Sudetens. France and Great Britain, fearful of war, abandoned Czechoslovakia and urged such concessions as have never been demanded of any undefeated country in history.

"The Czech government yielded, but no sooner had it surrendered than Hitler in his talks with Neville Chamberlain at Godesberg raised new and more difficult demands. He wanted not only the Sudeten area; he proposed, also, the Czechs understand, to march the German army into all other areas where there are German-speaking minorities and then, after a military occupation of three months, to stage a plebiscite whereby they would vote for union with Germany.

"This made the aims of Hitler clear even to Mr. Chamberlain. Gone was the pretense of defending the Sudeten minority. There, in stark nakedness, was the German plan to dismember Czechoslovakia utterly. Even Mr. Chamberlain recognized this as unacceptable and late yesterday the British and French ministers so informed President Beneš of Czechoslovakia.

" 'The Godesberg conversations have failed. You must take all the necessary precautions to defend yourself against an immediate attack by Germany.' This is what the British and the French diplomats told Beneš, according to the Czechs. That was the signal for mobilization. At 10:15 tonight the radio sounded that complete mobilization was ordered.

" 'Our struggle is just,' said the radio. 'Our motherland and freedom, long live Czechoslovakia.' As these words sounded, the thousands in the street uttered a single deep-throated cheer. It was the roar of people who say, 'Better to die on your feet than to live like slaves on your knees.'

"Trams were piled into; taxicabs and private cars commandeered. Thousands rushed frantically to clasp their wives, perhaps for the last time; to collect a knife, fork, and spoon, two days of food, and an extra pair of shoes. From the railway station, named after Masaryk, the late Czech President, and Woodrow Wilson, these soldiers fanned out in dozens of directions to stand under arms in their appointed places."

A sober, pacifist people, the Czechs were glad, nevertheless, to receive the mobilization order, as I tried to explain in the rest of my dispatch. Free for a brief twenty years, after nearly a century as a subject people, the Czechs were willing to fight. The mobilization order came as a relief after the announcement three nights before that Britain and France had abandoned them. There had been a peremptory notice by the British and French ministers to President Beneš that Czechoslovakia should agree to the immediate annexation by Germany of the Sudeten regions. In the gathering dusk loudspeakers over the city of Prague had suddenly blared this tragic announcement of the Godesberg ultimatum. In conclusion the radio spokesman had declared, "This case is unique in history; our friends and allies have imposed upon us such terms as are usually dictated to a defeated enemy." The people had come down into the streets to protest. Bowed low by their grief, they had marched in vast thousands down Wenceslaus Square, named after the good king of the carol. The crowd had been so orderly that even the fruit of a vender's cart, caught in the parade, passed safely through without one apple or pear falling to the ground. But now, three days later, the Czechs faced war. They were deadly grim, but in their hearts they were glad. Occasionally an individual lifted a cheer and hundreds around him smiled grimly, clear-eyed, with their shoulders back, conscious that though they might be going to their death they were going as a free people.

While the Czech mobilization proceeded—a miracle of quiet bourgeois efficiency—the French prime minister, M. Daladier, and his Foreign Minister, M. Bonnet, flew Sunday evening, September 25, to London, where General Gamelin joined them on Monday. General Gamelin complained that his report on the state of the French army had not been properly presented. Only its more pessimistic sections had been quoted to the authorities in London. M. Georges Bonnet, the French Foreign Minister, was a defeatist and he was connected with financial interests which were gambling on capitulation to Germany. General Gamelin told the British that the French army was in a position to fulfill its tasks successfully and to win ultimate victory. Later I learned that he made much of Germany's inadequate defensive positions along the Rhine and characterized the West Wall as "like marmalade." Then M. Daladier, as Premier of France, stated formally that if Czechoslovakia were attacked France would fulfill her treaty obligations to make war against Germany. In his turn Chamberlain pledged that, if French forces became engaged in hostilities against Germany, Britain would feel obliged to lend them support. Early in the evening of September 26 "an authoritative statement" was issued by the British Foreign Office.

It contained the following significant paragraph: "The German claim to the transfer of the Sudeten area has already been conceded by the French, British, and Czechoslovak governments; but if, in spite of all efforts made by the British Prime Minister, a German attack is made upon Czechoslovakia the immediate result must be that France will be bound to come to her assistance, and Great Britain and Russia will certainly stand by France."

Beyond the blunt warning of British intervention there was the intimation that at last London was in touch with Moscow. As Hamilton Fish Armstrong has pointed out, Chamberlain had given a pledge never given before; Daladier and Bonnet held in their hands the pledge which Poincaré and Viviani could not get from Grey in August, 1914—a pledge which then might have averted the first World War. This time France stood with England by her side from the start—"reluctant, still seeking a means to save peace, not well prepared, but reconciled to accepting France's decision if in her eyes it seemed necessary to risk a possible war to win a tolerable peace."

Had France stood firm, she could have preserved her honor, her independence, and her position as a major power. The geographic position of Czechoslovakia alone made that small state a formidable ally for France and a dangerous enemy for Germany. Bismarck had described Czechoslovakia as the "bastion" of the defense of Europe. "The master of Bohemia is the master of the continent," he said. She was more than that. She curled deep into the German Reich, like a claw, and from her airdromes the great industrial centers of Germany were only a few hours' flight. Bastion and claw, she was more besides. As the ally of France and the ally of Russia, Czechoslovakia served as the bridge between western Europe and the massed millions of the Soviet Union. Czecho- slovakia held together a coalition of powers which threatened the encirclement of Germany. These were the three strategic aspects of Czechoslovakia which inspired German aggression. Austria had been annexed only partially in order to add 7,000,000 Germans to the population of the Reich, but essen- tially because of Austria's strategic position, its mountain of iron ore, and its resources of timber and wheat. Czechoslo- vakia stood as the bridgehead between France and Russia, as the only terrain from which Germany could be effectively bombed, and as the well-armed and stubborn nation which could immobilize enough of the German army to guarantee the French a position of preponderant strength in the West. In addition there were the Skoda works at Pilsen, one of the world's greatest armaments factories. Hitler proved at Berch- tesgaden, Godesberg, and Munich that he sought not the annexation of the German minority of the Sudetenland but the destruction of the Czech state.

If France had fought before Munich, Germany would have enjoyed superiority in the air—but in nothing else. While German factories had already given Goering a formidable air force, French production was hopelessly bogged down and Britain's effort was still in the stage of factory construc- tion. Paris would have been hard to defend and London certainly had made no preparation against Goering's bomb- ers. The Royal Air Force had not been expanded and it was a well-known military secret that there were only eleven antiaircraft guns for the defense of the whole of London. While Paris and London would have to shiver their way through the first stages of such a war, Czechoslovakia had to face the possibility of her own total destruction in from three to six weeks. The German plan called for three weeks. Six weeks was the most pessimistic estimate of Czech generals with whom I talked. But the Czechs, and their generals especially, were willing to risk defeat in the confidence of final Anglo-French victory and their own ultimate resurrection as a free nation.

It must be remembered that in the fall of 1938 the German army had completed neither its training nor its rearmament. At best Germany could mobilize 140 divisions. Czechoslovakia had only 35 divisions. But the Czechs had the best system of fortifications in the world, scientifically built by Skoda with the cooperation of the French General Staff, so that they incorporated all the lessons of the Maginot line. Czechoslovakia was vulnerable, of course, on her Austrian frontier but the fort system through the Sudeten mountains was the most formidable obstacle to an army I have ever seen—more impressive to me than the Maginot line. Germany's total strength stood at 140 divisions, but France had three times as many trained reserves. To march into Czechoslovakia against 35 Czech divisions—the best-equipped army in the world—Germany would have needed 70 divisions as an absolute minimum. This would have left only 70 divisions to stand in the West against an overwhelming French superiority. Czech resistance—even if for only six weeks—would have brought Russian reinforcements through Rumania, according to Russian assurances which convinced President Beneš. If Germany attempted to cut these off by moving through Hungary, that would automatically have brought Yugoslavia into the war. Such was the Czech scheme and Czechoslovakia was no Poland.

What was the German plan and the prospect of its success? No more reckless gamble, based on one dubious contingency after another, has ever been envisaged. Immediately after the annexation of Austria—seven months before Munich—the German War Academy offered a prize for the best scheme of operations against Czechoslovakia and her French and Russian allies. The winning author was Colonel Conrad, chief of staff of the army corps with headquarters at Salzburg. Colonel Conrad outlined a three-week *Blitz* whereby Czechoslovakia's army was to be surrounded and overwhelmed. The success of the operation depended upon a timetable of three weeks because Colonel Conrad estimated that this would be the minimum period for French mobilization. He expected to return the German armies from Czechoslovakia to the western front before France attempted an invasion of Germany. He hoped that France, viewing the swift obliteration of Czechoslovakia, would abandon any attempt to invade Germany. Conrad assumed that Russia could offer no help because "in consequence of Stalin's methods, Russia for the time being is incapable of making war." He assumed that no interference need be expected from Great Britain. He assumed that the Czechs, "threatened by betrayal among their own ranks and confronted by superior power and attack from all sides, would morally and militarily go to pieces." The whole success of this German plan depended upon the destruction of Czechoslovakia in three weeks and had any one of the German assumptions gone wrong the swift defeat of Germany would have become inevitable.

Men like Chamberlain and Daladier—even levelheaded men like Mr. Hull—persuaded themselves that Great Britain and France were not prepared for war. Of course they were not. But they were better prepared for war against Germany in 1938 than in 1939—relatively. Time marched on the side of Hitler since he was rearming at the rate of two to one over Great Britain and France combined. Time marched at the side of Hitler because no armaments program undertaken by Britain or France could compensate for the destruction of Czechoslovakia as an ally and for the loss of Russia, since it was the final capitulation at Munich which drove Stalin to the unhappy expediency of a pact with Hitler. The argument that Britain and France were unprepared dismissed the well-trained and patriotic Czech army; its "Maginot line"; and its wealth of modern armaments, backed by Skoda. These arguments dismissed the role of British sea power at a moment when Germany's stocks of raw materials and food-stuffs were insufficient. Most important of all, they dismissed the mood of the German people in 1938.

In that year the Germans had not been taught by the British and French cowardice to believe that no one could stand before the mighty Third Reich of Adolf Hitler. In 1938 the German people never dreamed in their worst night-mares that Hitler was risking war. While millions in London, Paris, and Washington shivered through the Czech crisis, the German public had no sense that war was in the balance. In Berlin a few months before I had watched their fright and panic when they learned in midsummer the true details of the earlier Czech crisis of May, 1938. It was not until mid-summer that the German public learned that in the spring France and Czechoslovakia had begun their mobilizations after a decision to fight. The nationwide panic was all the more ludicrous because it came two months after the event. But it did not seem ludicrous to Hitler and the generals when the bottom suddenly fell out of the German stock market. From then until Munich itself, Hitler's propaganda machine carefully persuaded the public that Hitler was bar-gaining diplomatically but that under no circumstances would he risk war. Had Britain and France fought instead of going to Munich, the morale of the German masses would scarcely have stood the shock. October, 1938, was the last moment when opposition to Hitler and war by large elements within Germany might have been expected by the democracies.

"My God! I can't believe it. If Britain and France had stood firm, Germany would have gone into revolt after two weeks of fighting," a German colonel in the Sudetenland told

me shortly after Munich. I believed him too—only revolt
might have come after two years rather than two weeks of
fighting.

Their own lack of armaments, however, made the gamble
look too cruel to French and British statesmen who wanted
peace more than they wanted anything else and who believed
that "in war there are no winners." To men who know that
defeat is worse than war itself, it was plain that the odds were
better than they would ever be again. It was plain to Winston
Churchill in 1938. It was still plain to Winston Churchill in
1941. During his visit with Mr. Roosevelt, in December of
1941, Churchill said to a friend of mine, "Munich? It was
the greatest blunder in modern history. Of course, we should
have fought then. That ought to be plain to everyone now."

While the statesmen of France threw away the independence of their country and the British nearly lost theirs,
Hitler played a game of consummate skill. His nerves alone
stood the strain. France mobilized and the British fleet
steamed to battle posts, while gas masks were distributed and
trenches dug in Hyde Park. As always, initiative rested in
the hands of Hitler. He had told Chamberlain at Godesberg
when they talked on September 22 that his troops would enter Czechoslovakia on October 1. The clocks ticked inexorably and Chamberlain and Daladier steeled themselves to the
realization that it was war if Hitler acted. Monday, September 26, the British Foreign Office had issued the announcement that Britain would stand with France in war. The next
day Hitler spoke in the Sport-Palast. The whole world waited
anxiously for the hoarse, almost hysterical rush of gutturals.
Hitler denounced Beneš as a criminal and the animal roar of
the thousands in the Sport-Palast seemed to take the roof off
as they chanted "Sieg Heil! Sieg Heil!" But Hitler was a
calculating madman. Under the harsh language there was a
slight recession—such a recession as badly shaken wishful
thinkers in Paris and London could find when they looked
for it.

The door was not slammed. War was not inevitable. President Roosevelt made a dramatic appeal for peace. Chamberlain went on the air. With a break in his voice the Prime Minister of Great Britain said that he would labor for peace to the end but added, almost with a sob, that Britain would fight if "any nation made up its mind to dominate the world by fear of force." Just when he seemed strongest—frighteningly strong to himself, no doubt—Chamberlain displayed his own lack of will by sending back to Berlin Sir Horace Wilson, the Foreign Office official who invented appeasement. Hitler knew then that he was winning. He knew that the clock was ticking, ticking, ticking, until men of peace could scarcely bear the awesome noise. Mr. Roosevelt sent a second appeal and by then Hitler felt certain enough of his own position to reject it curtly.

Suddenly Hitler piled the blue chips high, threatening a showdown. He changed the expiration of his ultimatum from October 1 to 2:00 P.M., September 28. As panic swept Chamberlain and Daladier, Hitler held out an ersatz olive branch. His brilliant second, the badly frightened Mussolini, intervened to delay the zero hour from the afternoon of the twenty-eighth to the afternoon of the twenty-ninth. On the afternoon of the twenty-eighth the House of Commons met in the most momentous session since August of 1914. Chamberlain revealed that he had written once again, imploring Hitler not to precipitate a world catastrophe, urging Mussolini to hold back the German dictator. Through Chamberlain's speech there ran a sorrowful refrain: all this nerve-racking crisis concerned an agreement already reached in principle; all this fear of war came after Britain and France had already sacrificed Czechoslovakia. Hitler was not yet master of Europe, but he was able to manipulate this dramatic scene in the House of Commons like an impresario of genius. Suddenly a messenger crossed to the governmental bench. Chamberlain clutched at a piece of paper.

Falling again into the matter-of-fact tone which is affected in the Commons, Chamberlain said: "I have something further to tell the House. I have now been informed by Herr Hitler that he invites me to meet him in Munich tomorrow morning. He has also invited Signor Mussolini and M. Daladier. Signor Mussolini has accepted and I have no doubt that M. Daladier will also accept. The House will not need to ask what my answer will be."

The Four Power Conference was convened at Munich on September 29. Its deliberations were behind closed doors, with the emissaries of Czechoslovakia ejected. Hitler stood on his original date and it was agreed that on October 1 the Germans should begin the occupation of the four Sudeten districts, the annexation of additional regions being reserved for plebiscites under the supervision of an international commission. Germany and Italy agreed to join Britain and France in guaranteeing the new frontiers. Thus in a few hours the great democracies disposed of their twenty-year-old brother nation. Thus a black sheet was pulled over the only democracy in Central Europe, the only land where every school child in every schoolhouse had been taught for twenty years to recite passages from the Magna Charta, the American Constitution, and Lincoln's Gettysburg Address. Thus a French Premier disturbed the sleep of half a million of his countrymen in the bloody soil of Verdun and a British Prime Minister withered the poppies from Ypres to Chemin des Dames. Fighting a war of nerves alone, Hitler had turned the defeat of the Kaiser into Germany's greatest victory.

Arriving in England twenty-four hours later, Chamberlain murmured, "I think it is peace in our time"; and he was cheered madly by the crowd. Daladier, expecting to be assassinated, found an equally warm reception upon his return to France, where the people were oblivious of everything except the fact that war had been averted. Relief! Europe had waked up and the nightmare was not true. Outside Prague in his country home Beneš walked backward and forward in his small library, saying over and over again, like a maniac, "I can't believe the French did it—I can't believe the French did it." I stood in the streets of a Sudeten village which had been wrapped in swastikas, waiting for Hitler to come. It was raining. A German colonel and Edward Beattie, of the United Press, waited together. Hitler was late and we were cold. Beattie turned to the colonel. "How much longer are we going to have to wait for that pop-eyed bastard?" the correspondent asked. "Thank God," I thought, "that one man at least has retained a sense of proportion."

While the world had held its breath anxiously, Chamberlain and Daladier had played at poker. Hitler had won, but there was no war. The world looked around for new excitements, oblivious that its own fate had been at stake. Everyone forgot that in this, as in any other game, counters are required. The chips in this hand were human beings—the Czech and Slovak peoples. I never liked two peoples more. As Slavs they remained unaffectedly artistic, preserving their traditional dances and peasant costumes while they cultivated the higher arts. As moderns they were a thoroughly business-like and common-sense people. In attacking Spain, Hitler had called it red and people had believed him since the middle class in Spain was relatively new and uninfluential. Indeed President Azaña had said that democracy could never work smoothly in Spain until the country built up a middle class. Czechoslovakia was bourgeois to the core and it honored all the bourgeois qualities. Hitler described the country as red and communistic, but not even the credulous Western World swallowed that one.

If democracy depends upon the education of the masses, it is easy to understand why this twenty-year-old country proved so brilliantly successful as a democracy. Everyone read and almost nothing of interest was published anywhere without being translated at Prague. A book of my own which had flopped in America, and clung precariously to the bestseller list in England for three short weeks, was a sensation in Czechoslovakia. The Czech editions had been beautifully printed and I was both flattered and moved to find that waiters in restaurants, cabdrivers and army officers, and even censors brought me well-read copies, asking me to write them a few words. I was especially struck that everyone in the censorship office wanted autographs. I don't know how censors are selected, but in most countries they seem to be individuals chosen out of sheer perversity because they can't or don't read. In Czechoslovakia the chief censor was a professor of philosophy from the University of Prague. A more cultivated, charming, and understanding man I have never met. He was both profoundly shrewd and profoundly innocent. Truth to him was not something abstract in a philosophical system. It was tangible. He took great delight in any unusual or exclusive story we brought for his rubber stamp. In fact, this caused us some embarrassment. If he had been impressed by an exclusive story which you tried to guard secretly until its publication in America, he would tell all your colleagues about it and urge them to write it too. When I reproached him, he was honestly bewildered.

"But, my dear fellow, your story is true and it is interesting," he would say. "Surely you don't mean to suggest that in journalism there is a monopoly of the truth. Don't you want all the other newspapers in your country and in other countries to help you make the truth prevail?"

This is the kind of man, of course, that afterward the Germans slowly beat to death. This was the kind of mentality which enabled the Czechs to treat their minorities with moderation. The German-speaking people of the Sudetenland (which, incidentally, had never been German but had belonged to the Austro-Hungarian Empire) received better treatment than any other minority in Europe. The Czechs did to them none of the things the Italians did to 300,000 German-speaking folk in the Italian Tyrol. To the Italian Fascists it seemed natural to chip German names off the very tombstones; to the Czechs and Slovaks this would have been a ghoulish outrage.

Democracy, with its moderation and liberalism, does work. The Czech democracy had served as a living proof of the superiority of our system. A single example, perhaps, will suffice. In Slovakia the Prague government solved the Jewish problem as no other country solved it in the whole of Central Europe. The new government, set up at Versailles, found a deplorable situation in the small villages of Slovakia. In almost every village the Jews ran the inn, dispensed the drinks, and served as the moneylenders. The whole community was in debt to them and anti-Semitism was a problem. How did Prague face this? The Czechs set up state banks in each town with nominal interest charges, which, of course, meant the destruction of the Jewish moneylenders and of usury. But the Czechs were not anti-Semitic. They went to the moneylenders, explained their program and the reasons for it, and offered the Jews jobs in state banks at fixed salaries. As a result of this policy Maurice Hindus and I found twenty years later that this was the only region in Central Europe where there was virtually no feeling against Jews. The Jews themselves in several towns said that they preferred to work for the state institutions, that the whole community was richer under the new system, and that they themselves had flourished among friendly neighbors.

The discipline of the Czechs under German provocation made me marvel. The Germans had fomented disorders in the Sudeten region for many months. In the period after Hitler spoke at Nuremberg (September 9 to October 1) the Germans attempted armed rebellion in that region. They proposed to provide a pretext for their military occupation of the Sudetenland. The Berlin radio raged against atrocities, the mistreatment of Germans, and pitched battles in the streets of Sudeten towns. They employed the technique and the methods I had already seen in Austria and which the journalists were to see again at Danzig and in Poland.

Now it was the duty of a journalist to know and report whether these German charges were true. If the Czechs were terrorizing the German-speaking elements, that was news. If the two sides were fighting pitched battles, that was news. The Germans and Czechs alike poured atrocity stories into the ears of neutral journalists. I have always had two strict rules as a newspaperman. I don't announce the discovery of new gold fields. I report no atrocity story which I have not seen with my own eyes. Consequently, the only way to report atrocity stories in the Sudeten region was to go up and see what was going on. The Chicago *Daily News* already had Marcel Fodor to report political developments in Prague, and Fodor was probably the best authority in the world on Central Europe. I therefore drove back and forth between Prague and the German frontier—the dangerous and terrifying job of trying to be there when the shooting begins—a self-assignment as a professional innocent bystander.

There was a curfew, of course, and the Czech *gendarmerie* and soldiery could challenge your car or shoot without challenging, just as they liked. After having been shot at a few times, I used to turn the wheel over to a colleague and walk ahead of the car when we approached bridges or villages. The Czech soldiers were jumpy and just as scared as I was, so that some of those walks were very lonely indeed. Then you had to watch for areas in the roadways which were mined. Finally you had to guess at about which point you were going into the German-held lines, because it would have been unfortunate to have cried out to the Germans in the night the few Czech salutations we had learned. One night Sefton Delmar, of the *Daily Express* of London, parked his car in the square of one of those sleepy Sudeten towns. We went into the inn, since we might as well have a beer, we thought, as study our maps in the cold car. That was good beer. On the first sip we heard the rattle of a tommy gun. We found that the windshield of the car had been pulverized. That was just another German miss, but a miss which was as good as a mile.

The Sudeten Nazis were a pretty cowardly and uncertain lot. They had never wanted to be annexed to the German Reich and come under Nazi rule. But they did want autonomy from Prague. Consequently, German efforts to arm them and turn them into a fifth column were not very successful. The disorders in that region were fomented by armed invasion. Germany put some 20,000 troublemakers on the frontiers. Organized as the Frei-Korps, these fellows were tough and proficient in the technique of violence. They were superbly armed with tommy guns and grenades, and when they moved in force they used mortars and heavy machine guns. Their organization explained an unusual phenomenon which puzzled anyone with intimate knowledge of Sudeten towns. The German radio would announce that a certain Sudeten village "of two thousand souls" had risen in arms against the "unspeakable Czech terror." The trouble was that the total population of this village would stand at only 789 men, women, and children. This could not have been a remarkable phenomenon if it had not been repeated in one tiny village after another. I found that some two thousand soldiers of the German Frei-Korps would cross the frontier and attack a town, murdering everyone in the Czech gendarme station and searching out the mayor and other Czech officials of the town, while the local pro-German elements hid in their cellars or under their beds.

The moderation of the Czechs under such provocation astonished me. One day at noon I watched a pitched battle for such a village between 3000 Frei-Korps soldiers and a battalion of about 1000 men from the Czech army. Finding Czech soldiers were there to protect the village, the Frei-Korps fell back to make its getaway. The Czech soldiers sniped away at them with rifles. I expressed to a Czech major my astonishment that he used neither his machine guns nor his field artillery.

"I act under orders, sir," he said. "My orders are to avoid pitched battle and to answer the Germans with rifle fire alone. I suppose Prague has sound reasons for these orders. I suppose the government wants to give the Germans no pretext for invasion."

My blood boiled at this sort of moderation when I went into another village thirty minutes after the ejection of Frei-Korps raiders. There was still heavy rifle fire on the other side of the village as I slammed on my car brakes before the *gendarmerie,* and was suddenly yanked from my car and knocked down before my frantic squawk that I was an American correspondent stayed the butt of a gun raised over my head by a Czech soldier who meant to beat my brains out. He had thought that I was a Frei-Korps German and I shared his anger when I went into the *gendarmerie* headquarters. It was a two-story building and not a piece of furniture remained intact. The bodies of seven Czech gendarmes lay about in the *gendarmerie* station, where the walls and floor seemed wholly covered with blood. These seven men had tried to defend this little town against thousands of Germans. They had died at their posts in a hopeless battle, three shot, three killed by grenades—a messy business—and one bayoneted through the stomach and throat. We thought this last still breathed, but he was dead. After cleaning out the *gendarmerie* post the Germans had gone to the little post office in a baker's shop to pick up the baker and his wife, who served as the postmistress. The townspeople were torn between anger, shock, and fright when they told us the story. The Germans had put ropes around the throats of the baker and his wife and dragged them through the streets to an open-pit mine at the edge of the town. There we recovered their bodies. The woman· had been scalped as her head dragged the paving stones. The Germans had been successful, however. I never saw more frightened people than the people of this little town. I knew how they would welcome the next arrival of Germans. People with that kind of terror in their eyes would greet Hitler with a passion of hysteria. I could already hear them screaming, "Ein Volk, ein Reich, ein Fuehrer." These German-speaking villagers who in twenty years of Czech rule had never gazed on a scene of violence now learned what it means to oppose the onward sweep of *Groesser Deutschland*.

The day that Chamberlain flew to Godesberg, Knickerbocker and I heard a curious tip in Prague. The Henlein people there—Henlein himself had long ago fled into Germany for fear of being treated as the traitor he was—whispered that the Germans were going to kill all the Czechs in Asch. This little town, north of Eger, was situated in a Sudeten appendix which the Germans meant to snip off as a test of whether the Czechs would fight at the outright annexation of several of their towns in a moment when the British were coming to terms with Hitler. In Asch, Knick and I went directly to Henlein's headquarters. The Henlein group had been formally proscribed, but Prague, afraid of reaction abroad, stayed the prosecution of these traitors and we had no difficulty in finding their office. The only change was the removal of the sign over the doorway and the substitution within of Germans for Sudetens. Two Gestapo officers received Knick and me with a great clicking of heels and a to-what-do-we-owe-this-honor manner. We put our cards on the table. We said that we had heard from the Henlein people in Prague that the Germans meant to take Asch that night.

"Jawohl!" snapped the senior of the two officers, with startling frankness. "By dawn tomorrow there will be no Czechs alive in this town." He smiled knowingly. "Stay around," he said, "and see if anything happens to you."

Knick and I changed the subject to the general situation. Did the Herr Major know that Chamberlain had flown to Godesberg?

"Jawohl!"

Did the Herr Major not believe that Britain and France had decided at last to make a stand and that Herr Hitler would now decide upon a more cautious game? Rarely have I seen such scorn in a man.

"Absurb," he said. "Hitler will tell Chamberlain that we want all of the Sudetenland, that troops of the German army will march into that region at dawn October 1. Chamberlain will then know what he has to do. He will know that he has to prepare Britain and France for their humiliation."

This conversation took place at 5:00 P.M., September 22. Knick and I laughed at the German major. We were to learn many days later that he had been right and to marvel that a Gestapo officer should have known so precisely in advance the full terms which Hitler demanded of Chamberlain. We thanked the major for his frankness; we volunteered that we now intended to talk with the Czech gendarmes but that we would say nothing to them, naturally, of what he had just told us about the German raid planned for that night. As a Gestapo officer, he would understand that a point of honor was involved: we didn't bear tales from one camp to another. Perhaps he caught the note of irony in Knickerbocker's "as a Gestapo officer." Ushering us to the doorway, he grinned, clicked his heels, and said, "Oh, that's all right. You will find that the Czechs know about the fate which awaits them."

Four blocks away we found the Czech *gendarmerie,* very much on the alert. Machine guns and grenades were being issued to the men, clusters of whom were busily loading cartridge belts. The chief of the station was on the telephone, but we were ushered into his office and stood before his desk until he terminated a long conversation in Czech. After we had produced our papers and exchanged amenities, Knickerbocker asked if there had been any trouble in Asch.

"Trouble? We are waiting for trouble tonight," said the Czech. "The Germans are planning to come across the frontier in force. We have specific information of their plans. They mean to strike at midnight."

We asked when the Czech army would move into the town.

"Our troops are not coming in," said the Czech. "I have just telephoned Prague for the fourth time today. Prague declines to send the army to Asch because that would mean a pitched battle and that's what Berlin wants. The gendarmes know what to do. Our orders are categoric. We are to remain in the *gendarmerie* post and to return fire only if and when we are attacked."

"How many are you?" I asked.

"We are seventy-one men," said the chief, proudly and defiantly. "Not a one of us will come out alive. But I think we know how to die."

The fatalistic chief of these Slav policemen shook our hands and excused himself. He wanted to talk with his men and make certain dispositions for their defense. Knickerbocker and I went to the little hotel in Asch, more moved than we liked to admit by the resignation of these men. We lay in our beds fully clothed, but we did not even bother to cut the electric lights. Neither of us could sleep, waiting for the first sound of firing. Nothing happened. Both of us must have dozed because we woke suddenly at 6:30 to the sounds of a village coming to life again. For some reason the Germans had not attacked. Something must have happened at Godesberg, we reasoned. We passed by the *gendarmerie* and congratulated the chief and his sleepless men upon their survival, and drove back to Prague. Six days later the Germans stormed this *gendarmerie* with mortars and hand grenades. Not a Czech survived, we learned.

This is the sort of thing the Germans did night after night in towns like Eger, Asch, Grazlitz, and Heinrichsgruen—beautiful mountain towns in the wooded country along the frontier, set among hop fields with pine-forested mountains for background. Once the Frei-Korps had subdued a town, the Gestapo arrived. They raced automobiles and motorcycles, mounted with machine guns, along the winding roads beside the beautiful trout streams. Out of the cars they dumped hundreds of swastikas and vast heaps of black and red bunting. The townsfolk were told to decorate the town in honor of its early inclusion in *Groesser Deutschland.* The Gestapo agents immediately undertook a house-to-house search for Czech officials and "Communists." They were shot out of hand. The Gestapo had another trick. All Sudetens of German origin who had married Czech wives were kidnapped and taken across the frontier. When the Czech troops went back into these towns to liberate them and restore the Czech flag, they showed a discipline and moderation which seemed incredible to me. I went back with the Czechs, for instance, into Heinrichsgruen. The Germans had left snipers on rooftops and in windows. The Czechs would not use their tanks or artillery for fear of further destruction and killing in the town. As a result, all the odds went to the German snipers. We restored Czech sovereignty, but the Czechs lost seven dead and thirty-one wounded. We found only three German dead.

After watching the behavior of the German Frei-Korps for a month, I thought I knew what the German occupation would mean. But it was worse than I had imagined. The same methodical, systematized murder is still going on in the fourth year of occupation. The Germans came into Czechoslovakia in four stages, first entering a zone along the Austrian frontier at dawn on October 1. Knickerbocker, Virginia Cowles, and I were the only journalists who saw the first entry of the German army. The three of us were sentenced to death together with a Czech gendarme in the mountain village of Oberplan, due south from Budweis, the home of the famous beer. The Gestapo charged us with being Czech spies and ordered our summary execution. Mr. Moto never talked as fast as we did. Mr. Moto, moreover, never did his talking with a tommy gun held against his spine, as I did. While we argued with the Gestapo officers in the town hall, a crowd outside roared for our blood. We had seen five murdered Czechs on the pavement in front of the town hall and we knew that this crowd meant business. Oberplan was a village, like most in the Sudetenland, composed entirely of village idiots. These Sudeten Germans are an inbred race, caught in mountain pockets, passed over by the civilizing force of Vienna. Hitler has Sudeten antecedents and it is no figment of a heightened imagination that I saw his face here and there among the crowd. Many of the Sudetens affect his mustache and brush a lock of hair over the brow. They have the same pale eyes and, tasting blood, as they had, these people looked wild-eyed and ridiculous at the same time. Once they were armed by the Gestapo they felt themselves fiercely heroic before the unarmed Czechs whose superior education, moral code, and self-discipline had been a constant reproach for years to the inhabitants of Hitler's Tobacco Road.

This was the tragedy of the initial German occupation. These mobs, given schnapps and arms by the Gestapo, killed savagely in the interim between the withdrawal of the Czech troops and the arrival of the German army. Their night of the long knives lasted roughly from 7:00 P.M. to 6:00 A.M. At nightfall the Czech army began to retire from the Sudeten zone, a tragic defile of men beaten without having been given a chance to fight. They withdrew in a drizzling rain, hauling back in every column mile after mile of magnificent field artillery, great trucks pulling 155 mm. guns, tanks grinding and roaring along the roadways. These columns were a study in grief. Closed up like the well-trained troops they were, the columns gave you the feeling of an army with its backbone broken. The men marched with their heads down on their chests, rain drizzling down the backs of their necks, and they neither sang nor raised the sound of orders being passed along by junior officers. They knew only too well what their orders were. They were coming back into Czechoslovakia, behind their magnificent system of fortifications, back to where they would have no chance to stand when the Germans struck again. Their backbone had been broken at Munich. And once they were withdrawn the killing among their own people began. The German army was too proud to permit indiscriminate murder of civilians in the streets. But the German army did not march in until eleven hours after the Czechs had gone out. You can shoot a man in the split second it takes to pull the trigger. As many Czechs were murdered in one village or another throughout the Sudeten mountains as there are split seconds in eleven hours.

In the midst of this terror we three Americans saved our hides. And we frightened the Gestapo officer into sparing the life of the Czech gendarme. Stupidly the Gestapo officer had given us his name, when we demanded it with a great show of huff as outraged Americans. Threatening to use all sorts of imaginary friendships in high place in Berlin, the three of us swore that if he killed the Czech we would see that Himmler killed him. All German bullies can be cowards. We watched every hesitation and doubt on the part of the Gestapo officer, and we pressed them home until he became at first unsure of himself and then frightened. Two hours before, he had not hesitated to slap my face. Now we demanded and got an apology from him. Better still, Virginia, a cool little cucumber, demanded gasoline for my car. The Gestapo officer got us half a tank of that precious, rationed fuel. Being American journalists who had interviewed Hitler, gone to the Nuremberg Conference, and met big shots like Goering and Himmler and General Blomberg, we were able to bluff for ourselves and the Czech gendarme.

But we were ashamed of ourselves. I was ashamed after Munich to be an American, to come from a democratic country, to be a friend of the British and French, and to have had any acquaintance with the Germans except that of fighting against them in trenches. I had a feeling that I wanted to do something violent, a feeling that I never heard expressed properly until nearly four years later. Mr. Churchill expressed it when he said, "What kind of people do they think we are?" I wanted to try to snatch a gun from the Gestapo officer and shoot him down. I wanted to go out into that crowd of village idiots below—not harmless but savage idiots—and say to them, "Listen, you swine, we aren't all the kind of people who went to Munich. We aren't men to stand by in impotence and cowardice and watch you shoot down unoffending and unarmed Czechs." I did nothing of the sort, of course. I shook the hand of the Gestapo officer, climbed in my car, and went on about the business of covering the entry of the German army and getting back to Prague to file my story.

Back in Prague the grief of the Czechs had a nightmarish quality. They knew what had happened. They were going once again to be a subject people, after twenty brief, bright years of freedom. I served as the go-between to arrange that President Beneš should take a professorship with the University of Chicago. Beneš felt that to leave by airplane was to abandon his people in the lurch. He was persuaded that no purpose would be served by his waiting until, captured, like Chancellor Schuschnigg, he could be slowly tortured to madness. Beneš would not leave, however, until he had exacted certain promises from those Czechs and Slovaks who would be compelled to treat with the Germans.

"Books are going to be burned, newspapers suppressed, Jews beaten, and trade unions dissolved," said Beneš. "Against this we can do nothing. We must carry out German orders when German orders come, but one thing we can do. We can see to it that no Czech or Slovak initiates such things on his own. The rats will try to come out now. Keep them down. See to it that no Czech burns books, suppresses newspapers, persecutes Jews, and attacks the trade unions unless he is compelled to under German orders."

It is a tribute to the steadfastness of the Czech people that this admonition has been their watchword through four years of hell. Two hours before he left by special plane Beneš sent me word that I could quote him on his final advice to those who remained. With the bitter irony of an old and wise race he said, "We must cooperate in the onward march of Germany. Her progress lies down a magnificent highway, comparable to the *Autobahn* built by Hitler. We Czechs must help the Germans go down that highway—all the way to the precipice."

This was in October of 1938. Six months later Hitler marched into Prague, occupying the rest of the country and destroying the state utterly. In arranging the annexation of the Sudeten regions at Munich the British and French governments had guaranteed the new frontiers. Would they honor this guarantee? Hitler knew the answer. As he was marching into Prague, March 15, 1939, the Federation of British Industries was completing in Duesseldorf far-reaching negotiations with the *Reichsgruppe Industrie* to replace "destructive competition" by a series of Anglo-German cartels. Counting on the venality of big business, the German revolutionaries were undermining British nationalism and capitalism just as they were negotiating in the same period cartel arrangements on artificial rubber with Standard Oil and similar American corporations.

March 15, 1939—six years after Hitler had seized power and only six months before Great Britain and Germany were to be at war—the British government was still dominated by the business-as-usual mentality. Speaking in the House of Commons on March 15, Mr. Chamberlain discussed the destruction of Czechoslovakia with the measured moderation which had distinguished his analyses of British budgets. He regretted Hitler's action. He said that a trade mission which was ready to go to Berlin would not leave. He argued that none of the signatories at Munich had contemplated this development. He concluded that the aim of his government then, as always, was to substitute the method of discussion for the method of force. And that was that. Mr. Chamberlain defended and maintained the policy of appeasement.

And then two days later Mr. Chamberlain did an abrupt

about-face. Speaking in his native Birmingham, March 17, he said that his hopes had been shattered. What had become, he demanded, of Hitler's declaration of "no further territorial ambitions," of his assurance that "we don't want Czechs in the Reich"? Had Hitler taken "a step in the direction of an attempt to dominate the world by force"? Mr. Chamberlain demanded. Then he warned that Britain would be willing to fight to defend "the liberty that we have enjoyed for hundreds of years and which we will never surrender." This speech meant the abandonment of appeasement. It was followed immediately by the introduction of conscription, and six months later when Hitler invaded Poland, with which a pact had been signed, Mr. Chamberlain took Great Britain to war.

What had happened between the two speeches? Hungary on March 16 had annexed Carpatho-Ukraine, the easternmost appendage of the now-dismembered Czechoslovak state. This sparsely settled mountain region was the strategic pathway to the Russian Ukraine. Because Germany renounced it many observers concluded that Hitler had given up any thought of war against Russia. Other observers, struck by the coincidence of this renunciation falling between Mr. Chamberlain's two speeches, concluded that it was responsible for his reversal of policy. They reasoned that Mr. Chamberlain believed at last that it would be impossible to embroil the Nazis and the Communists in war and that he feared consequently that Germany would attack Britain. This is an interesting speculation except that there is no basis for it. Mr. Chamberlain knew no more about the Carpatho-Ukraine than the man in the street. Mr. Chamberlain knew about votes.

Indignant when Hitler marched into Prague, the British electorate was shocked when Mr. Chamberlain maintained his policy of appeasement before the House of Commons. The British people are slow to judge and they are temperate in their attitude toward the men who carry the heavy responsibility of high office. The typical American who disliked the President was saying in that period, "What does that so-and-so know about the heating and roofing business?" The typical Englishman who was opposed to appeasement had been saying, "Well, after all he is the Prime Minister. He is a rum one, but he has access to information we haven't got." But by the spring of 1939 the British people were thoroughly alarmed. They counted them off on their fingers. Manchuria. Ethiopia. The Rhineland. Spain. Austria. Czechoslovakia. Where would this thing end? Was Chamberlain going to hand over the Houses of Parliament to Hitler? Did that German bastard want Westminster Abbey or just one of the little Princesses? The London Cockney added American slang to his bitter humor and sang, "Britons never will be slaves. . . . Oh, yeah?"

Mr. Chamberlain's lame oratory on March 15 enraged a public already thoroughly alarmed. The voice of simple England rose over the dart games and the beer and ale of the pubs. And the members of Mr. Chamberlain's own party heard the voice of the electorate. One Member of Parliament after another came to tell the Prime Minister and the Tory Whip that the Chamberlain government risked being swept out by the nation. Individual members, after consulting their constituents, threatened that they would not follow the Whip on the next vote of confidence. This was a dangerous threat. The left-wing of the Tory party, the younger and more energetic members, had long been opposed to Mr. Chamberlain's conduct of foreign affairs. I knew of several instances when they had lined up as many as two hundred members who promised to vote against their own government only to be dissuaded by the Tory machine in the end. This time the threat would be carried through. Speaking in Birmingham, Mr. Chamberlain reversed himself to save his government and party. He abandoned appeasement.

Mr. Chamberlain was no Machiavelli, slyly working with a "Cliveden set" to balance Germany against Russia and destroy communism. He was no "perfidious" Englishman with ice water in his veins who calculatingly threw the small countries to the German wolves. Nor was Mr. Baldwin before him. Both were manufacturers who believed profoundly that Britain needed "good government," by which they meant "a businessman's government." Their kind of Tory—the newer industrialists as opposed to the older aristocracy—felt that a sound financial policy, protectionism for trade, and the restoration of British industry were the primary needs of their country. Otherwise, they thought, Britain would revert to depression and out of hard times the inexperienced and callow Marxist intellectuals would fashion a proletariat movement which would mean social unrest and strife. Such a movement of the masses was utterly repugnant to what they called "British common sense," but then they had been frightened by the assumption of office by the first Labor government and by the general strike of 1926. They had rid Britain of Ramsay MacDonald's government by the dual expediencies of a financial crisis (in which they maneuvered the abandonment of the gold standard) and a "national" government. The rise of Hitler was embarrassing and it complicated their task enormously. But what was their task? Well, it was to make Britain strong. That is the way they put it to themselves. If you could avoid social strife by sound financial and trade policies, you could make Britain strong. If Britain was strong internally, she need fear no foreign foe.

This led Baldwin and Chamberlain alike to the conclusion that first of all they had to keep the Tory party in power until it had performed its task. That led them in turn to the notion that it was patriotic to play vote-getting politics—not a novel idea to politicians either of the right or of the left. During the Ethiopian War, Mr. Baldwin played to the pacifists at home by invoking economic sanctions against Italy though he appeased the Fascists, first, by arranging that sanctions were not to become effective and, second, by attempting the Hoare-Laval settlement. Equally concentrated on internal improvement, Mr. Chamberlain exploited British pacifism in precisely the same way and sought at any price to avoid a crisis in foreign affairs. Just as the Tory party needed time to consolidate its position so Great Britain, too, needed time, he thought. Mr. Chamberlain had a business-man's mind and he contrasted the wealth of the British Empire with the resources of Hitler's Germany. At first it was inconceivable to him that Great Britain could be endangered. Any businessman knows that money talks. Any revolution-ary—German or Russian—knows that real wealth consists in the productivity of the nation's man power. When Mr. Chamberlain finally saw the danger during the negotiations before Munich he became panicky. He was like the president of a bank who discovers that the assets are no longer liquid: he feared that if he revealed this he would start a run on the bank.

That is the explanation of Munich. Mr. Chamberlain suddenly saw that Hitler meant war, but Mr. Chamberlain thought he could not say that to the British public. The Prime Minister knew that at the time of Munich there were only eleven antiaircraft guns for the protection of London. This meant more to him than General Gamelin's assurances that France, backed by Britain, could defeat Germany. What frightened him most after the specter of war was the thought of what the British electorate might do if it discovered the inadequacy of Britain's preparations—the full measure of the bankruptcy of his own leadership. Like most men he rationalized. Had France not been weakened by sudden changes of government in periods of crisis? Even after Munich, Mr. Chamberlain could not persuade himself to put the facts bluntly to the British people. He behaved like Mr. Roosevelt and Mr. Willkie, who made election promises not to send our boys overseas when both knew that America would lose its independence unless it went to war and promptly. Playing politics instead of providing the nation with leadership, Mr. Chamberlain had not been able to per-suade British industry to convert its plant rapidly for the rearmament program. He had been afraid both of starting a "run on the bank" and of causing severe economic dislocations. London behaved as Washington did later when the American automotive industry, instead of being converted immediately to war purposes, was permitted to make new automobile models after Dunkirk. Having played so long to the pacifists and the industrialists, Mr. Chamberlain lost his own confidence in the British people and in British democracy.

His Minister of War, Leslie Hore-Belisha, summed up for me the attitude of the Chamberlain government in words more precise and revealing than any used by the Prime Minister. In the last months before Munich I was arguing that time was on the side of Hitler and that if Great Britain let Germany destroy Czechoslovakia she would lose her own last chance to fight a successful war.

"You may be right," said Hore-Belisha gravely. "But what can you do in a democracy? In a democracy you can't take the initiative. You have to wait for your enemy to make moves until your people are aroused and willing to make the necessary sacrifices."

What people did Mr. Hore-Belisha mean? Did he mean the Federation of British Industries, which was negotiating with Germany, or the simple man and woman who stood against the bombs with unparalleled heroism once they found a Prime Minister who had the courage to talk honestly and to lead?

Mr. Chamberlain's belief that it was necessary to keep the Tories in office, his fear of causing dislocations in industry, his incapacity to take the initiative, and his lack of confidence in the British people took his country not only to Munich but to Norway and Dunkirk, Greece, Crete, and Singapore. His tragedy, and the tragedy of little Czechoslovakia and the mighty British Empire alike, lay in the lack of vision and courage which characterized an otherwise able and well-meaning man. That old white-maned champion of a virulent, aggressive people's democracy, David Lloyd George, said to me, "That businessman from Birmingham has a retail mind and wholesale problems."

VIII

BREAK NO EGGS FOR THE OMELET

THE speaker is General Maurice Gustave Gamelin, supreme commander of the British and French forces. The time—a year after Munich and a few weeks after the conquest of Poland—is late. The place is the great hall of the Elysée Palace. Once the home of Pompadour, of Bonaparte, of Napoleon III, the Elysée is now the residence of the President of the Republic. Ordinarily the cabinet convenes in the office of the Premier. For full-dress meetings it goes to the Elysée, where President Lebrun presides. This is such an occasion. Premier Daladier has asked the French General Staff whether, in view of the lessons of the German victory in Poland, the government ought not to reconsider the military measures taken for the defense of France. The General Staff has been given two weeks in which to prepare a formal and detailed statement. General Gamelin puts on his pince-nez glasses, clears his throat, reads slowly from a lengthy, typewritten paper. His uniform is immaculate, his body compact and trim; his features are classic Gallic under the close-cropped gray hair, and his manner is one of studied dignity with only a hint of the supercilious.

M. Gamelin concludes: "The French General Staff does not believe in the efficacy of mechanized warfare where proper defensive dispositions have been made. We do not believe in the tank and the dive bomber. It is our considered opinion that German tank columns could not reach the frontiers of France in peacetime if the bridges were blown. Be tranquil. Trust in the simple soldier of France."

General Gamelin sits down. There is quick and polite applause. General Georges, speaking informally, agrees with his chief. This visibly impresses the politicians. General Georges has been shockingly critical of Gamelin in the *salons* and many army groups have urged that the younger and more dynamic man should replace Gamelin. President Lebrun, after a few appropriate remarks—as felicitous and empty as if he had been speaking at a country fair or a flower show—closes the session.

In the anteroom Premier Daladier shrugs his shoulders in weary resignation. He is not satisfied with the statement of M. Gamelin. The Premier is worried about the tanks in Poland and the superiority of German planes. He believes that France must extend the Maginot line along the Belgian frontier to close the vital hinge to the Channel. "But what can one do?" he demands in a petulant, tired voice. "What can one do when the military offer such assurances?"

For nearly three years—since June of 1936—Daladier has been Minister of National Defense and now he is Premier with dictatorial powers. Son of a baker, professor of history, master politician, Daladier has labored day and night over the army of France, the sincerity of his consecration to that task having made it possible for him to bridge the widening gap between the men of the left and the men of the right. A leftist himself, Daladier has been willing to work with the reactionaries and he has made one political concession after another to gain their confidence. Champion of French democracy, Daladier has followed, nevertheless, the advice of that semi-Fascist, Marshal Pétain, vice-president of the Permanent Committee on National Defense and of the High Military Committee. Pétain and the other generals have twice scaled down the military budgets in the period of preparation. Pétain in 1934 declined to strengthen the fortifications at Sedan (where the Germans were to break through in May, 1940). In the same year Pétain cut the military appropriations from 600,000,000 to 400,000,000 francs. Not believing in the airplane as a striking weapon, the generals had reduced the budget demands of Air Minister Pierre Cot, whose leftist politics they abhorred; but Daladier, by his moderation and suasion—some would say his weakness—has been able in actual wartime to reconcile the reactionaries and to lay down an enlarged program for aircraft. He is also arranging the purchase of planes from America, though he will not finance the expansion of American factories.

Much of Daladier's program is still in the paper stage; "mais cà marche quand même," says the Premier when he lets himself feel optimistic. But now he is worried and alarmed. The magnitude and speed of the German victory in Poland is disturbing. Paul Reynaud, the Finance Minister, insists again on a hearing for Colonel Charles de Gaulle, a bumptious advocate of the armored division. "But what can one do in the face of the military clique . . . how can one go against the advice of the experts?" demands Daladier. He is not satisfied with the statement of Gamelin. The generals seem defeatist. Denied Russian help and the possibility of forcing the Germans to fight on two fronts, they refuse any initiative and think only in terms of the defensive. But what can one do? Daladier does nothing. He goes to the home of Madame la Comtesse, who listens sympathetically to the tired Premier of France.

This is the version of a historic cabinet session given me by one of those who was present—the Minister to whom Daladier confided his misgivings in the anteroom. Because of the French censorship and the inability of the members of the government to escape after the German occupation, the story of this decisive decision to do nothing has never been published before. The day's discussion faithfully reflected the formal attitude of the French General Staff. Members of the staff had their doubts and they were divided. But, facing the politicians, they stood united as "the military." There has been a cleavage of caste between the generals and the politicians since before the days of Dreyfus.

The attitude of the generals went far down among line

officers as well. I remember a conversation of Robert J. Casey, correspondent of the Chicago *Daily News*, with a French colonel in the Maginot line. It was six months later, in the period of the "phony" war. We journalists talked continuously of offensives—German and allied. The colonel grew impatient.

"There aren't going to be any offensives in this war," he said. "This is a war of attrition. We are going to sit the enemy out and win by blockade."

Casey said in his direct and humorous way, "You're loony as hell."

"Mais dites donc," retorted the colonel. "There will be no offensive. Ecoutez. There is not an officer of the French or German General Staffs today who was not a combat officer in the last war. Now a combat officer in the last war knows what an offensive means. He knows what it means to butcher a million men in three or four months of struggling backward and forward across a position marked with flags on a map. Eh bien? You do not think it necessary to break eggs to make an omelet if you yourself have been an egg."

Responsibility for the military defeat of France rests squarely upon the shoulders of the generals who did not believe in mechanized warfare and the colonels who did not believe in breaking eggs to make an omelet. Both failed to measure up. In the *simple soldat* they had a magnificent fighting man—the son of the Frenchman who in 1916 contained the full fury of the German assault on a single front for week after week from February to September, muttering "They will not pass" and piling nearly a million French and German dead before Verdun without breaking. They took these stubborn peasants and armed and trained them with the weapons and tactics of another generation. They sent the *simples soldats* to fight when they themselves no longer had the will to win.

And yet France suffered more than military defeat. France suffered collapse. It is not enough to examine the shortcomings of the French General Staff. If Clemenceau was right in holding that war is too serious a business to be entrusted to generals, the collapse of a great nation is too complicated to be explained by generalship alone. If Waterloo was won on the playing fields of Eton, where was the Battle of France lost? It is too soon for an observer to offer more than a tentative explanation. And yet certain contributing factors are already clear. Some 40,000,000 Frenchmen, attached to the soil, highly individualistic, and profoundly democratic, lived on the frontiers of Germany—a nation of 80,000,000, industrialized, regimented, and militaristic. France failed to prepare herself, though, unlike Great Britain and America, she had neither the narrow Channel nor the broad Atlantic between her and the fact of modern, militarized Germany. If I have understood France, there are four reasons why she showed no more foresight than the other democracies. In the first place, the French played the fool by remaining on the defensive and leaving all the initiatives—ideological, political, and military—to the enemy. In the second place, they played ostrich. In the third place, they played politics. Finally, as a result of an irresponsible belief that a people can endure by maintaining the *status quo,* they found themselves too soft; they could not stand the blood.

The defensive mentality of the French army merely reflected the mentality of the whole nation. Imbued with the idea of security and the maintenance of the *status quo,* the French felt as safe behind their Maginot line as Americans felt behind the Atlantic Ocean and they cultivated the mentality of defensive resistance as naturally as Americans talked about "continental defense." Their Maginot line, moreover, was no mere Atlantic. It was one of the prodigious accomplishments of all military history. The French poured 100,-000,000,000 francs into its construction. Figuring the French franc at the 1928 mean of 3.92 American cents, it will be seen that France spent some $3,900,000,000 on the Maginot line. France could have built with this sum nearly eighty battleships of our dreadnaught class. Had this vast effort gone into naval defense, France could have built a force of battleships equal to the combined British and American fleets—and been equally defenseless before Germany.

A Maginot line, like warships, is no better than the men who man the guns. Militarily a fort has never been anything in itself; it merely serves to reduce the number of effectives, or fighting men, required to hold a given front because it affords them a fixed refuge and supply base as well as the advantage of firing over prepared terrain. But the fighting men, not the forts, matter. Hitler was said to have improvised secret weapons which reduced the vast *ouvrages* of the Maginot forts. His only secret weapon was the superiority of German morale to that of the French, denied confidence in their leaders and kept eternally on the defensive. The Germans felt out the Maginot line for points of weakest resistance. They dropped specialist parachutists against *ouvrages* where there was slight response to their fire. Once into forts abandoned by certain French units, the Germans had little difficulty in destroying resistance to either side. Where the French stood and fought, either inside or outside of their forts, they beat the Germans to a standstill. One of my best French friends commanded a division which feared neither tanks nor dive bombers nor the myth of an invincible army. His division destroyed two German divisions before it was finally driven from the lines. But my friend's division was exceptional. Most of the French armies fell back in confusion before they had even begun to fight. They had lost faith in their own victory and they had lost faith in France.

How could the French soldier have believed in anything? In seven years of uninterrupted successes by Hitler there had been only a bewildering chaos of successive governments in Paris, each showing itself incapable of leadership. Manchuria had gone, and Ethiopia and the Rhineland and Austria and Spain, and finally Czechoslovakia—with the active assistance of the British and French governments. Then even Russia had been lost. During that dismal period when had France taken the initiative once? Where had one blow been struck by the Third Republic? And then Poland went in a matter of weeks. And Finland. And Norway. Who struck first in Norway? These are the thoughts which Daladier and Gamelin left to idle soldiers sitting in the boredom of an underground forts system through the fall, through the winter, and into the spring.

They might have conditioned their army to offensive action by an immediate invasion of Italy. But half the Frenchmen liked Italian Fascism anyway because they had been taught to fear Communism as the alternative, and the other half were genuinely concerned with the possibility of French casualties. Daladier and Gamelin pondered the excessive losses of the World War and the futility of offenses designed merely to move General Staff flags. They did not want to break any French eggs to make an omelet. Had they attacked Italy in the first weeks of the war, while Germany fought in the East, they could have knocked Mussolini out, brought the whole of the Balkans and the Near East into the conflict as French allies, and sent back to the western front a hard corps of seasoned men who would have learned their soldiering in the only school of military science that matters—the school of the battle line. Action in the Italian peninsula and the Balkans would have conditioned the French home front as well. The public would have been given headlines and victories and some reason to believe in the destiny of France. But French democracy—under the dead hand of the aged—had become too conservative to take risks.

I watched the morale of the French army change under my eyes. Never men for false heroics, the French are businesslike soldiers and in the first six months they were keen for action and danger. I remember the thrill that ran through the mess of a crack air squadron when the pilots found that the Messerschmitt fighters, though avoiding Curtiss pursuit ships, were giving fight to the Morane, an outmoded French plane. The pilots literally fought to take up this inferior fighter in order to get a crack at the Germans instead of having them turn tail as they were ordered to do in that period. Everywhere there was impatience at the restraints. The Ministry of Marine is in the Place de la Concorde. I was talking during the period of the "phony" war, aboard a French destroyer, with an officer who had already got one submarine and wanted permission to raid the German coast. "No damned salt water ever gets into the Place de la Concorde," he said. "We ought to wash those politicians over the rail and begin effective offensive action by land and sea." This was characteristic of the fighting men in the first stage. This keenness to get at the enemy went to pieces under an enforced defensive attitude. Similar inactivity in the last war had brought the Italian collapse at Caporetto. After nearly a year of waiting on the defensive almost no army is fit for the line.

When the Germans broke through the French front, the world at large forgot the mental attitude of the French army. The world was impressed with the superiority of German tanks and planes. Why didn't the French know about these new weapons? What had happened to allied intelligence services? Why were Britain and France unprepared for such an army as Hitler put into the field? The dismay was worldwide and comparable only to the shock two years later suffered by millions who before Pearl Harbor, Singapore, Java, and Burma had underestimated the hitting power of the Japanese. France had underestimated Germany for the same reason that America underestimated Japan, and the simple Frenchman like the simple American asked, "Why didn't they tell us?" The answer is that the French had been told just as the Americans had been told. But the whole French nation played ostrich. Frenchmen would not believe what their ambassadors, their military attachés, their journalists, and their spies reported from Berlin. Every political move by Hitler, every new tank and airplane built, and every new division of troops put under arms was duly reported to Paris. I have known French ambassadors who were in Berlin and I know what they reported. Paris had facts.

The French did not disbelieve these reports: they disbelieved what they meant. When you added them up, the reports meant only one thing—a brutal attack of Germany against France. France stood as the symbol of the *Diktat* of Versailles. France represented the democratic system and France lay directly and immediately athwart Hitler's path to world power. The French blinked the facts because they were no more willing than Americans to suspend the manufacture of automobiles and electric refrigerators because "interventionists"—*bellicistes,* they were called in France—warned of war. The cry of one French politician after another reflected the popular aversion to war. The exceptions were few, if notable. Paul Reynaud, standing like a bantam rooster in the cockpit of the Chamber of Deputies, sounded warnings in his harsh, strident voice, but he was as lonely in France as was Winston Churchill in England. The individual Frenchman closed his ears to the wingbeating of this ugly little Gallic cock.

Hitler, the shrewd political psychologist, was quick to reassure the French. Giving the lie direct to his program as outlined in *Mein Kampf,* Hitler assured the French that he had no quarrel with them, that he renounced his claim to Alsace-Lorraine, and that he sought a bilateral understanding that peace between the two neighbors should never be troubled. Intelligent though they were, the French welcomed these assurances. Blind self-confidence in the ability of France to improvise her preparations before Hitler would be ready for war marked the thinking of highly placed Frenchmen up to the day of war—even through the last year of peace (1938–39), when Germany was producing 1500 airplanes a month and France only 52. "Time always works for the democracies and Hitler will think twice before he goes up against the Maginot line," said the average Frenchman.

In reasoning thus the Frenchman reflected the essentially conservative mentality that has characterized and almost destroyed the great democracies in our time. Profound philosophical and psychological differences exist between the man of the totalitarian state and the man of the democracy. It is a matter of outlook, aggravated by the fact that the democrat is at peace while the totalitarian is at war in the period before frontiers are crossed. The average, or typical, citizen in a democracy lives in an economy of plenty, has the mentality of great expectations, and thinks in terms of security, unknown to Germans, Italians, and Japanese in recent years. Thanks to their governments, even the petty party officeholder in Germany, Italy, or Japan ate less well than the Frenchman on relief. The industrialist in Germany, Italy, or Japan had his profits limited, his labor rationed, and his reserve capital arbitrarily turned into any enterprise which pleased the whim of the state, while the French industrialist still thought in terms of future profits. In the totalitarian states the individual had become desperate and he saw no way out of his individual predicament unless, as his leaders said, the country could be enriched by wars of conquest. Long before the invasion of Poland, many of my German friends were saying with apathetic weariness, "Why not war? The Fuehrer has been right so far. If we don't have war, everything will crash around us anyway and we'll have Communism. We had rather take a chance with war." In startlingly similar language some Italians were telling me in the weeks before their own intervention, "It is war or internal collapse. We are so poor that war could not be much worse." The Japanese echoed this same philosophy of rule or ruin when they prepared their attack at Pearl Harbor.

The Frenchman, on the other hand, was a thrifty sou pincher, a born conservative. Essentially a nation of peasants, the French farmed their own land, tilling it well and profitably, with raids on the public treasury in years when it took the equivalent of American farm legislation to pull them through. The working classes achieved collective bargaining and the forty-hour week and, like the peasants, they were as loath as bankers or industrialists to believe that war would come to upset the national economy. Thus, while the German and Italian said, "Maybe I can get somewhere by war," the Frenchman said, "I will be all right if we can just avoid war." Sure of the docility of their own peoples, whom they had debauched politically, Hitler and Mussolini exploited the very virtues of the democratic French, shrewdly plotting each new conquest to create the maximum of surprise and then lulling them with new reassurances. And the French public unwittingly played into the hands of the dictators' propaganda. By the definition of their democratic laissez-faire system they were optimists and they believed in progress. The individual Frenchman for the past seven years had been saying, "Next year my income is going to be considerably higher . . . next year we are going to throw those political bums [*les salauds*] out of office . . . next year Jean is going to buy me a fur coat . . . next year I think we can afford that Renault car."

This was the mentality of the French until the day of general mobilization. Against this mass psychology of a whole nation which acted less from comprehension of national interest than from the individual's dream of bettering his own position, the trained expert who knew something about power politics and Hitler's preparations got nowhere at all. No American who knew him would have questioned the honesty of the late Senator Borah. And yet a few months before the invasion of Poland, Senator Borah challenged the prediction of European war which President Roosevelt had made on the basis of expert advice. Too many French politicians were like Senator Borah. They had played ostrich until their shoulders stooped. I remember dining one night with two French politicians and Henri André François-Poncet, Ambassador first to Berlin and then to Rome. The Ambassador over a period of years had accurately forecast the creation of the German conscript army, the occupation of the Rhineland, the invasion of Austria, Czechoslovakia, and Poland. The politicians argued with him, incredulous as he assured them that Italy would attack France. He was a pessimist, they said.

"My friends, you are stupid," said François-Poncet with asperity. "You do not believe in a devil any more. But the devil exists. He exists, he exists, he exists!"

But for the French nation, rich in the good things of this life, right and wrong were only relative, one "truth" was not much better than another, and the devil did not exist. Business and politics could go on as usual if you did not let yourself get alarmed or if, as a good 100 per cent Frenchman, you did not worry about what happened to Chinamen or Austrians or Spaniards or Czechs. "What happens to them can't happen to us with the Maginot line between France and Germany." All this scare stuff came from ambassadors and journalists—professionals in the business of crying havoc and loosing the dogs of war.

Americans have been shocked by the partisan strife of French politicians and the venality of the French press which in rare instances received outright subsidies from German, Italian, and Japanese sources. It seems to me that both have been exaggerated in the American mind. Certainly the French parliament played politics with the future of France. But the Chamber of Deputies in its lowest moment never sank to the level of an American Congress which declined to fortify Guam and which agreed in 1941 to extend the selective service by the margin of only one vote. Several French newspapers—prior to wartime censorship—spread distrust of Great Britain and demanded querulously why Frenchmen should die for Poland. But no French newspaper publisher ever went so far as some American newspaper proprietors have gone before and since Pearl Harbor. The French public made no show of its patriotism, avoiding parades and demonstrations and music in the streets; but had a French newspaper printed such articles and editorials as appeared in the Chicago *Tribune*, for instance,—including the publication of military secrets,—a French mob would have smashed the printing presses and lynched the publishers.

Americans know that political strife raged unabated in France from the day Hitler came to power in 1933. We are inclined to attribute the blame to the Popular Front and this version has made considerable headway thanks to the propaganda of Nazis and Fascists, who have made "red menaces"— real or imaginary—the pretext and excuse for everything from their own seizure of power internally to their wars against the democracies. The groups that came together to form the Popular Front in France reflected the political weaknesses of the whole French democratic system. The blunder of the Popular Front, like that of every other group, consisted in their determination to "save democracy at home" before facing up to foreign affairs—a laudable idea in the abstract but one which in practice proved merely an effort to save their own notion of democracy or the patronage and power of their own group. Trying to "save democracy" when France, rather than its political system, was in danger cost the French people both the fatherland and democracy. When the right-wing reactionaries were in power, the left groups argued that France could not be saved until a more representative government took over. And when the Popular Front came to power, the rightists refused to cooperate with them precisely because they *did* reflect the overwhelming mandate of the masses. Thus France was in political deadlock throughout the period of Hitler's military preparation and his successive coups. For seven years the French governments which fell in and out of office with dazzling rapidity had no more real authority and power than an American President who has a congressional majority against him. There is also a fundamental weakness of executive power in the ministerial system. Instead of electing the executive director and giving him vast power for a four-year stewardship, as in the American system, the French elect deputies who in their turn create and dismiss governments. Consequently, the Premier came from the parliament, suffered from the parliamentary tradition of logrolling, and rarely had the advantage of administrative experience.

The headline personalities of the French right during the period of Hitler's preparation for war were Pierre Laval, Etienne Flandin, Colonel de la Rocque, and M. Caillaux. Behind them was the power of the "two hundred families," the banking interests—such vested groups as the *Comité des Forges,* which brought together the arms merchants and the masters of heavy industry generally. They had the support, too, of Catholic and royalist groups. No one of these individuals acted as if he foresaw the inevitable struggle between the totalitarian and the democratic systems as a fight to the finish in which one or the other must be destroyed. Indeed they were inclined to Fascism, and their programs varied between concessions to the dictators and an outright program for a Fascist France which could ally itself to Germany. These groups were supported by military leaders like Pétain and Weygand, who attributed all France's ills to democracy and dreamed of a semi-Fascist military dictatorship. Of all these men the most intelligent and sinister was Laval.

A dark-skinned little peasant, Laval affected white bow ties of the washable variety as the last reminder of his humble beginnings. The exigencies of riding the band wagon have taken him from left-wing radicalism of the Communist kind to his post-armistice position as an ultrareactionary Nazi tool. As a journalist once remarked, Laval's politics are like his name; they read the same from the right or the left— L-A-V-A-L. In this opportunistic career Laval accumulated a considerable fortune, but wealth never cloyed the venality of a man who enjoyed recounting some sharp bargain in which he had once again skinned a tenant or a rival company. Thus his signal contribution to the strengthening of French democracy against the rise of the dictators was a "bargain" in which he skinned France. He won Ethiopia for Mussolini, a victory which saved Fascism in Italy. Having made a deal with Mussolini in Rome nine months before the invasion of Ethiopia, by secretly selling out Great Britain and the League of Nations, Laval kept his word and saw to it later that sanctions against Italy were never made effective. Laval believed in Italo-French cooperation and he thought the Italians would be grateful. Instead Mussolini, strong after his African victory, scoffed at the obligation and turned against France in open hostility. I last saw Laval in his old-fashioned office in Paris—a stage-prop office for the skinflint in a melodrama. It was a few months before Hitler invaded the Lowlands and he was smoking one cigarette after another through nicotine-blackened teeth. There was something feline about Laval and he would remind you of a cat if his raven hair were not so greasy, his fingernails so dirty, and his teeth so black. The cat is a cleaner animal. Laval told me that he had no political hopes for the moment. He was biding his time until after the war.

"Democracy is a failure," he said. "And the war is making Frenchmen realize it. My time comes after war. I will reorganize France on Fascist lines. Of course France will never be like Germany. Frenchmen aren't Germans and we will eliminate the abuses which mark the authoritarian state in Germany and Italy."

By "after the war" Laval then meant after the defeat of France. He was already in touch with Berlin through the Italians, who were technically nonbelligerent, and between the invasion of Norway and that of his own country Laval completed the terms for the betrayal of France. The Marquesa Capomazza, of the Italian Propaganda and Foreign Ministries, gave me categoric information in Rome, June 9, 1940—the night before Mussolini's declaration of war. Capomazza said that Laval had already assured Rome and Berlin that he "and others" could force the resignation of the government and ground French arms. Tentative armistice terms had been discussed for a "soldier's peace." "Within a month," added Capomazza, "Laval guarantees a French declaration of war against Great Britain." Laval's secret negotiations with the enemy were known to French military intelligence for many weeks before the collapse of France, but the Paris government hesitated to act against him for fear of precipitating general opposition from rightists. By shooting Laval and his associates French democracy might have saved itself.

Quarreling with rightist leaders, Laval's associate, Flandin, posed as a champion of democracy against Fascism long enough to win the confidence and the votes of the left. It was during his premiership in 1935 that Flandin and Laval were persuaded to sign the Franco-Soviet pact. The French General Staff forced this policy upon the two politicians, but military considerations could not change Flandin's prejudices and alarms; he promptly veered right again. Before the ink dried on the pact with Russia, Flandin began to blame Communism for all the ills—real and imaginary—of France and the world. If Moscow's influence were destroyed, Flandin argued, France could live in perpetual peace with Germany and Italy. He joined Laval in blocking sanctions against Italy and when, as a direct consequence, Germany marched into the Rhineland he opposed French mobilization.

The fundamental policy-making of Flandin and Laval grew out of their fear of a "New Deal" in France. Consequently they persuaded themselves that Russia rather than Germany endangered France. They were the men who alienated Stalin and drove him to a policy of isolation. This in turn created a defeatist element within the French General Staff. The majority of the generals had always felt that war should not be waged against Germany unless it could be turned into a war of two fronts. Unless the Russian masses could divert and contain a large part of the German forces, 40,000,000 Frenchmen could not stand up against

80,000,000 Germans long enough for Great Britain to equip and train a land army, it was argued by those generals who minimized the efficacy of the Maginot line. In addition to shaking the confidence of many generals by their alienation of Stalin, Laval and Flandin did a further disservice to the army. They were the men who named General Gamelin to the supreme command. Since the Laval-Flandin conservatives were seeking an understanding with Hitler, they were anxious not to provoke him. They were admittedly afraid to name Weygand—a disciple of Foch, whose military philosophy was summed up in the famous dispatch from the first Battle of the Marne: "My right is exposed; my left is heavily attacked; my center is unable to hold its position; I cannot redistribute my forces. The situation is excellent. I shall attack."

Colonel de la Rocque was an honest but not politically intelligent French patriot. He thought France could be saved from political paralysis by Fascist military discipline and he appealed to the French equivalent of the American Legion. An honest man, la Rocque knew that he was ill-qualified to become the dictator and he looked about him in vain for a Frenchman with a mustache or bulging eyes. Street thugs and German agents abused the good name of the *Croix de Feu* organization; the riots of February 6, 1934, alarmed true lovers of democracy, and the subsequent excesses of the *Cagoulards*, or hooded French Ku Klux, who received funds directly from Berlin and Rome, compromised the la Rocque type irrevocably. His chances, but not his followers, were obliterated long before the arrival of the Germans.

Joseph Caillaux was the classic reactionary who served the cause of big business. Born during the American Civil War, Premier and Finance Minister before the first World War, Caillaux represented the dead hand of the very aged on French life. In 1917 Caillaux, posing as a pacifist, had attempted to negotiate through Switzerland with the enemy.

His fifth-column effort to arrange a negotiated peace had been discovered by Premier Clemenceau, who promptly imprisoned him for conspiracy. The old Tiger did not give Caillaux time to betray France. By 1924 Caillaux was a free man again and as the political agent of François de Wendel and the other arms manufacturers and industrialists who controlled the *Comité des Forges*—much too powerful a group of financiers to be the French equivalent of the National Manufacturers Association—Caillaux was quickly returned to political life despite the hostility of the democratic parliament. His powerful masters made him Finance Minister twice again; but when he failed to produce any plan whatever to save the franc and handed over in abject, but unadmitted, failure to Poincaré, Caillaux was placed in the Senate. The old man's ugly sneer and firmly clenched umbrella came to be the very symbols of the upper chamber, which, under outmoded constitutional provisions, had become altogether unrepresentative. Led by Caillaux, the Senate exercised such vetoes as Roosevelt feared might have characterized a wholly conservative Supreme Court of the United States.

A financial "expert" with a caustic tongue for any budget maker who had progressed beyond his own income-tax provisions of 1906, Caillaux boasted that he was vindictive, unyielding, and unfair. He struck out savagely at the Popular Front government even when its financial measures had been amended to meet every one of his own suggestions! In the end he destroyed Blum and the Popular Front out of sheer political hatred at a moment when rightist deputies and Blum's bitter foes were rising in the Chamber to applaud the patriotism, generosity, and courage of Blum's concessions—concessions which abandoned the electoral promises of the Popular Front in a belated effort to placate the obstructionists and prepare France against invasion. On that tragic occasion Caillaux hissed the word "Jew" at Blum, but what he could not forgive him was no mere matter of race. Blum had proposed to collect taxes from the rich. He offered no "soak-the-rich" program, but on the contrary he presented a measure which would have scaled down the existing tax rates. The French rich, represented by Caillaux, had always been tax evaders—letting their taxes slide for five or six years at a time and then settling for a fraction of their obligations —and Blum had the temerity to propose that these loopholes be plugged. Caillaux and his kind feared taxes more than they feared the Germans and they hated the Popular Front more than they loved France. They were the men who had no shame in saying to me and other foreign observers, "Better Hitler in Paris than a Jew like Blum."

But what of the left? Their leaders—Edouard Herriot, Léon Blum, and Edouard Daladier—had one merit at least. They knew that an understanding with Hitler was impossible. Like the masses they felt instinctively that the world could not endure half totalitarian and half democratic. And yet, knowing that France faced a struggle for her very survival, they failed to prepare her. The men of the left, as parliamentarians, were prisoners of the political party system and their machines confused internal politics and party patronage with the destiny of France. This weakness grew almost inevitably out of the nature of the Radical-Socialist party. Neither radical nor socialist, this party represented middle-class bourgeois France—the France of the little businessmen; the farmers; the schoolteachers; and the civil-service officeholders, who were legion in a country which, like the rest of the world, had moved inevitably toward bureaucracy. This party ruled France for as long as the Republicans ruled the United States in their infrequently interrupted tenure of office from the Civil War to the New Deal. Moreover, the countless governments formed in France during the 1933–1939 period of Hitlerism were most frequently Radical-Socialist governments or coalitions built around that party. During and after the rise of Hitler there were only two general elections in France. One brought the Radical-Socialist government of Herriot in 1932, while Bruening was still Chancellor of Germany; the other brought in 1936 the Popular Front, of which the Radical-Socialists were the bulwark.

Herriot, the perennial mayor of Lyons, is the French liberal at his best. A self-made man, Herriot is a scholar, an author, a professor, and an orator of the first rank. At one and the same time, he is a master of machine politics and an idealist. He has faith in Rousseau's notion of the universal brotherhood of mankind, though he thinks, of course, that all the men who compose that brotherhood are French and therefore rational human beings who believe in fraternity, equality, and liberty.

I can remember lunching with Herriot in 1932, when he was Premier and Foreign Minister. He was working desperately to save the Disarmament Conference—and peace— by giving Germany equality of armaments within a scheme of general security—so desperately indeed that had the Germans been rational men they would have come to terms with France and prevented Hitler's rise to the chancellorship. Putting a quarter of a pound of butter on his beefsteak and downing a pint of beer before turning to the *vin rouge,* this hearty Frenchman talked with candor.

"I am determined on a policy of concessions to Germany," he said. "But I am reading a book by that General von Seeckt who has rebuilt the German army. He explains with passion and cold hatred just how Germany is to invade France again. . . . Ah, mon cher! The thought that my concessions may undermine the security of France keeps me sleepless at night. It is too heavy a responsibility before history for one Frenchman. And yet I mean to take it. I will gamble for peace."

Herriot gambled in vain. Hitler and the generals quit the League of Nations and the Disarmament Conference. The Germans withdrew from Geneva in order to make the French policy of conciliation impossible.

This sentimental, heavy-jowled, hearty Herriot lost office because he insisted on paying the war debts to the United States. It was political suicide with America isolationist and Germany bent on rearmament. Waiting in the lobby of the Chamber of Deputies, before Herriot put the fateful vote, the journalists told him so. "Oh, I know that," said Herriot. "But look at my fat bottom. I was cushioned to fall out of office." And this is the way M. Herriot, with no false heroics or breast smiting, sacrificed his career for a principle. Except for Blum, he was the last of the Premiers to think the times too grave for statesmen to play politics in the unprincipled fashion which marks our times.

Other Radical-Socialist governments succeeded Herriot for the next two years, each more mediocre than its predecessor —Hardings and Coolidges faced with the problems of Hoovers and Roosevelts. The *annus horribilis* 1934 was too much for even the perennial Radical-Socialists. The Stavisky scandal broke that year and was closely followed by the riots of February 6; between the two the Radical-Socialists were badly compromised. They lost office and right-wing reactionaries, led by such men as Flandin and Laval, ruled through two disastrous years during which Hitler consolidated his power, built a mighty army, and invaded the Rhineland. Mussolini conquered Ethiopia and prepared the Axis alliance. France wrangled about internal corruption and putative revolution.

France was only moderately corrupt by American standards, though it rocked along for years with the Tammany system of "fixers"—or lawyers with political connections who were called in to arrange governmental contracts, tax cases, or even tickets for traffic violations. There was nothing to resemble the refinements of the Washington lobbyists with their streamlined farm bloc. Beside the Teapot Dome scandal or the peculations of the Huey Long machine, the few connections which Stavisky, the crooked pawnbroker, enjoyed with certain Radical-Socialist politicians were of negligible significance. The French public was sick, however, of the logrolling spinelessness of the Radical-Socialists, and people generally were ready to be shocked and indignant. The Fascist leagues which were then beginning to flourish exploited the Stavisky scandal to make political capital of it. By comparison with the pillage and plunder which marked the Nazi and Fascist systems in Germany and Italy, France was lily-pure; but the Fascist leagues (operating on Hitler's admonition that the bigger the lie the more credible it becomes) urged Frenchmen to emulate the "discipline" of Berlin and Rome.

To the charges of indecision and spinelessness, already brought against the French democracy, the slur of corruption was added. Popular confidence was further shaken. The Fascist leagues began to feel their oats. Young thugs marched through the streets—most of them hired, many of them sincere converts to Fascism—and there were fist fights and scenes. Feeling ran high and the Communists put out their thugs too. Everybody seemed represented in these brawls but the decent element of hard-working, sober, middle-of-the-road Frenchmen. There were secret societies, caches of arms, and talk of seizing the government by sudden coups. Fascist groups made one abortive attack on the Chamber of Deputies and almost succeeded in setting it afire. When they threatened to throw Herriot into the Seine, he said, "Oh, no, you will have to take me back to Lyons and throw me in my own river." The troublemakers got out of hand on February 6, 1934. There was rioting in the streets of Paris, with autobuses and buildings fired and hundreds beat senseless; and as the cry went up to march against the government, order was restored only after the famous *Garde Mobile* fired into the populace and charged with drawn sabers. There were dead, and the Fascists lifted the charge of "assassin" against Premier Daladier.

This Radical-Socialist was called the "Bull of Vaucluse" because he came from that region and his friends described him as a strong, silent man. In this moment he lost his head and, instead of ruling firmly, resigned office in dead funk. Daladier was guilty only of indecision, but for the Fascists that constituted proof that he had planned to shoot into the populace. He was first decried as a ruthless assassin and then ridiculed as the "Veal of Vaucluse." As Daladier's political stock sank to zero, that of the Radical-Socialist party went down with it. The bankruptcy endured nearly two years— two disastrous years in which the rightists truckled to Germany and Italy while provoking Russia. Finally with something approaching alarm the country went to the polls in April and May of 1936. The Radical-Socialists made common cause with Léon Blum's Socialists and Joseph Stalin's Communists. Thus was formed the Popular Front. This coalition swept to an electoral victory which reflected reaction from the harsh policy of financial deflation of Laval and his associates, fear of Fascism, and the sudden awakening of national determination to "save France."

The Popular Front received the mandate of the French nation as truly as the New Deal leadership of Roosevelt reflected the aspirations and confidence of the American people in 1932, 1936, and 1940. Léon Blum was their man as much as Roosevelt was ever America's, and the social reforms which the Frenchman attempted were demanded by the public vote and authorized by the legislation of the parliament. They were not emergency improvisations.

Léon Blum is probably the greatest Jew in politics since Disraeli. An aesthete and drama critic in youth and an eloquent, crusading journalist all his life, Blum recognized early in his career that there was no range for his vast talents except in politics. His tall, slightly stooped, elegant figure with the broad forehead, the drooping mustaches, and the shrewd, kindly eyes had long seemed the one permanent fixture of the Chamber of Deputies when Hitler revived anti-Semitism, just as Caillaux's scowl and umbrella had become the symbol of the Senate. Intellectually he was a

giant and, with a complete mastery of the tricks and tradi-
tions of parliamentary practice, this veteran floor leader of
the opposition towered over his fellow deputies. The Socialists were the victors within the Popular Front coalition
and Léon Blum at last became the maker of governments,
not their critic. Coolly analytical, intellectually rather than
oratorically persuasive, and forceful in the strength of his
own integrity, Blum became the Premier of France. There
has rarely been an abler Frenchman or a more unsuccessful
Premier.

Once they had inducted Blum into office the various factions with him and against him conspired to make it impossible for him to rule. Within the Popular Front the
Radical-Socialists wanted immediate control and the premiership ultimately in the hands of their own party, while
the Communists, under orders from Moscow, loathed a
Marxist who was much too intelligent to be doctrinaire
and much too patriotic to be amenable to Moscow-controlled
Communist influence. Outside the Popular Front it was decided that the whole attack of the right should be concentrated against the person of Blum. He was decried as a Jew
and a Communist; the vilest lies and calumnies were circulated against his personality, and his political programs
were distorted and perverted in German-financed propaganda. Blum soon found himself caught between two mill-
stones—the determination of the right to make it impossible for government to function and the insistence of the
trade-union movement that the Popular Front had to carry
through social legislation or be dissolved under the wearing
force of the sit-down strikes. And when he tried to satisfy
the workers—ill-timed as the moment for that may have
been—the financiers and industrialists, resorting to blackmail, denied his government the appropriations and the
cooperation necessary for the construction of airplanes.
When civil war was organized by the Fascists in Spain it was
vital for France to pick the winner—either side would have

been better than neither, from the point of view of power politics, since France, already wedged in between Germany and Italy, could not risk a third hostile power on its frontiers; but Blum's public was bitterly deadlocked and the Premier could only devise nonintervention, the one policy which made an Italo-German victory in Spain possible.

But of all the tragedies deliberate sabotage by the financial interests was the least excusable. In the moment when Blum was trying to save the currency and start the rearmament program, the investing classes of France began a flight from the franc. The country's gold holdings—second largest in the world—suddenly disappeared overseas. There were three reasons. First, many investors were genuinely alarmed by the Italo-German propaganda of a Communist revolution, which, in the opinion of this observer at least, was never even remotely threatened. Second, when Blum offered a financial program which actually reduced tax rates but made it possible for the first time to collect them, the reactionary elements cynically organized a strike of capital to drive the Popular Front from office by proving that rearmament under Blum was impossible; it was this movement which paralyzed industrial expansion in a country which was twenty years behind its neighbors technologically and even lacked a machine-tool industry because of the essential timidity and conservatism of the capitalist class. Third, individuals— shamelessly selling France short—lined their own pockets out of manipulations of the national currency. Blum was an unyielding and doctrinaire democrat in the face of tactics which made democracy unworkable and he blundered by refusing, the moment he took office, to decree currency restrictions and prohibit the export of capital.

The end was inevitable. The right drove the franc down, the left retaliated with a new outburst of sit-down strikes, and the Senate wantonly rejected Blum's financial program. Blum pleaded in the Senate that his laissez-faire financial solution embraced all the demands of the conservatives and represented the sacrifice of Socialist ideas in a final effort to stand at bay against Germany. Caillaux's opposition was personal, said Blum. "Yes," sneered old Caillaux in a voice which chilled the galleries. In an effort to break the deadlock and make government possible, Blum then resigned after a year in office. The leadership of the government thus went in June of 1937 to an innocuous group of Popular Front nobodies. By January of 1938 the Popular Front had gone to pieces on the financial and Spanish issues and Blum, the patriot, gallantly took office again for a brief interim. Finally, in April of 1938, Edouard Daladier, who had failed so miserably in the moment of the February 6 riots in 1934, became Premier with the unsavory Georges Bonnet as his Foreign Minister. French democracy had failed to discipline itself and the Popular Front had failed to rule, but patronage belonged to the Radical-Socialists again.

They were back and, assuming the posture of the ostrich, France began to play politics by the old formulas. Daladier held office longer than any of the other Premiers in the Hitler period, taking his country to Munich and later to war against Germany. For nearly two years he enjoyed dictatorial powers in the least dictatorial of all countries. Moreover, he held for a long time the genuine respect of the man in the street. Daladier was a plain man, not smart but not dumb, and he resembled a certain type of Southern and Western Senator in America in whom you sense a kind of wholesome mastiff-dog manner. He played middle-of-the-road politics. By conniving to throw Blum out of office, he won the reactionaries even though they had called him "assassin" during the 1934 riots. Because they were now thoroughly alarmed about Hitler, he won the center and the left. He promised to play the strong man and yet he went to Munich. Daladier did not understand the issue when Neville Chamberlain led him off to Munich, but he comprehended the tragedy of France when at last he was confronted by Hitler. A Frenchman who accompanied him told me that Daladier flew back to Paris expecting to be stoned and mobbed by an angry and humiliated nation. He could not believe his eyes and ears when he was met at the airdrome with applause.

If French relief at being spared war thus expressed itself spontaneously, it was short-lived and the common sense of the French was quick to assert itself. In a matter of weeks after Munich the French knew that war had become inevitable. They knew at last that it was too late to play ostrich, too late to play politics. Approaching national unity for the first time in six years of Hitlerism, France turned to Daladier and gave him the support of the nation for want of a better man. A life spent in the Senate or Chamber of Deputies makes a hand brake rather than a spark plug out of a man. Daladier had two definite weaknesses. He got tired if you talked at him long enough. Brain fag started if he was kept on a short ration of sleep for several days. And this led inevitably to his second weakness—a lack of decision. Daladier changed his mind—as I can avow from personal contact—not less than twice a week every week for months on the vital decision whether to send French expeditionary forces to Finland or Norway, nearly maddening General Staff officers. They were still being told "Maybe yes, maybe no" when the German invasion of Norway began. This was typical, not exceptional.

The great achievement of the Daladier regime was the return of confidence in the franc and the rebuilding of French finance. This was accomplished largely by the Finance Minister—a hardheaded little patriot named Paul Reynaud, who was finally to turn against his chief and throw Daladier out of office. Reynaud thought Daladier was too weak to win. The last Premier of free France, Reynaud promised Churchill that France would make no separate peace. If Paris fell, Reynaud planned to fight on from the provinces and then from France's African colonies if necessary. Hitler's success depended on quick victory before his supplies were exhausted, and Reynaud was confident that the tanks and planes could be slowed down and that the allies could win the war. Reynaud was the kind of squat, stubborn Frenchman who made the Miracle of the Marne and cried "Ils ne passeront pas" at Verdun. Such a Premier might have saved France, but Reynaud was not a Radical-Socialist and he came too late. His speeches over the seven years before he became Premier seem remarkably prescient if reread today. He foresaw Hitler's every act and he cried himself hoarse calling upon his countrymen to bury their internal differences.

Reynaud was a man of the right, but he was never a reactionary and indeed the force of events compelled him to adopt the political thinking of the left. As an independent without a major party Reynaud was never built up as a public idol, though men in key positions were asking for his leadership and politicians were importuning him to intrigue against Daladier, whom he cordially hated. I remember talking with Reynaud in his office in the beautifully designed and appointed Finance Ministry. He said frankly and bitterly that he had done his job as Finance Minister and that what France needed now was an "economic dictator" to coordinate the various home-front efforts but that Daladier was jealous and refused to grant him such powers. I asked if he would wrest the premiership away from Daladier in order to undertake this task of coordination. Reynaud broke into English, which he speaks well. "I do not believe, as you say in America, in shooting the piano player," he said. I never heard a less convincing declaration.

When Reynaud finally took the premiership, Daladier had lost the confidence of the people and Reynaud believed that he had become an unconscious defeatist. Reynaud was aggressive. He knew that France had to regain its belief in democracy and fight for it with passion. He knew that wars are not won by remaining perpetually on the defensive. He had seen eye to eye for five years with General de Gaulle. Reynaud wrote the preface to de Gaulle's book calling for armored forces capable of independent offensive action against Germany. When other statesmen were busy playing politics, Reynaud, with de Gaulle's notes before him, demanded in 1935 the immediate creation of eight mechanized divisions for the French army. Germany had already equipped four *panzer* divisions and planned four more. The French politicians turned a deaf ear to little Reynaud. Had France possessed these eight divisions five years later, Hitler's armored columns could have been cut in the rear in the spring of 1940 and France today might be victorious and free.

But France in 1940 did not have the armored divisions. She only had tanks. In actual numbers there were more French than German tanks, but they were dispersed with infantry units and driven by crews trained in the outmoded tactics of 1918. Only in airplanes were the French hopelessly outnumbered—opposing no more than 2000 to Germany's 14,000. While the French tanks floundered aimlessly and the French infantry searched the skies in vain for interceptors to protect them against the *Stukas*, the German armored divisions drove straight through to one objective after another, knifing past the centers of French resistance and surrounding a large Anglo-French army. Gamelin, whose notions of static warfare had brought this disaster, was summarily removed by Reynaud and Weygand, the disciple of Foch, was ordered home from the Army of the Orient. Then the Germans got, and made the most of, their final "break"—a fortuitous climax to the allied blunders of driving forward into the Lowlands, of assuming that tank divisions could not come through the forest of the Ardennes, of failing to complete the extension of the Maginot line.

Without waiting for Weygand to arrive from Syria, the British high command elaborated directly with General Billotte, the French commander in Flanders, plans for a joint Anglo-French counteroffensive by which they hoped to break through the German lines. Billotte was killed in an automobile accident before he could order the French advance, and the British forces launched an operation which failed for lack of French support. Meanwhile Weygand, ignorant of this plan, arrived in Flanders with his own operational scheme for a counteroffensive only to learn that any chance of its success had been doomed by the gallant, but isolated, British attack. The fight went out of Weygand, who waged one battle, halfheartedly, after Dunkirk, and as the Germans pressed on Paris the French government fled toward Bordeaux. Having abandoned the capital, which he had promised to defend house by house, would Reynaud stand in the south of France and, failing to halt the Germans there, would he carry resistance to the vast African empire? In short, would Reynaud honor the solemn engagement he had taken with Churchill that neither ally was to make a separate peace with the enemy?

At the Château de Cangey, June 11, Reynaud's government heard General Weygand. The "Battle of France" had been lost, he said. It was imperative to sue for an armistice. Several versions of this historic cabinet meeting have come from ministers who were present. They agree, first, that Weygand said that "the only possible reason for continuing this struggle would be for the honor of our arms and our flag" and, second, that he declared, "I must also be concerned about the maintenance of order in the country . . . to avoid the danger of communism, which so often follows in the wake of military defeat."

Before Reynaud or other ministers could intervene Marshal Pétain, who had entered the cabinet as vice-president of the council, took the floor. "We must speedily ask the victors to state their terms, so that hostilities can be stopped before our armies suffer complete defeat. We shall thus be able *to throw the weight of our remaining intact forces into the negotiations,*" said the Marshal.

Thus spoke Weygand and Pétain, the one seventy-two, the other eighty-three, both Fascists in personal politics. Throughout the period of Hitler's rise to power and Germany's preparation for war such antidemocratic generals had been primarily concerned "about the maintenance of order" in France. And nothing else! They had opposed preventive war, believing that a rearmed Germany would prevent the spread of Communism. They had vetoed demands in the parliament for the extension of the Maginot line. They had cut down successive military budgets. They had blocked Pierre Cot's plans for the expansion of the air force and the training of parachute troops. They had killed the efforts of de Gaulle and Reynaud for the creation of armored divisions and a professional army, which might have smashed the Siegfried line while Hitler was invading Poland. They had declined Daladier's demand that the whole strategy for the defense of France be reconsidered in view of the lessons of the *panzer* divisions and the *Stukas* in Poland. Finally, clinging to the notion of static warfare, they had kept the armies of France idle and destroyed the morale of the *simples soldats*. And now in the moment of military disaster, instead of falling on their swords, they uttered not one word of self-recrimination.

In the hour of France's agony Gamelin sat in the garden of his Paris home unimaginatively composing memoirs to justify himself, while Weygand and Pétain, blaming democracy for their defeat, conspired to strike it down. Dismissing "the honor of our arms and of our flag," these men, who feared the threat of Communism more than the advancing Nazi tide, saw only justification for their own twenty-year contention that what France required was a Fascist military dictatorship under their own direction. History will measure these men against Napoleon's generals, the revolutionaries who created the Jacobin France of which the Weygands and the Pétains were so contemptuous.

The fear of Communism in France was rooted in conservative notions of class and property. But a general can cherish these notions only if he loves honor more—"the honor of our arms and of our flag." Class? Marshal Lannes understood better than Weygand and Pétain the meaning of the "officer class." Seeing his troops waver before the walls of Ratisbon, Lannes seized a scaling ladder himself. "I will let you see that I was a grenadier before I was a marshal," he screamed. Property? Listening to a friend who envied him his wealth and his estates, Marshal Lefebvre showed generals how to measure property rights. "Very well," said Lefebvre to his friend. "Stand here in the courtyard and let me fire twenty shots at you from thirty paces. If you live, you may have all this. I have stood at closer range to have a thousand times that many balls fired at me to get my wealth and fame."

In face of the two generals Reynaud tried to stand firm. He demanded time; he sent General de Gaulle to London; he conferred again with Mr. Churchill; he made a final appeal to President Roosevelt for American intervention. But the self-destruction of the French Republic was foreshadowed when Pierre Laval joined Pétain and Weygand in Bordeaux.

These conspirators were denounced before the cabinet by César Campinchi, the Minister of Marine. "There are traitors in our midst," said Campinchi. "These people want to take advantage of the miltary setback to further a political scheme at which they have been plotting for years." Raoul Dautry, the Minister of Armaments, who had impressed me more than any other Minister with whom I had talked in France's wartime Ministry, reduced the issue to stark reality. "Be careful, Messieurs," Dautry said. "Our choice lies—and don't forget it—between an Anglo-Saxon and a Germanic civilization."

But Camille Chautemps and other weaklings in the cabinet were won over by the little clique which had made its choice long before the Council of Ministers agreed to sue for an armistice. The vote was thirteen to eleven. Paul Reynaud, who had failed to measure up in the moment of crisis, immediately resigned. Marshal Pétain was ready and drew from his pocket a list already drawn up which named General Weygand Minister of National Defense, Paul Baudouin to the Ministry of Foreign Affairs, and Admiral Darlan to the portfolios of Navy and Commerce. France at last was Fascist and the victory of Hitler was complete. Going to the nation over the radio on June 20, Marshal Pétain consciously, or unconsciously, admitted that the people were ready to fight on—just as the people of Madrid had fought and as the people of London and Moscow later were to fight.

"From June 13 the request for an armistice was inevitable," Pétain said. *"The blow surprised you.* Remembering 1914–1918, you sought the reasons for it." Remembering the Miracle of the Marne and Pétain's own Verdun, the people were not beaten; they were willing to fight on, hoping for and believing in another miracle. But Pétain—an old man who no longer dreamed dreams—told them that they were defeated and the reasons for this defeat, he said, were "too few children, too few arms, and too few allies." ("Trop peu d'enfants, trop peu d'armes, trop peu d'alliés, voilà les causes de notre défaite.")

Not the French birth rate but the infant mortality caused by social conditions which the right refused to remedy, not democracy but Pétain's own reductions of the military appropriations, not the Popular Front but the policies of the Laval-Flandin Fascists which drove Russia into isolation, were responsible for the shortcomings which Pétain attributed to the parliamentary system.

When the radio brought the mournful news of this capitulation, I recalled my conversation in Paris three months before, with a French General Staff officer—a brilliant man whom I had known for years. No defeatist himself, this colonel, who fought later with great distinction, said that France would be beaten within six weeks of the coming German offensive. I believed in the people of France and, though I knew the superiority of the German army, I insisted that my friend was too pessimistic.

"No. France is doomed. France is betrayed," the colonel said. "Only one thing can save us, but neither the politicians nor the General Staff have the courage to do it. We can save ourselves by shooting fifty prominent men in twenty-four hours. We must begin with Pétain and Laval!"

I shook my head in amazement and dissent.

"Oh, yes, I know that we both disapprove such methods," continued the colonel. "And yet democracy must defend itself. These men are not traitors by the old definition of 1914 —1918. But they are traitors by the definitions of total war. They attack the Premier—first Daladier and now Reynaud. They destroy confidence in the army. They say that nobody wins a war. They whisper that we were pushed into this blood bath by England and that Hitler will give us honorable peace terms. All we need to do to have peace, they say, is to rid ourselves of anti-Hitlerian democracy. Among them there are editors, bankers, and many great industrialists. They are undermining the will of the army to fight and the will of the nation to maintain itself. They are led by Pétain and Laval. And why have they been carrying on this whispering campaign? Because Pétain and Laval, through Spanish and Italian emissaries, are negotiating with Hitler. Positive information is in the hands of the Deuxième Bureau [Military Intelligence]. When the French army fights at the front these men plan to stab it in the back. We can save ourselves by shooting only fifty men."

The capitulation gave me hindsight and it gave the words of my friend a terrifying eloquence. The men who betrayed France in 1940 were willing to betray the country in 1917. Standing in the Chamber of Deputies in 1917, Laval, without explaining how it came into his hands, read a report from Pétain on the mutinies in the French army.

"Make peace at once!" Laval screamed. "For, if you don't, the soldiers will come back from the front with their guns in their hands, and they'll force a revolution on you."

In that period "Tiger" Clemenceau was Premier of France. The associate of Pétain and Laval was Joseph Caillaux and he was found to have discussed a negotiated peace with the enemy. Clemenceau arrested Caillaux without a moment's hesitation and by that action cowed the Lavals and the Pétains. In 1940 neither Daladier nor Reynaud was a Clemenceau. Among the servitors of French democracy there were too many men in high places who believed neither in the people nor in the democratic principle. And among those who held the faith there was no man of iron will to stand traitors against the wall.

IX

FRANCE IS AN INVALID

"FRANCE must be treated as an invalid—an invalid slowly recovering from a very serious operation. You must bring her fruit, not admonish her. You must tiptoe into the sickroom, not pound at the door and berate her for her weakness."

These are not the words of a Fascist, a collaborationist, or an appeaser. They were uttered to an American journalist by General Charles de Gaulle, the leader of the Free, or Fighting, French. He commands as yet only about 40,000 soldiers; but he is the ablest living field commander of a country with a glorious military tradition, and around his person he will be able ultimately to rally 40,000,000 Frenchmen if he can learn to forget his preoccupation with personal prestige and that he must cooperate with President Roosevelt and Mr. Churchill. During the first World War de Gaulle was wounded three times and, after his capture in the heroic Verdun fortress of Douaumont, he attempted five times to escape. During the twenty-year lull he pleaded in vain for the mechanization of the French army, and when the second World War came he justified his theories by smashing a German army at Laon with his tank brigade. He in no way resembles the men of Vichy. He expects ultimately to eject them and deliver his country. Meanwhile, however, General de Gaulle knows that France has lain prostrate and delirious after Hitler's blow, for the men of Vichy have been the slaves of Germany—not free agents.

It was inevitable that the American invasion of Morocco and Algeria should have been opposed—not welcomed by Vichy. A similar German move would have found a government at Vichy that had neither the will nor the power to resist, a fleet whose officers were divided politically, and an empire through which thousands of German agents had filtrated. The defense of a beaten, disarmed, and partially occupied country rested in the hands of Marshal Pétain—the eighty-four-year-old defeatist who betrayed his people with the false armistice. This man was nevertheless the hero of Verdun, and conquered Frenchmen generally felt that they could find no more honorable leader who would be acceptable to the Germans. For in dealing with the Nazis, Pétain had two ace cards and he used them for all that they were worth. Whenever the Nazis threatened to go beyond the terms of the armistice, Pétain intimated that he could release the fleet to the British and order the French colonial troops in North Africa to go over to their former allies. He could say, "If you violate the terms of the armistice we can violate it too."

These two threats were ace cards so long as Pétain did not play them. For neither threat could be carried through successfully unless Anglo-American expeditionary corps landed in North Africa. Force remained the decisive and final arbiter in beaten France and Hitler disposed of that force until the dawn of the first American landings, November 7, 1942. And yet it was because Pétain brandished these cards that a maximum of illusion was created, so that many Frenchmen in Vichy, and a few in occupied Paris, remained unaware of the destructive nature of collaboration with a "master race" which feels neither respect nor pity for Frenchmen. These ace cards, moreover, created popular illusions even in America, where few people understood the realism with which the White House and State Department played to Pétain's hand by sending agents to Morocco and negotiating with Vichy even after General Weygand was relieved of his colonial command. Washington knew that the fleet could not be handed over to us until we gained a preponderance of power over Germany in the Mediterranean and

South Atlantic, but Washington hoped to strengthen Pétain's refusal to surrender the ships to the Nazis. Washington knew that Hitler held more cards than Pétain and that Berlin's game was both patient and clever, for Hitler stacked the cards and gave himself trumps when he divided France into occupied and unoccupied zones. Just as the division of France by internal political dissension had enabled Hitler to beat it at war, so the division of the country geographically has enabled him to rule it in defeat with a minimum of opposition.

The line of demarcation cut through everything—the national economy, the transportation system, the interlocking factories, the circulation of the newspapers, the churches, the families, and the political party organization. On one side of the line lay French wheat; on the other, the country's meat. Even to make a symbolic sandwich the French had to plead for permission to cross an arbitrary line. The Germans opened and closed that frontier ruthlessly and cleverly. Without permission Frenchmen could not cross the line to attend a funeral. The Vichy government could not reopen the line to send back undesirable refugees shoved across by the German Gestapo. While I was at Vichy the Germans shunted across nine boxcars filled with 119 lunatics from an insane asylum. Vichy could not send them back. Vichy had to take them, find asylum for them, and learn again to laugh at the German sense of humor. It is no wonder that even Pétain, long-suffering and silent, full of illusions and hope, cried out, "The line of demarcation is a halter around the throat of France."

The Germans designed the demarcation line as a halter and they have had a genius for knowing when to tighten until it chokes. Not the least of its harmful effects, of course, has been the division of Frenchmen in face of "ces messieurs," the conquering Germans. The people in the occupied zone who feel the weight of the German heel cried out that Vichy let them down in order to spare itself trouble and persecution; Vichy said that the people in the occupied zone, thinking only of their own misery, forgot that Pétain had to play a patient and diplomatic game with the conquerors.

Hitler's second card has been reparations levied on the excuse of the army of occupation. The French were compelled to pay 400,000,000 francs a day for the cost of occupation. At this rate the French have disgorged some $3,500,000,000 a year to Germany.

The charge against the French is based on the cost of an army of occupation numbering 8,000,000 men. Actually the Germans have never quartered more than 3,000,000 men in France. Thus two-thirds of the sum charged is pocketed by the Germans. The stolen two-thirds has been used to buy control of French factories from French shareholders. This provides a tremendous loot for the Nazi higher-ups who now own most of the French factories working for Germany. Fifty per cent of French industry is at work again, it is estimated, and of this only 5 per cent works for French consumption. Groaning under such a burden, the French have alternately hoped that it would be lessened and feared that it would be increased. The cost of occupation has proved an effective weapon in German hands as well as the most colossal instance of looting in modern history.

The final and most important of Hitler's weapons was control over 1,300,000 French prisoners of war, of whom only 50,000 had been returned as the war entered its fourth year. There is scarcely a French family that does not wait for some loved one. Whenever he has wanted to shake the French, Hitler has either hinted that these prisoners might be released or reminded the French that they can still be held. In the main the prisoners are under the supervision of German officers who were prisoners in the last war and know the prisoner's psychology. But some are in camps under the more vicious type of Nazi storm trooper. Any or all of the prisoners may receive the most brutal treatment at any moment. Except for a favored few in model prisons, the

French prisoners are given an inadequate diet. I saw several hundred released prisoners come back into France. Sallow, emaciated, and in many instances tubercular, they were a pathetic sight.

Many a Frenchwoman, with the shrewdness which characterizes her, knows that the only hope for France is revolt in an effort to facilitate an Anglo-Saxon victory over Germany. Many a Frenchwoman knows that Hitler's promise of the early return of prisoners is a cynical and cruel propaganda lie. But almost every Frenchwoman forgets these things if she has a husband or a son in a German prison camp. A mother always nurses the illusion that her boy is coming back; a wife always knows that her man is still alive.

These three cards sufficed. Great Britain and America had always to fear sudden moves by Vichy, but Hitler only infrequently feared that Pétain would send the fleet or the empire to his enemies. Vichy handed over French Indo-China to Japan with a *pro forma* protest but disputed bitterly de Gaulle's effort to land at Dakar and the British entry into Syria, which was undertaken to forestall a German occupation, as well as our own occupation of French Africa. With his three aces Hitler divided Frenchmen geographically, disunited them politically, and paralyzed their will. In beaten France, as a result, no national sentiment has crystallized. Sitting in Berchtesgaden, Hitler must have chuckled to see how well his technique worked—the technique employed in the Saar, the Sudetenland, and even in the fifth-column propaganda in America. It is the technique of exploiting the individual's personal fears and personal aspirations, turning class against class and race against race until, in the general despair, loyalty to the national interest seems too costly and too risky. It is a technique based on the rule that nothing succeeds like success and the fear of the individual that, whatever he may do, nothing his country can do will stand before "the wave of the future."

I asked Admiral Leahy, President Roosevelt's special envoy in Vichy, what single thing caused him the greatest difficulty in his effort to persuade France to an anti-German policy. He thought for a long while.

"I think the greatest difficulty is the Frenchman's affection for his own army, an affection increased by its defeat," he said. "The very fact that a million and a half men from this army are in German prison camps makes the average Frenchman refer to it as 'the army of heroes.' Thus the French search for any explanation of defeat except that of the inferiority of their own army. They blame the British. They blame their own politicians. But not one word must be spoken against 'the army of heroes.' And, consequently, the Frenchman has come to believe that the German army is unbeatable. Any army is unbeatable that proved superior to the French army. Thus very few Frenchmen believe that essentially unmilitary peoples like the British and Americans can fashion and put into the field an army able to beat the Germans."

Equally important in the creation of the new French mentality was the absence of British and American victories. Continued American neutrality until Pearl Harbor influenced French thinking more than anything done by Hitler and the German General Staff. The average Frenchman felt certain that Britain could not win alone and he viewed developments in America with dismay. In the United States he saw the ostrichlike posture and the same internal wrangling of isolationists and interventionists which had brought his own defeat. We denied the Frenchman hope.

The first critical moment for the Axis came after General Wavell's victory in Libya. Then Frenchmen felt that the moment had come for them to invade Libya from Morocco and Tunisia, robbing Germany and Italy of their vital African supply base at Tripoli. German propaganda ended this threat, thanks to the American isolationists. The remarks of men like Lindbergh, Wheeler, and Nye, and the editorials of Hearst and McCormick, were used by the Germans to fill the front pages of the French newspapers and to provide hours of antidemocratic propaganda for their radio programs. With this ammunition the Germans persuaded the French that America was divided, as France has been divided; that we had learned nothing from the lesson of Europe; and that our conquest was inevitable. The Germans persuaded the French that, having lost the war once, they should not make a move which would mean that they were to lose it again. However sincere or well meaning they may have been, men like Lindbergh and Wheeler reconquered France for Germany and strengthened Hitler's control over Spain and his influence in Turkey, just as they persuaded the Japanese that we could be attacked with impunity. Had these men worn the uniforms of German field marshals they could have rendered Hitler no greater service. No field marshal has conquered so much territory.

What this picture of America did to the Frenchmen who would have fought again was best illustrated by a French general who held a most important position in Morocco.

"We are the soldiers of a beaten army," he said in 1941. "We think as soldiers and we think as beaten soldiers. In Morocco we view our problem as essentially military. We believe that we could successfully resist an Italian invasion of North Africa. We believe that we could resist a Spanish invasion. With luck we might contain a combined attack of the two. But against two German *panzer* divisions we could not stand for more than forty-eight hours. We are armed and equipped as a colonial army. Against modern mechanized columns we have neither the tanks nor the airplanes with which to stand. Consequently, we cannot oppose the Germans.

"You in America—seemingly blind to the danger of your own conquest—ask continually what *we* will do. It seems to me that America is not a great country. Finland and Greece are great countries. America is only a big country. Words from your President and your State Department—after the words of Lindbergh and Wheeler—strike us as lacking the reality of a single German *Stuka* or tank. We would be impressed if one day we saw in Morocco American tanks, planes, and troops. Within two seconds of their landing we would no longer be the soldiers of a defeated army. In two seconds we would become the sons of France again, three times invaded by Germany within the memory of the living, proud to take up again the struggle against our enemy."

What this general said, millions of Frenchmen thought, until we actually struck in Africa and brought, together with the brilliant victory of General Montgomery, the second crisis for the Germans. That period without victories explained, along with the demarcation line, the costs of the army of occupation, and the presence of 1,250,000 Frenchmen in German prisons, the position of Marshal Pétain. Even the Frenchman who most despised and disliked the policies of the old Marshal persuaded himself that Pétain represented dignity and honor—as opposed to anarchy and German reprisals. In this tragic period the soul of France cried out deliriously for "dignity and honor." Pétain could give France neither, but he could give Frenchmen certain illusions. All human beings cherish illusions, and the French are no more logical than the rest of us. As a French friend of mine once remarked, "We reason logically, but too often we start from a false premise." Who should govern the soldiers and women of a beaten army if not the hero of the defense of Verdun?

The French knew that Pétain was false to their notion of France, but whoever governed France in the period of the armistice must be acceptable to the Germans. Pétain was better for France, they reasoned, than anyone else the Germans would approve. Who else could prevent the collapse of the country into chaos? This is why 85 per cent of the French people supported Pétain while 90 per cent were opposed to his policy. Certainly not more than 10 per cent of the people sincerely believed in the policy of collaboration which Pétain represented. And there is a contradiction in Pétain himself which made it possible for him to rule. Believing fanatically in the Catholic hierarchical notion of authority, Pétain abhors democracy and yet he listens attentively to public opinion. His strongest argument with Hitler has repeatedly been "The French people won't stand for it." So long as Pétain could prevent Laval and his like from handing over the French fleet and Morocco to the Germans, he was sure to have the support of the French public even though that public perfectly understood the true character of the old Marshal and his humiliating collaborationist policy. His motto for France, carried beneath his photographs which were prominently displayed all over the country, was embraced in the phrase "Dignité, l'honneur et la patrie." The average Frenchman repeated "Dignité, l'honneur et merde," but he supported the government of the Marshal. Thus, even one of the Vichy Ministers, who works in close collaboration with Pétain, said to me, "Vichy stinks. Once the Germans are defeated we must blow away every building, plow the town under, and sow it with salt."

Pétain's associates debated bitterly whether he was ga-ga. For two hours or so each day the Marshal seemed bright and surprisingly energetic. For the rest of each day he was a tired old man with slight strength or energy. Then his mind was likely to wander. A man who served as one of his secretaries, when Pétain was Ambassador to Spain, shortly before the collapse of France, explained that the Marshal was remarkably well informed and had a retentive memory for anything which happened before and during the war of 1914–1918. The events of the past five years seemed to defy him. He had little grasp of them and it was very difficult to brief him. For instance, the Marshal's secretaries used to spend two hours with him each night going over the list of Spaniards he was to receive the next day, explaining their political predilections, their attitude toward France, and the like. The next day the old Marshal, showing a certain irritation, would ask all over again about each of his callers. In this way much went on in France of which the Marshal knew nothing. The American Embassy, for instance, sent repeatedly unsuccessful messages to Pétain protesting that an American Red Cross ship, which had brought bread and milk to the French, was being detained at Marseilles in direct violation of a Vichy undertaking. When Americans finally reached Pétain himself, the old gentleman cleared the matter in two hours. The Germans controlled many of his lieutenants and prevented questions from reaching him direct. The Marshal himself was likely neither to remember nor to act on a written memorandum, and he objected to taking up important business verbally.

The true character of the Pétain government in the first phase of collaboration lay in the strength of the shrewd but cynical Laval. Unlike Pétain, Laval espoused complete collaboration, believing that by concessions he could release the French prisoners and obtain some relief from reparations. Laval hoped that Paris would be restored as the seat of government and he was willing to sign a definitive peace treaty with Hitler. Laval also proposed to defy the old Marshal by raising him above the vicissitudes of political strife. To use a less elegant American phrase, Laval planned to kick the old gentleman upstairs so that the real power and authority would rest in his own hands. This conspiracy of Laval and the Nazis came at a moment when French public opinion was thoroughly sickened of Laval and could no longer stomach him. Laval had groveled before the Germans with so little sense of shame that General Weygand blurted out, "Laval wallows in defeatism like a dog in its own vomit." Pétain decided to strike down Laval. The story was best told by Laval himself to a friend.

"The Marshal called the cabinet together and asked for our collective resignations," said Laval. "We tendered our resignations, walked out of the room, and came back after an appropriate interval. Then, to my astonishment, the Marshal accepted my resignation alone. The rest of the cabinet remained.

"I am not thin-skinned. I have never been one, either, to stand on what are called points of honor. But I have a certain pride. When Pétain's new cabinet had ended its deliberations, I was waiting for the old man. I said to him, 'You can't do this to me.' The Marshal was ashamed of himself and embarrassed. He said, 'You have deceived me. You have carried on every sort of negotiation with the Germans behind my back. You have not troubled even to keep me informed.' I said to the Marshal, 'I have told you in advance of every move I have contemplated and I have informed you regularly of each development. Is it my fault if you have no memory of what I tell you?' The Marshal asked why I did not give him written reports on each development, saying that verbal reports were not sufficiently precise. I explained that in Vichy there were no secrets and that I could not risk the failure of negotiations by leaving about memoranda which would fall into the hands of anybody and everybody. The Marshal drew himself up with a great puffing of his cheeks and said, 'Any written document you hand to me could be put in that safe, the combination of which is known to me alone.' I laughed in Pétain's face. 'You don't know the combination. Open the safe for me if you do,' I said. The Marshal could not bluff it out. He admitted that he did not know the combination and that he did not know which of his secretaries had access to the safe."

Laval is not a trustworthy witness, but I credit his version of how the old Marshal dropped him. Certainly Laval's contempt for Admiral Darlan is fair, despite Laval's jealousy of the man who temporarily succeeded him only to yield to him again and finally to play an ignominious role in Africa when he changed over to the American side and finally went down before an assassin's gun. Darlan was the son of one of the consummate politicians of France and in his own career as a naval officer he navigated more political corridors than salt water. Indeed, in the first World War, his greatest exploit was the command of a gunboat on the Rhine. For all his preoccupation with politics Darlan was a man who remained extremely unsophisticated in his prejudices and his principles. Vain to a fault, he was panicked into following German orders whenever the Nazis suggested that otherwise he might be removed from the Vichy government. Bitterly unfair about the British attacks on French warships at Oran and Dakar, he was childlike and vociferously articulate in his jealousy of the British navy. He gratuitously indulged this feeling in an early meeting with Admiral Leahy. "The British have ruined seven generations of my family," said Darlan. Ambassador Leahy asked him if he would be precise and explain just how the British had ruined seven generations of Darlans. The Admiral turned on his heel and walked off in a huff.

The Admiral's abberrations stemmed from two things—a great ignorance of the world beyond France and absolute confidence in German victory over Great Britain and America. As often happens with a politically naïve man, Darlan's very simplicity of purpose sometimes took him too far. At a press conference in Vichy, Darlan was gushingly enthusiastic about the results of his effort at collaboration some months after he had taken up where Laval had ended. He told the press that he wanted to make an important announcement as proof that his policy was working to the benefit of France. Germany was sending down wheat from occupied France to Vichy France, he said. This was a thrilling earnest of Germany's good will and generosity, said the Admiral. It was too much even for Marshal Pétain, who intervened.

"I think it ought to be clear," interjected the old Marshal, "that this wheat, which is being sent down by the Germans, is French wheat, grown in French soil by French peasants.

It is part of the wheat seized by the Germans. I think we ought to make that point clear."

What Darlan said about the "generosity" of the Germans— that was his favorite word—was less important than what he tried to do about the French fleet. He charged that the British were preventing the arrival of ships with food for France, despite the fact that many came through regularly from Africa and America though 82 per cent of their cargoes were transshipped directly to Germany. Darlan's distortion of the British blockade was made even more preposterous to the French public by the Germans. Their censorship forced every newspaper in France to publish simultaneously the headline: "No bananas for little French children." Few Frenchmen could read that headline without understanding the German stratagem and without laughing, however bitterly. But whether Darlan understood it or not, he proposed to assemble the French fleet and convoy all French cargo ships. The Germans wanted this because it would have made armed conflict between British and French warships inevitable and actual war very likely. Pétain had to restrain Darlan.

Other German orders were carried out by Darlan without the knowledge, or interference, of the Marshal. The Axis forces in Libya have been reinforced by troop-carrying aircraft flown directly from the Marignan airdrome at Marseilles, and supplied by ships which have abused the territorial waters of Tunisia and used such ports as Bizerta. Similarly Darlan brought the *Richelieu* from Africa to Toulon, the great Mediterranean base, where it lay more readily to hand for the Germans, and only the eve of our invasion he handed over valuable merchant shipping. From the day when he came to power Darlan worked to put his own men into key positions. Thus collaborationists found their way to the command of French warships, but even Darlan could not set aside the patriotism of the French naval ratings, admirable sailing folk from such regions as Bretagne, who remained steadfast in their desire for the ultimate defeat of Germany. Darlan failed and the Germans put Laval back in power over the angry but futile protest of Pétain.

Two equally unrepresentative Frenchmen worked with Pétain in an effort to turn France into a corporative state, in shoddy imitation of the Fascist regimes of Mussolini and Salazar. The first was Pierre Pucheu, the Minister of Interior, who transformed the French police system into a Gestapo. Pucheu was both shameless and ruthless as he terrorized the French public with his leather-jacketed, Nazi-minded gangsters. He fought against sabotage and what is called "communism," a generic term for anything from the possession of arms to belief in democracy. It is thanks to his terrorism that 50 per cent of the factories of France are running again, though it must be repeated that they work almost wholly on orders for Germany with only about 5 per cent of their production going into French consumer goods. The second henchman was Paul Marion, a former Communist, who was placed in charge of the press and radio. He ground out the steady stream of hatred for "Americans, Englishmen, and other Jews and Communists" which is the daily diet of the Frenchmen living in Monsieur Pétain's Fascist heaven. The excesses of this regime are best reflected in the press, which has lost any pretense of fair-mindedness or generosity. Even the arrival in France of food shipped by the American Red Cross would bring the editorial warning throughout the "French" press: "Mr. Roosevelt must not think that we can be bought with a few tons of flour and a few tins of condensed milk." The Germans used the same technique in Spain, where, upon the arrival of a wheat ship, the newspapers wrote a heart-rending story which depicted a gaunt and sour-faced American Protestant tearing off bits of bread which he offered disdainfully to Spaniards, only to find that the very beggars—having a sense of what it means to be a hidalgo—declined the gift. Pucheu and Marion were aided in their efforts to make France Fascist by the "Legion," a uniformed party army created among ex-servicemen of the last war (servicemen of this war are still in German prison camps). The "Legion" helps in witch hunts and devoutly upholds the moral codes of certain Catholic clerics. It also spreads the typical slogans "Support for de Gaulle is support for the Jews" and "Soviet money is behind the de Gaullists."

It is clear that the regime of the old Marshal was Fascist. Many Americans, consequently, especially certain left-wing elements, attacked the American State Department for what was described as a policy of "appeasing our enemies." This charge was too glib and ill informed. Robert Murphy, former American chargé d'affaires at Paris, was sent to French Morocco, where he agreed in conversations with General Weygand to send oil and certain foodstuffs required if Weygand's army of 150,000 men was to remain intact as a stabilizing force between German pressure on the one hand and the danger of Arab revolt on the other. It was obvious that as a *quid pro quo* Washington expected Weygand to resist German invasion or German demands that his army come over to the German cause. In proof of French sincerity we have the widely known diplomatic secret of Pétain's instruction to Weygand. Wide currency was given the fact that Pétain told Weygand, "With or without telegraphic instructions from me, you will know what your duty is if the Germans violate the terms of the armistice." Mr. Murphy's mission to General Weygand did not prevent Vichy from handing French Indo-China over to the Japanese. It did not prevent Vichy from opposing the British entry into Syria, though General Weygand himself declined to go to Syria to organize resistance. So long as Weygand remained in command in Morocco—ultimately, of course, the Germans forced his dismissal—Washington could say that North Africa and the French fleet were not in German hands.

In diplomacy what happens ultimately is not always the vital consideration. As Jay Allen has said, "In these times an optimist is a man who believes that the future is uncertain."

Ultimately the issue of Morocco and the fleet was determined by force. That it would be so was always plain to Washington. Morocco and the fleet could be gained only by the arrival of an American expeditionary force. Given the isolationist sentiment of the American public and the irresponsibility of the American Congress, it was the duty of the American State Department to devise a policy to gain time. Appeasement was never a substitute for an expeditionary force. It was, however, better than a do-nothing policy or a rupture of relations with Vichy, either of which might have driven the fleet and Weygand's army to Hitler. Thanks to this realism, we kept Germany from getting the French warships at a time when Great Britain was in peril and alone just as we removed a similar danger that the Japanese might use them to overwhelm our own one-ocean navy in a moment when it carried on a seven-seas war.

American policy was also based upon a sound appraisal of French psychology. President Roosevelt and Sumner Welles have believed that a distinction must be made between the Pétain regime and the French people. Washington recognized that 85 per cent of the people supported Pétain but that nine out of ten Frenchmen were opposed both to collaboration with Hitler and to any program which would genuinely assist German victory. In short, the French masses are beaten but they are not changed in their hearts. The French people have had no arms with which to make revolt, but revolt is what they want. They were betrayed by Pétain, Laval, and the other defeatists who precipitated a premature peace. These false leaders believed that Great Britain would capitulate. The French people as a people believed this too. But today the people are glad that Britain fights on and that Russia and America have come into the war. They do not know whether Germany can be beaten. But now they have hope. They are still without arms, but now at last faith stirs in the towns and the villages. Once an American expeditionary force moves up from Africa and reaches the shores of

France proper, our soldiers will find that Frenchmen have not been changed by Marshal Pétain's shoddy Fascist state. Those of us who have been in France since the occupation have found it so. Proof abounded on every hand in a multiplicity of incidents—little in themselves, but significant.

Clendenning Robertson, of the American Red Cross, went to a restaurant where it was said that one could eat well despite the ration system. The waiter shrugged his shoulders and said that he had nothing to serve. Robertson finally persuaded him to prepare an omelet. After one bite of obviously spoiled eggs, Robertson put down his knife and fork and called for the patron. "Here I've been working for months with the American Red Cross," he said. "We have brought milk and bread to your children. Here I come in and ask you for a meal and you serve me rotten eggs."

The patron cuffed the waiter. "Imbecile!" he screamed. "I've saved those eggs for five weeks in order to serve them to a German."

Jeanne Preece and Polly Peabody, American girls who had driven ambulances for the French, stood in Brest during a British air raid many months after Vichy had embarked upon a program of collaboration. As the British bombers rained down destruction on this important naval base, the men and women of Brest stood in their doorways. With tears of joy streaming down their faces, they cheered the British planes. "We are willing to risk the lives of our wives and our children," said a middle-aged man, "if the British can destroy the sales boches."

In Lyons I ate in a restaurant with a French general. It was hard to get a proper meal and he wrapped up a little of his own scanty serving to take home to his children. We were bitter that German occupation had made it so difficult for people to eat in the province of plenty and the beautiful city which had once been the gastronomic capital of the world. I asked whether he thought America should support the British blockade or schemes like Mr. Hoover's for feeding France.

"Don't feed us," said the general. "Starve us. A people that isn't willing to die hasn't the right to live."

It is still impossible to write freely about the French. It only enables the Germans to search out the good ones for the firing squad. I cannot write about the French men and women who risk their lives every day. But thanks to them the Germans found it necessary, week by week, to move the depot where they stored and loaded bombs for the air raids against England. When commandos landed at Saint-Nazaire the whole town rose against the Germans. Later in raiding Dieppe the British radios warned that no invasion was being attempted. There are French organizations that murder German officers, and the German officer who rides alone in an automobile in any part of France today is a fool.

Nor is it possible to write about the French who are responsible for the escape of literally thousands of British prisoners. It is enough, perhaps, to point out that British soldiers have found food and hiding in almost any French home to which they have come in the night. I remember two Scots lads who told how one French family after another moved them steadily toward the Spanish frontier over a period of five months. Their experience was, perhaps, typical. They had been with some twenty-odd fellow prisoners when their German captors turned the tommy guns on them. Both lads fell and shammed dead. Their journey began when a French family gave them clothing and burned their uniforms. They had taken a rowboat and were preparing to cross a river when two German officers stopped them. They thought their number was up but stalled with broken French and found that the Germans only wanted to cross the river too. "We paddled them across," said one of the Scotsmen, adding without a trace of humor, "and charged them five francs each for the trip."

Americans know about France only what is passed by the German and the Vichy censors. We have slight comprehension of the quiet hatred which the French feel for "ces messieurs." From the beginning of the occupation the French, except for a few traitors and Vichy folk, have had no relations of a human kind with the Germans. When the German army marched up the Champs Elysées and desecrated the Arc de Triomphe with their haughty presence, every blind and shutter in the streets of Paris was drawn. No Frenchmen stood at the pavements of the broad boulevards of the City of Light. The Germans had brought prostitutes with their army and stood them at corners. Since then German officers have eaten alone and danced alone except for the company of prostitutes. A few international families—unhappily the wives are American—have opened their homes to "ces messieurs."

Reports censored by Vichy or by the German military authorities in Paris tell us nothing of the time the two German soldiers went into the farmhouse, ordered out the woman whose husband and son were in a German prison camp, and took only two of her six chickens. This case could be multiplied one hundred times. The censored reports tell us nothing of that bright afternoon when the Germans took the two horses from the little farm. There was no gasoline for the tractor, and the mother and one boy of fourteen were trying to work the farm with these last two horses. This, case could be multiplied a hundred thousand times. From the censorship we know nothing of the boats beached all along the Mediterranean and Atlantic coasts and the old fishermen watching the hunger of their people, standing on the quays unable to put to sea because the Germans have seized all French reserves of *mazout*, the fuel for these fishing fleets. Nothing is told us about the Germans confiscating, for use elsewhere, seed for spring planting. Nothing is told us about the peasant women and their boys, who in the absence of a million French farmers, harvested the wheat and then found that the Germans had refused to let the French manufacture or import binder twine.

Nothing is told us of the arrival in southern ports of French foodstuffs brought in from French Africa but "bought" up in advance by the Germans. "Ces messieurs," who are always "très corrects," used French francs they had stolen to outbid Frenchmen in the markets for every ton of this foodstuff. The censors let us know nothing of the cumulative effect of malnutrition on the French. The censors would not pass what I heard from one of the leading baby specialists of France.

"The Germans have made it impossible for us to keep official statistics," said this doctor. "They don't want us to understand and meet our problems. But we doctors are getting figures together among ourselves. Do you know what the average weight of babies in France is today? If you add the stillbirths, it cuts the figure down. The average weight of babies at birth—the dead and the living—is four pounds. Ah, we know well today that the Germans are the master race. We doctors believe, though of course our figures cannot be scientifically exact, that the German program is methodical. The Germans are trying to halve the population of France, about every twelve years, until they destroy the French nation."

We learn from the censored reports that sabotage is not very effective in France, which was manufacturing more arms for Germany than we were shipping to Great Britain under Lend-Lease before Pearl Harbor. In Lyons I found French workers at French looms using French war stocks of silk to make parachutes for German pilots. There was no sabotage. Similarly I learned that, near by, the French were making collapsible rubber lifeboats to be put in German planes. The men of France are afraid to put pinpricks into parachutes and collapsible rubber lifeboats. They are afraid of "ces messieurs." They are afraid of what will happen to the women and children of France. The Germans know how to take away the ration card of the wife and child of a French worker. They are just as clever at this as they are at taking away the factory of a French industrialist.

The owner of a French aircraft factory told me that he

refused for months to permit his factory to make planes for the Germans. His workers applauded his courage. Then the Germans took him to Berlin. They locked him up for three weeks in a concentration camp. Still he refused, so they took his factory from him. They handled the workers just as easily. The factory was closed down. The wives and the children of the workers began to starve. The airplane factory is working for the Germans now. The climax came, of course, when Hitler demanded 150,000 slave workers. These instances can be multiplied many times. They are like the first time that a German soldier forgot to be correct. For months the German discipline was severe. Then one night a German soldier raped a Frenchwoman in one of the suburbs of Paris. He had forgotten to be correct. This case could be multiplied a thousand times.

The censors let us read a little about the shooting of hostages. We know that the Germans arrest thousands of Frenchmen daily for traffic violations. If you forget and walk against the red light, the Germans arrest you. When a German is shot in the night, they take you and a hundred like you and stand you up against a stone wall. This is the system of hostages, unknown in civilized times. The censors don't tell us how they search out "Jews, communists, and de Gaullists." This is a curiously efficient system. In every medical association, in every group of lawyers, in every group of storekeepers, in every police force, there are three or four men endowed with more courage and intelligence than their fellows. They are leaders. It is these men that the Germans label as "communists." These are the men they search out to be shot as hostages. If you kill the three or four "stout fellows" in every group, you reduce that group to nothingness as a center of resistance. You also destroy the future of France.

We know so little about these things. The French know all about them. Some, like General Henri Giraud, escape to join the American and British armies. Others bide their time. They prepare the day of reckoning. That is why men like Pétain and Laval must continue to believe in German victory. For in the moment of German defeat the French people will take their kind to the lampposts. Once the blackout is over, the street lights of Paris will reveal the dangling bodies of every Fascist who has betrayed French democracy. For France remains France despite the Fascist government of Marshal Pétain and the Nazi occupation of Herr Hitler.

Disarmed and robbed of hope, the French could do very little. Waiting for Russian resistance and American intervention, they could only resign themselves to their fate. They could only tell themselves that here it was again—the fate known to their forebears under the Hun, the Moor, the English, the Spaniards, the Austrians, and once a coalition of all Europe. The Germans alone had occupied France in 1814, 1815, 1871, and 1914. The German foe was back again. They resigned themselves to the fate explained to me by a Frenchman whose grandmother lived in the north. Told in 1914 that the Germans were crossing the frontier, the old lady finished her knitting before taking her place in the long streaming line of refugees. "The Germans are coming again," she said, "comme d'habitude." And in 1940–41–42 the French resigned themselves—the Germans had come again, as was their habit.

Under the Nazi occupation the French found themselves represented this time by no Adolphe Thiers, who fought stubbornly and with imagination against Bismarck, the Iron Chancellor. From old Marshal Pétain they heard a pathetic plea that they should sing only the last verse of the "Marseillaise" because the first verse "breathed bloodthirstiness and hatred." And so they sang the last verse. They sang the last verse and they thought back on their history. They remembered the Hundred Years' War, when France shrank to petty dimensions and when, as André Maurois has reminded us, the Armagnacs and the Bourguignons split the people and fought as bitterly as the right and the left had fought in the last years before the German invasion. And they remembered that something in Frenchmen had been deeply stirred by "the great pity of the Kingdom." There will be no Joan of Arc now, but someday General Charles de Gaulle or General Henri Giraud, backed by the man power of America and Great Britain, will land on the coast of France proper. That will be "the Day of Glory" of the "Marseillaise." For the French people belong in the company of the United Nations—and they will prove their right in the day of their deliverance.

X

THERE'S NO ONE LEFT TO LET US DOWN

After the collapse of France the defeat of Great Britain seemed inevitable. Like Hitler and Mussolini, the military experts of the world were unanimous in believing that capitulation was only a matter of weeks. For in truth the British Isles were defenseless. It was all very well to talk about fighting on from Canada. The French had talked that way too. But can a nation fight on with its bare fists against the greatest mechanized power in military history? Having brought off less than 200,000 of their own troops from Dunkirk, the British were without an army. The Royal Air Force was outnumbered two to one and behind its front-line strength there were scant reserves. The navy—primarily an instrument for blockade—could do nothing against a Third Reich which now exploited the continent of Europe. The capacity of the arms industry was wholly inadequate. Mr. Neville Chamberlain had spent only $2,000,000,000 for arms in 1938, when Hitler spent $7,000,000,000, and, incredible as it seems, he had not improved the armaments position during 1939, the year of the "phony" war, when Britain felt secure behind the Maginot line and the infantry divisions of the Third Republic. Facing the ultimate doom which overtakes all empires, the British could not raise up a youthful leader to take over from the old man with the umbrella. In their desperation they turned to Mr. Winston Churchill, nearly seventy, a die-hard Tory imperialist, who reflected the dead past of Victoria in the style of his oratory no less than in his outlook. The decline of this empire was no longer debatable. The world—with mixed feelings—awaited its fall.

What had been the strength of England? What had toppled it from its pinnacle? From Napoleonic times England had been supreme. An energetic people, the English had achieved a measure of political development far in advance of their neighbors and they had made the industrial revolution their own. Shipping the world its staple industrial products and accepting foodstuffs and raw materials in return, the English had brought an expansion of trade, an improvement in the standard of living, and an increase in the birth rate throughout the whole of the civilized world. Exporting more than any two rivals, England evolved the two-power naval standard, maintaining a fleet superior to the combined forces of any two powers. The prevention of war was in the British interest, and the instrument of naval power was in their hands; they established the rule of law and gave the world a period of relative peace for a hundred years. No people is perfect. They misruled Ireland out of prejudice and blundered against the Boers, but their system and their rule nevertheless were the most enlightened in the history of the world.

Inherent in the philosophy and economics of nineteenth-century England there were forces which ultimately would destroy the nation's hegemony. Coal, machines, ships? Free trade, easy credit, equality of opportunity? England taught the other nations of the world how to utilize them. By 1913 the United States and Germany equaled Great Britain in exports, not together but singly. German production equaled and American production doubled that of Great Britain. By 1918 the British position was worsened by the exhausting efforts of a war into which the British threw the whole of their resources—a war to which the Americans had made a negligible contribution though we persuaded ourselves that our entry was decisive. At the peace the British, though victorious, recognized the facts. Far from maintaining the two-power naval standard, the British admitted virtual parity with two powers—the United States and Japan. As the world's greatest creditor, Britain had been compelled to sell foreign investments during the war and afterward the interest on the remaining investments was required to right the balance of payments. The British recognized that financially as well as politically the capital of the world had been shifted to North America. This was plain to everyone except to the Americans. Writing in Germany in 1918, Max Weber held that America's hegemony was "as inevitable as that of Rome in the ancient world after the Punic War." But in the United States we repudiated the Versailles Treaty, the military guarantee to France, and the League of Nations. We were the supreme power of the world, but we were led into isolationism. We declined to assume our obligations.

Britain's postwar leaders consequently were faced with a dilemma. Collective security was the only sound policy for Great Britain since London lacked the economic and military strength to impose its own will and dominate the recalcitrant nations. But the United States, by declining to accept its responsibilities in the League system, made collective security a myth. The British, after a brief collectivist effort at Locarno, fell back consequently on the nineteenth-century notion of the balance of power. In Europe the British attempted to curb the influence of the most powerful continental military state, France, and sought not only to win the gratitude of Germany but to strengthen that power as a counter first against France and subsequently against the increasing strength of Communist Russia. In the Far East the British sought collective security through the treaties of the Washington Naval Conference, but the Pacific policy of isolationist America became increasingly a policy of balance of power because of our distrust of Russia and China's successful effort to play America against Britain. The relations of the two Anglo-Saxon nations in the Far East is accurately summed up, I believe, by Edward Hallett Carr in his suggestive *Conditions of Peace*. He writes:

"After 1931 Great Britain was patently unable by herself

to curb the power of Japan. The United States, lacking the psychology of leadership and taking refuge in the irrelevant point that British financial interests in the Far East were larger than American, were unprepared for any concrete action. In 1932 American diplomacy by half-promises of sympathy and support busily encouraged Great Britain to act, and discredited the British government for its failure to do so. But in 1937, when British diplomacy more cleverly declared itself ready to participate in any action initiated by the United States, the latter developed the same inertia as Great Britain had displayed five years earlier. From 1936 onward American opinion severely condemned Great Britain ,for her failure to intervene effectively in the affairs of Europe. But this condemnation did not imply on the part of the United States any corresponding readiness to act themselves."

In short, Britain's postwar politicians, like those of the United States before the election of President Roosevelt, provided no leadership. The Liberal party disappeared as a political force with the century which it had, made so dynamic, and the Labor party, under the old-fashioned leadership of Ramsay MacDonald, proved too timid to evolve twentieth-century solutions for twentieth-century problems. Conservatives like Baldwin and Chamberlain reflected the pessimism of an electorate which saw that Britain no longer enjoyed its old prestige. Writing of the period 1895–1914 Halévy had already remarked that "England felt an increasingly powerful conviction that her vitality was less than that of certain other nations." By the time of the 1929 depression this feeling was general. Thus the public turned to the Tories. Attempting a realistic acceptance of Britain's weakened position, the Tories cold-bloodedly returned to "splendid isolation." They proposed to set their own house in order with a minimum of interference in continental affairs. Class-conscious, they interpreted world events in terms of a revolution between the right and the left instead of seeing the nationalistic nature of the new and dynamic Germany. They defined their task as one of obviating class struggle by rebuilding British trade. They planned to do this by classic conservative methods. Thus they left innovations in internal problems and the initiatives in foreign affairs to the aggressive and antidemocratic forces in Japan, Germany, and Italy.

Thinking of class struggle and envisaging palliatives in terms merely of money and industry and shipping, the conservatives were afraid. Not one of them had the political acumen to understand either Mr. Roosevelt's profound assertion that we have nothing to fear but fear or Herr Hitler's comprehension that wealth consists not of money and industry and shipping but of the productivity of the men and women who make up the nation. They ignored, but Hitler acted on, the assumption that no nation's accumulated wealth, in capitalistic terms, represents more than about five years of the nation's productivity. Baldwin and Chamberlain would not substitute welfare for wealth. They would not substitute national armaments for wealth. They put private business first. Once again it became sacrosanct. American production mounted with the impetus of Roosevelt's program of welfare. German production mounted with Hitler's notion of sacrificing everything to the demands of the state. But in Great Britain neither Baldwin nor Chamberlain was able to undertake a successful rearmament program. At the time of his resignation Mr. Chamberlain had contrived to put only 10 per cent of the nation's wealth into the armaments effort. He had persuaded himself, the majority of the conservatives, and the leaders of Germany, Italy, and Japan that Great Britain was decadent. It was upon this assumption that Germany made war. After the fall of France the world at large was ready to agree that Hitler's estimate of the British had been sound. The decline of the British Empire was apparent; we awaited its imminent fall.

One foreign observer proved exceptional. President Roosevelt. After the fall of France one of Mr. Roosevelt's ambassadors flew to Washington. He urged the President to intervene immediately because otherwise, he argued, Great Britain would fall in a matter of weeks and the United States, isolated and without allies, could not stand against a combined German and Japanese attack. The President replied that the American people were not interventionist and that he did not propose to attempt to lead them to war.

The ambassador then spoke with considerable vehemence and he quoted the President's reply as follows: "The danger you point out is real. All my military experts agree that Great Britain cannot stand. I don't agree with you or them. I feel it in my bones. The British people will confound the world."

President Roosevelt meant, of course, that the British were not the people we had seen under Baldwin and Chamberlain. The President understood the people of a democratic country and he knew to what heights of sacrifice and heroism they could be led in a people's war. He saw what Hitler once had seen in the British, what Hitler had written and pondered, until Baldwin and Chamberlain persuaded him of British decadence. For in *Mein Kampf* Hitler wrote:

"The spirit of the British nation enables it to carry through to victory any struggle which it once enters upon, no matter how long the struggle may last or however great the sacrifice that may be necessary or whatever the means which have to be employed; and all this though the actual equipment at hand may be utterly inadequate when compared with that of any other nation."

The simple men and women of England knew the truth of this assertion. They, too, felt it in their bones. Baldwin and Chamberlain? Well, they were done with them and well rid of them too. In the words of Lloyd George, "Hitler has got more brains in his little finger than the combined governments of Baldwin and Chamberlain." The House

of Commons destroyed the political prerogatives of big business in an hour's sitting, voting the government such powers
as even Stalin did not enjoy. "At last," sighed the British
people, "the war effort will come first." The fall of France?
That was a hard blow and bewildering but, as a simple
woman expressed it, "I finds it improvin' on the whole—
there's no one left to let us down."

The first World War and the transition from one century
to the next may have destroyed the preeminence of British
capital and British trade. It improved the lot of the simple
men and women who are England. Their financial position,
relatively, was improved, and so were their health, their housing, and the educational opportunities afforded them. They
had had enough of rule by the Birmingham businessman.
Now the war was up to them and they felt worthy. All they
asked was honest leadership. Mr. Chamberlain had talked
to them like the director of a company when its assets are
no longer liquid; he was afraid that the truth might start
a run on the bank. "It's time for Winston," the people
cried. Winston had told them the truth about the rearmament of "that bastard Hitler," sounding off in the Commons
year after year like a bloody Cassandra, he did. And he had
told them the truth about Munich. Mr. Churchill was a
member of the Conservative party like Mr. Chamberlain,
but he was different. He believed in the people and the
people could believe in him. The reason lies in the peculiar
British notion of an aristocrat. The secret of that notion
is reflected perhaps in something said many years ago by
Mr. Churchill's father, Lord Randolph Churchill. "The
English upper and lower classes are bound together," said
Lord Randolph, "by a common love of immorality and a
common detestation of the middle class." Mr. Chamberlain
was a middle-class Birmingham businessman. Mr. Churchill
was an aristocrat. And from the moment he took over, Mr.
Churchill pleased. He surprised the nation and the world

by an elasticity of mind which showed itself promptly when he offered union with France, later when he turned to America, and finally when he, the red-baiter, made an alliance with the Soviet Union. Philip Guedalla has quoted Macaulay's essay in which Pitt says, "My Lord, I am sure that I can save this country and that nobody else can." That was Mr. Churchill too, confident of the empire, the people, and himself—just as confident in 1940 as he had been when he first went out to Kipling's India, a young cavalry subaltern, insufferably proud to be a hussar and thrilled by the "soothin', jingle-bump-an'-clank" of the horse artillery.

Having brought off 186,587 British troops (and 123,095 Frenchmen) from Dunkirk, Mr. Churchill had to build an army in the very moment when he was fighting Goering's *Luftwaffe* and expanding Britain's laggard war industries. The British trained and equipped 1,500,000 men for the regular army. And out of homes, fields, and factories they brought another 2,000,000 boys and old men to form the Home Guard, somber civilians who amused us journalists by the intensity with which they simulated the repulse ot invasion forces. The Home Guard stood with fixed bayonets around 3000 miles of island coast, ready to serve a cup of tea to a German parachute jumper or equally ready to garrote him. The Home Guard knew that the parachutists and the air-borne infantry would serve merely as a screen for the major effort. For Hitler planned to land full armored divisions, each with four hundred tanks, from thousands of flat-bottomed Diesel-driven barges. Flat scows could be driven against the shore until guns and tanks were rolled off, because the scows are held there by enormous outboard motors of the type first used for barges on some American canals. Consequently the Germans would not need jetties and docks to land. The British planned to meet these landings by counterattacks, the regular army fanning out against each German bridgehead. These improvised defense torces knew what they were up against. The *Luftwaffe* would try to protect the first German landings against the nominally superior forces at the disposal of the British. In addition, it was fairly certain that they would use gas in order to regain the element of surprise and to achieve superior driving force, as they attempted to penetrate to key points and to disrupt the British defense.

The German technique in the use of gas was a matter of tactics. If there are five roads fit for armored columns leading from the coast to a key defense point, the Germans would gas three of them. The invading German forces would know which two roads had been left free of gas and were, therefore, open. Thus they would know exactly where the gassed areas began and ended, while the British would have to find out. The Germans would be able to roll forward immediately, but the British would have to spend hours, perhaps decisive hours, discovering which regions were gassed and trying to neutralize these contaminated areas. British troops moving into roads covered with mustard-type gas would know that their clothing had to be changed within four hours.

While fighting the *Luftwaffe* and building an army against invasion the British also faced the problem of production. Mr. Churchill's first act upon becoming Chamberlain's successor was to draft Ernest Bevin, Britain's labor leader. Working together, the two devoted 60 per cent of the national income to war expenditure as against scarcely more than 10 per cent under Mr. Chamberlain. British production figures remain secret, but there are certain general indications of its progress. The production of all kinds of army supplies was tripled after Dunkirk and by mid-1942 stood at roughly ten times what it had been when Hitler first marched against Poland in the fall of 1939. In the last quarter of 1941 British shipyards launched four times the tonnage in warships that slid down the ways in the three months before Hitler's aggression, and twice as many merchant ships. The production of airplanes was tripled. This prodigious effort was undertaken when the British found German planes overhead ninety days out of every one hundred and when they were bombed nightly through twelve months except for thirty nights alone. This accomplishment can be judged against production in America, where there was no bombing attack. During the year 1941 America was able to send Great Britain 200 tanks and 2134 planes. During the same year Britain sent abroad to her own fronts and to Russia about 3000 tanks and 9781 planes. Thus it will be seen that for every bomber and fighter plane that Great Britain acquired from America during 1941 she produced and exported five. For every tank we sent her she produced and sent abroad fifteen. Of the planes that defended the British Isles against the *Luftwaffe* 89 per cent were British-made. Of the planes that fought for British forces overseas 75 per cent were British-made. The British made the planes and they flew them. Of the total casualties among airmen 75 per cent were borne by the United Kingdom alone. The British, moreover, had shot down by 1942 some 9396 German and Italian planes.

"After all, we have a navy," said Mr. Churchill. "Some people seem to forget that we have a navy. We must remind them." Occasionally the navy made a headline, as at Taranto or when it hounded down the *Bismarck,* but generally it was as quiet as it was efficient. The Royal Navy kept 600 ships continuously at sea in all kinds of weather, bringing 40,-000,000 tons of foodstuffs and raw materials to British workers and factories every year. The navy brought the convoys safely into port with their losses held down to less than one-half of one per cent—held down to one ship out of every two hundred. It was the navy that took 30,000 war vehicles and more than 1,000,000 tons of other supplies to the Middle East alone. Before Pearl Harbor the British navy accounted for 86 per cent of the German and Italian surface war vessels sunk, 89 per cent of their merchant vessels sunk, and 94 per cent of all the enemy submarines destroyed by the United Nations.

Great Britain's most bitter trial came in the air, an element which the Germans claimed that they had made their own. Great Britain's strength in first-line fighters, with French combat planes included, was about equal to Germany's 1500 aircraft. Germany's second-line fighter strength of 2700 was a thousand stronger than the combined British reserve fighter strength. Britain's weakness after the defection of France can be imagined. In bombers the German first-line strength stood at 2500 and was three and a half times as strong as that of Britain. In reserve Germany had 4500 bombers or about two and a half times the British reserve strength. The British public scarcely dreamed what awaited it. Through the "phony" war Lord Beaverbrook's newspapers, the *Daily Express* and the *Evening Standard,* agitated to have the blackout regulations lifted on the argument that they interfered unnecessarily with retail trade! The truth was never put to the British until Mr. Churchill took over. The man in the street never dreamed that in the period between Danzig and Dunkirk the Germans were building at least seven Heinkels for every British Wellington bomber. And yet, as often happens, a British weakness proved a British strength.

Weak in quantity, the R.A.F. was strong in quality. "British goods are best." That has been the boast of the British businessman through generations. In aircraft, too, they demanded the best. The R.A.F. might have been numerically stronger if it had accepted a lower standard of quality or if it had mobilized all the resources of the aircraft industry for standard types instead of permitting a part of it to continue with adaptations and improvements. Consequently the pilots of the Hurricanes, Spitfires, and Typhoons knew that they had the best fighting craft in the world. Their planes were superior in speed and guns. They proved themselves superior as pilots, just as their high command proved superior to Goering and the other leaders of the *Luftwaffe*. The German bombers came over, 200 and 500 at a time. Their object was to wear down and destroy the British fighter strength. Husbanding their woefully inadequate handful of planes, the British Fighter Command showed from the beginning remarkable efficiency at interception. In exercises an average of 30 per cent interception had been thought satisfactory and 50 per cent was described as good. In the summer of 1940 the percentages rose to 75, 90, and 100. As David Garnett discloses, the controller of Number Eleven Group ordered up 21 squadrons on September 27, and each was able to report having sighted the enemy and having made a successful interception. This is what saved Britain in 1940 as truly as Nelson saved her at Trafalgar. On September 15 the Germans made their all-out daylight bombing in undoubted preparation for invasion. The British shot down 185 German aircraft, losing 25 R.A.F. planes. On September 27 the Germans sent 900 planes and lost 133; on September 30 they sent 600 and lost 49. The morale of the *Luftwaffe* could not bear up under such casualties. Consequently the Germans went in for night bombing where they could start fires so that pilots at great altitude could rain down bombs indiscriminately. The mass daylight attacks during July, August, and September had failed to overwhelm the British fighters, who inflicted casualties of five to one on an enemy inferior in everything but numbers.

The indiscriminate bombing of men, women, and children failed equally to terrorize the British nation. The Germans made two grave psychological blunders. They bombed London first. Had they bombed the provincial cities, carefully avoiding the capital, they might have given some meaning to the propaganda of Lord Haw-Haw and others that the British people were forced to fight on only because of the "warmonger" Churchill. The people of the whole country, however, had watched with anguish and horror the trial of London before they took their own particular form of hell at Coventry, Bristol, Plymouth, Birmingham, Dover, and the other cities and towns of the kingdom. In the second place, the Germans twice bombed Buckingham Palace while the royal family was in residence there—bombings which were unmistakably deliberate. In that moment the King and Queen became one with the simplest man and woman in the land. The little princesses were children too. These blunders put the British public on its mettle. The people knew that the Germans were trying to break their morale. So that was their game, was it? The simplest Briton felt himself to be in the front line, felt that the defense of the empire rested on his own behavior. As many as 6954 civilians were killed and 10,616 wounded in a single month. A German pilot, talking over the German radio, described looking down on docks and ships which provided a tempting target. "But I had other orders," he said. That was the game.

The Germans were bombing for panic. The British people knew how to behave in the face of that sort of thing. They inspired the R.A.F. and the R.A.F. inspired them. I remember talking with the leader of a bombing squadron at a British airdrome. He took me to the pilots' quarters and showed me a pile of bricks under his bunk. "That's all that is left of the house in which they killed my mother and father," he said. "I'm going to take a brick along with the bombs every time I go to Germany." The same bitterness characterized the fighter pilots. They were the lads who broke up the German formations by diving into them, crying, "Tally ho—here we go." The superlative quality of the youthful pilots was matched by their senior officers. Against night bombing the Air Ministry devised radio detection which registered the position of a German plane and ultimately set British guns going automatically when the enemy bomber was in range. Similarly they evolved schemes for dummy fires, so that the German planes loosed many a bomb-load on open fields. The senior officers used their planes and men sparingly and to maximum advantage. Mr. Churchill has offered his eloquent tribute to the R.A.F.: "Never in the field of human conflict was so much owed by so many to so few." I prefer the cartoon in *Punch*. A young British pilot was being congratulated by a fellow officer as he stepped from his plane.

"After all, old chap," the pilot said, "I outnumbered the Germans one to five."

This pose of superiority, insufferable and sincere, was possible in young men who had behind them the uncomplaining courage of simple men and women standing in the streets of every city, town, and village of the United Kingdom. I went out into the provinces to try to understand the nature of a struggle in which every civilian is a fighter and every home a front line. I went to Birmingham and Coventry and Dover and Bristol. I went to Plymouth too. I went to Plymouth because Lady Astor, my fellow Southerner, persuaded me that Plymouth was truly typical of England. The English are as proud of "our town" and as blatant in its praise as the Chamber of Commerce in any American community. Each town argues that it has been bombed worse than any other. The man who has stood with his neighbors through the fearful horror of bombardment—fought the fires, rescued the living, buried the dead—and then seen his own kind come out with their spirits undaunted believes that there are no people quite like them in the world.

Before the Norman conquest Plymouth was described as a "mene thing, an inhabitation of fishars." And after more air raids in a year than there are days in a year Plymouth, though its population approximates 200,000, is a "mene thing" again. The "old Church" of St. Andrew is gutted, but the 1460 tower still stands. The imposing Gothic Guildhall, which spread over two blocks and lent a quiet dignity to the town, is blasted and burned out. The retail shopping center that served the workers of the shipyard, the arsenal, and the naval station, which make Plymouth the great port of southwest England, is a blackened desert of rubble and waste as far as a man can see. The homes of Plymouth—the beautiful little gray stone houses in the quiet streets—are wrecked by the thousands, square mile after square mile of them. The Germans have destroyed 51 churches and every auditorium. There is no hall left which will seat more than 300. But in this "mene" place I found Main Street, England.

Plymouth is the living illustration of what the British mean by tradition. Hitler's invasion of Britain has never come off because every preparatory phase of bombing has failed. It has failed to break British morale. Plymouth folk took six days and six nights of bombing without interruption. They were dead beat from want of sleep. They were so jarred and shaken by the explosion of bombs that few could keep food on their stomachs. And yet they carried on. Every man and every woman, whether his station was high or low, felt that the morale of Plymouth and the survival of the empire rested on his own shoulders. That is tradition—pride of place and manner, handed down from generation to generation. When the *Mayflower* sailed on September 6, 1620, Plymouth's fame had already been carried to the far corners of the earth by Hawkins, Raleigh and Gilbert, Cavendish, Frobisher and Oxenham. It was to Plymouth—heart then as now of simple England—that the "invincible" Armada sailed and it was on the turf of Plymouth Hoe that Lord Howard and Sir Francis Drake played bowls when Master Fleming brought news that the Spaniards approached. Drake persuaded Howard to finish the bowling. "There's plenty of time," he said, "to win the game and thrash the Spaniards too." Facing an armada of the skies, the folk of Plymouth today preserve the same unperturbable calm. They are the breed that sent Drake to circumnavigate the globe and the Pilgrim Fathers to plant in America the life spark of the greatest nation in the world.

In the ruins of Plymouth's bombed-out railway station we had tea at a canteen. Soldiers, sailors, and civilians are served there together because in English towns like Plymouth civilians are combatants too. A pretty little woman behind the counter chaffed Lady Astor.

"Only one spoon of sugar for you, Milady," she said.

"Give her more; she's a growing girl," said a sailor.

The whole crowd roared, because the youngster could have been her grandson.

"You wouldn't be saying that," laughed Lady Astor, famous as a prohibitionist, "if you hadn't been polluting yourself in the pubs. Own up. Answer me now. You've had a morning's beer already, haven't you?"

The laughter of the crowd was turned against the cleareyed youthful sailor. He shook Lady Astor's hand and she patted him on the back.

"Savior of his country, he is," she said, and the crowd roared.

The youngster blushed, tears of laughter in his eyes.

We were stopped by a woman of the shopkeeping class, well dressed, with a blue hat which brought out the color of her clear, defiant eyes.

"Did you ever see such beautiful raspberries, Milady?" she said, proffering the basket. "I'm forgettin' my troubles when I look at them berries."

"Go on with you," said Lady Astor, "you've got no troubles."

"Haven't I now? They blitzed my shop. I've got no more business. They blitzed my home. I went to my daughter's. They blitzed that. Regular Jonah I am. I'm livin' with my sister now, but she says I'll be bringing a blitz on her house too. I'm a Jonah all right, but look at them berries. Prettiest I ever did see. When we get berries that pretty we're doin' fine, I says."

A well-knit, heavy-shouldered man with gray around his temples doffed his cap.

"Excuse me, Lady Astor," he began. "Seeing as how you're my Member of Parliament—though, if truth be known, I didn't vote for you—I want to be asking you something. I had experience in the last war, all through—Ypres and the Somme. Now the government won't let me sign up. Say I got to stay working in the dockyards. I've got no family and I'm wanting to be back in the army doing my bit."

The Member of Parliament explained patiently that workers were just as important as soldiers and that the government under its emergency powers had to decide arbitrarily that men of certain age remain at industrial tasks.

"That's all wrong, Lady Astor," said the workman. "I'm seasoned timber, I am. Meaning no disrespect to the young ones, for fine lads they are; but they'd never have quit Dunkirk if they'd had seasoned timber there like me and my kind."

A lame old woman with a "Queen Mary" hat perched on her greasy mop of hair and a "Chamberlain" umbrella under her arm stopped us. She was plainly excited.

"Me old man turned on me, Milady. And I wuz so exasperated I hit him in the face. He wuz ailing after Tom's death; killed at sea Tom wuz, and the finest son that ever lived, Tom. All we had, Tom wuz. Then we wuz blitzed out of our house—been living in one of the communal rest centers since. It got me old man down, it did. 'Molly, we ought to commit suicide, sez he,' me own husband. I hit the old un across the head with my pocketbook, fetched him a blow to bring him to his senses. 'Wot?' sez I. 'Kill ourselves and let Hitler win? Not I, nor you,' sez I. 'Hitler's a criminal and I mean to live to see him dead, I do.' "

Farther down the street we stopped a young couple wheeling a pram.

"Yes, he's seven weeks old, a real blitz baby," said the pale little mother. "Ain't he the darling?"

"Awful hard it was on the missus though," interrupted the proud father. "She in the shelters for three nights straight, then to the hospital, and he born with Jerry giving us the merry."

"But he's not one bit nervous," I said.

"Oh, yes, he is," replied his mother. "He's all right, but he's nervous. All blitz babies are. A shame for them to be born in such conditions. But he's none the worse for it, only nervous."

"Now, now," said the husband. "Things can be worse. That's what I always say."

I stopped to talk with an elderly man in one of the twenty-seven communal kitchens.

"Yes, I'm eating here," said the old man, "because they blew in my house. It's really more diverting getting out with people. This food's as good as I ever et only it's spiritual food we want nowadays and you need more than pease and potatoes in these times. You see, when they blitzed my house they destroyed my books. But I'm not downhearted. I'm not complaining. I've got my books in my head—right here between these two big ears of mine. And they're a comfort to me."

I visited the arsenal, the navy yard, and the docks. Every part of all three had been blasted by bombs and fire, but the whole works rang with the reverberating roar of riveting machines, the heavy, clanging thud of drop-forges, and the creaking noise of cranes heavy enough to pick up entire gun turrets. Where roofs were blown or burned away men worked in the open air, though in such roofless plants the lights must be switched at night after an alert is sounded. One group of workers, cursing Jerry roundly, showed me how a battleship they had reconditioned got another bomb through the deck just as they were ready to float her away from the drydock. "All in the game," one observed. Elsewhere patterns were laid out and steel plates were being cut. And with this roaring, hammering sound of men and machines at work on steel for mile after mile down the water front there mingled the cries of the workers themselves— "Steady . . . Hold 'er . . . Damn yer soul . . . Easy there . . . " These men worked with a will, and noisily, while antiaircraft crews lounged around their guns and telephonists sat with earphones to the distant listening devices.

"We rarely go to the shelters now," said a supervisor or foreman. "We just let Jerry drop his eggs and we go on with our job unless the raid is really big. You see, there's many a man here had his kiddy or wife killed by the Hun laying bombs down row after row of workin'men's houses. The men all agreed they preferred to go on with the job. The Hun has to be hittin' bloody hard before the men'll take to the shelters."

The only labor problem was absenteeism—workers missing a day or more from work.

"That's understandable among civilians," said the naval officer. "Men want to find new homes for their wives and children when their own houses are blown out." A worker agreed. "But the men are back on the job soon's they've taken care of their womenfolks. Of course, sometimes men knock off for a few days after they've had a whole week of bombings day and night with no letup. But not many. Our absentees have never run 10 per cent, my supervisor says, even in the worst blitz periods."

The English have an extraordinary sense of property values and the bitterest men I saw were the hard-bitten dockers. They unload the ships after the convoys have brought them the slow, long, zigzagging, roundabout journey through U-boats and Focke-Wulf bombers. It is heartrending to comprehend the difficulties of the long Atlantic voyage, to unload the stores in backbreaking work—sometimes under enemy bombing—and then to see a million dollars' worth of tobacco or tons of Argentine beef or a warehouse full of powdered milk go up in unmanageable flames. These barrel-chested men, the best-organized union labor in the world, clench their fists and spit when they say "Jerry." Only it's generally four words said as one. "Jerry-the-bloody-bastard," they say.

In a vast open meadow, before the cricket pavilion, I

watched the Lord Mayor, the Lady Mayoress, the Regional Commissioner, and the Aldermen of Plymouth hold a lawn party. The reception honored two thousand A.R.P., or civil defense, workers ranging in age from boys of sixteen to one gentleman of eighty-two, George H. Foster, Plymouth's oldest warden. I stood on the fringe of the crowd as the oratory began.

First speaker: "We must hope for the best and prepare for the worst. . . . If things do not go well with the Russians, Plymouth will know what it is to be in the front line again. . . . The whole United Kingdom congratulates and praises you on still being very much alive and a going concern.". . .

Second speaker: "What is the spirit of Plymouth? I can give it to you in a sentence. Sympathy for others and courage on our own. . . . People who once adopted a patronizing tone now recognize the A.R.P. workers as guides, philosophers, and friends once the sirens blow.". . .

Third speaker: "There are still five thousand school children who are not evacuated from Plymouth. That isn't mother love; that's 'smugger love,' complete selfishness. We all know that living conditions for the evacuated children are as perfect as we can make them. . . . I put it to you as neighbors—should these children be here when Plymouth is blitzed again?"

Fourth speaker: "I pray that this war is not won until the United States is in. If so, reconstruction will be very difficult. There is no reason why if, after the war these two nations get together, we could not build a world where war on a large scale would be impossible. . . . When we Plymouth folk say that we hate war we know what war is.". . .

Fifth speaker: "What kind of freedom will there be if we let down our side? . . . Yes, my friends and fellow townsmen, Plymouth is fighting in the front line and fighting proudly. . . . We are fighting for this thing we call freedom —freedom even to grouse and complain, freedom not to like a thing if we don't like it . . . freedom to say our say to any blessed mother's son in the whole cockeyed world.". . .

As the sixth speaker, Lady Astor said: "I've been talking with foreigners. I've talked with foreign correspondents. Do you know what they're saying? They say that people all over the world thought when France collapsed that Britain was beaten. I told them the idea never occurred to any of us. Is that true?"

The crowd mumbled its astonishment. Men lifted their eyebrows. Women shook their heads in puzzlement. I am convinced that for nine out of the ten of the two thousand souls standing on that cricket ground the idea of Britain being beaten was presented to them then and there for the first time. I like to think that this quality in them comes less from what is called British phlegm or stupidity than from the tradition and habit of behaving well.

I met Colin Campbell, town clerk and A.R.P. controller. A tall, slender, well-dressed man of forty-five who looked like any automobile dealer in an American town, Mr. Campbell was grousing about three members of the Board of Aldermen who had not turned out for the lawn party. I asked this taxpayer who was indignantly berating politicians to tell me about the A.R.P. problems.

"Well, sir," said Mr. Campbell, "the national government puts up the antiaircraft barrage, the balloons, and our fighter aircraft. Our problem as citizens of Plymouth is mainly fire-fighting and rescuing our wounded and our dead. Before the war Plymouth had twenty firemen. With so much stone in our houses we don't have bad fires normally. Now we have got five hundred all-time, paid, professional firemen and two thousand volunteer firemen. We've also got the step-up system, of course, by which we tie in with near-by towns. If we're getting all the blitz and the whole town is on fire, every town for fifty miles around that isn't being bombed rushes us apparatus and men. We do the same, naturally, when a neighbor town is taking it and we're on the quiet.

Yes, sir, these volunteers are everything from lawyers and bankers to dock workers. Naturally everybody who can turns out to fight fire in his own neighborhood, but we've got never less than two thousand volunteers on duty. Some are on duty this very minute. Yes, that's a pretty terrible drain especially on men that have worked all day. They have to take turnabout sleeping at nights except when we get a solid four or five days of blitzing without a letup.

"We've built a wonderful organization—on paper, that is. Everything's easier on paper. The trouble is Jerry upsets things. For instance, we get our fire watchers all perfectly scattered and our fire fighters waiting in every part of town and our apparatus stored where we think it's safest from bombs and yet handy. Then everything may go all right, or, as frequently happens, the very first bombs may blow out vital water mains or the telephone lines in half the town. What do we do then? Why, it's just like war at the front when the field telephones go. You've got to send couriers through and plenty of them so that no matter how many get killed the message comes through."

Mr. Campbell suddenly called to two young boys whose mouths were full of buns. He introduced me to Thomas Puley and William Collister, both aged sixteen.

"They've carried messages for us on bicycles," said Mr. Campbell. "This is Tom Puley's boy. Step up, Tom, and tell the gentleman what you did."

"Why, I took the messages through," said Tom Puley, and that was all that he would say. He and Collister were plainly embarrassed by this fuss and the presence of a strange questioner.

Dismissing them, Campbell explained: "Little Puley there carried seventeen messages in a single night—every one of them carried through with bombs exploding in every street of Plymouth. He was blown off his bicycle twice, and the last time the bike was ruined and he came in on foot.

"Oh, yes," continued Mr. Campbell, "bombs do funny

things without hurting you. The Presbyterian minister had a funny one. He was running down the street screaming a warning to his neighbors that a land mine was falling. A land mine comes down on a great parachute, slowly. You can see them falling and if you can run a hundred yards away the blast will blow over you and not injure you. But you especially want to be in the open because the blast of a land mine will bring down a whole block of buildings or houses and you don't want to be crushed under them. Well, the clergyman was warning his neighbors—running as spry as a dog, with his preacher's coattails out in the wind behind. The land mine blew him head over heels. He came up uninjured, but the blast had clean cut away his coattails. People stopped to laugh with him right in the middle of houses still coming down. I laugh now when I think about it. A Presbyterian preacher without his coattails is like a rooster with his tail feathers gone.

"People behave splendidly even when their homes are destroyed and their families killed. It's a funny thing, but the only people who complain are the ones with little problems. A man with his windows blown out can make more trouble than a man whose house is gone.

"But this blitz business can be pretty grim. You get exhausted, you know—exhausted emotionally as well as physically. Sometimes you think you can't take any more. Most of the A.R.P. workers are like me; they get to worrying about their own loved ones when they are digging out the maimed and mangled bodies of others. It's a bad thing to hear the big ones come bumping down and the whole town rocking and shaking. And when the fires are going Jerry just opens the hatches and lets them fall, anywhere, everywhere. Jerry mixes up incendiaries and explosives until it makes you giddy. And you get sick of the sound of the incendiaries tinkling down—that damned tinkle all mixed up with the crash of bombs and the roar of the antiaircraft flack. It fair puts the wind up you.

"It's all right when you're too busy to think. But when you're waiting to go into action in your part of town, you think about your own family, miles across town, under the bombs. One bad night I heard by telephone that a land mine had been seen coming down toward the end of Devon Road. That's a routine call; we spot them all. Only it wasn't routine to me. My house is the only house at the end of Devon Road. I called my wife—she was in the house with my three babies—and the telephone was dead! It was seven hours before my duties let me get home. I found my own loved ones all O.K., but, believe me, I sweat blood that night. You ought to see some of the babies we dig out. As long as I live I'll remember the severed head of one infant. There was a rubber teat clenched in the mouth and a smile on the poor little fellow's face."

Mr. Campbell introduced me to one of his fire fighters who had just come out of the hospital after the amputation of a leg.

"Dunkirk was quite a show," he agreed, "but I'd go through Dunkirk twice again as soon as one of Plymouth's bad blitzes. In Dunkirk you knew where they were coming from and you felt like you could get away. But no, sir, not in these towns. I spent three months in hospital with wounds after Dunkirk. I've been in hospital with a leg taken away after Plymouth. I was bringing in a lorry with fire apparatus with bombs falling all around. Never knew where the one came from what got me. Blew my lorry clean into a crater."

A bell rang out sweetly in the distance. All that remains of the 1460 church, the "old Church" of St. Andrew, is the belfry and the bell. It is the same bell that proclaimed Drake's victory. Everyone started away. It was the signal for dancing on the Hoe. We were off to join the dancers.

"Of course, we risk our people being machine-gunned and bombed by German planes," explained Lord Astor, "but the Aldermen and I have agreed that the risk is worth it."

To the people already dancing to the American jazz of the

Royal Air Force band the risk was certainly worth it. Best dance of all was a "Palace Glide"—first for the grownups, then for the children. The children were timid until the ice was broken; then they had as much fun as children at their first dances anywhere in the world. Their shrill laughter was ringing loudest of all when the sun sank beyond Plymouth Harbor below the Hoe and turned the silver balloons of the barrage a soft and warming red. British patrol planes whined, too far overhead to be seen, as the people of Plymouth returned to their homes or their communal rest camps to wonder—as they always wonder—whether Jerry would come in the night.

I slipped off into an open-air pub—open-air thanks to enemy action—to have a drink with Mr. Percy Cole, air-raid warden and director of the Plymouth morgue. After four hundred bombing attacks within twelve months Mr. Cole spoke quietly in tones blended of profoundly distressed compassion and the undertaker's habit of professional sympathy.

"What's worst in a blitz is when the bodies can't be found," said Mr. Cole. "That upsets the relatives so. Sometimes you know that there were twelve people in a house, but you can recover but nine bodies. In such cases we have taken apart the whole ruined house out of consideration for the relatives, but often as not it's been in vain. You shore up and climb into the wreckage and you bring nothing out and people are so frightfully upset. You can't hardly blame them. I remember a sailor who helped us look for his wife and two little children in a house which took a direct hit of high explosive. We couldn't find any tangible remains. The sailor was pretty good. He asked the rector to say a funeral service over the blasted rubble. Then he tore off a few square inches of wallpaper from plaster lying in the ruins. 'Paper's off our bedroom wall,' he said. 'Want to keep it as a remembrance.'

"Take the greengrocer's drayman, Tom Fellowes. Known

young Tom and his family all his life. One afternoon after a bad blitz night when I had had no sleep he came into the morgue. 'I thought you were fifty miles away from here, serving in the army. When did you get leave?' I asked Tom.

" 'I got only eight hours' leave and got to be back in two hours,' Tom said soberlike. 'I'd be grateful for a favor. I heard Plymouth was blitzed mighty bad and I got leave to come into town.'

"Tom pulls a parcel out of his right coat pocket, all wrapped up in paper. He pulls another parcel out of his left pocket. He puts them both on my desk.

" 'This is all,' says Tom, 'that remains of my father and all that remains of my mother. They was sittin' both sides of the fireplace in rocking chairs. I like to think that they had their hands together when the bomb hit. But I don't know. There ain't enough of them left to know. I'd be thankin' you, sir, if you'd see that they got decent burial. I've got to be back to my unit.' "

The director of the morgue paused.

"It's not a jolly life, you know, with bombs bumping down," he continued. "What's hard is certifying the dead. I personally have certified more than one thousand dead and everyone of them a neighbor, most of them known to me all my life. Those are hard lines. I was really grateful to the Lord Mayor when he took me in hand and told me I had to take a week off. Only letup I've had in a year of bombing. Only fine thing is the way the people of Plymouth behave. Ruddy heroes, they are, one and all."

The next morning the scene on the Hoe was a strange contrast. The children and the soldiers and sailors and airmen and young girls were there again. But all the old men and old women of Plymouth were there as well. More than five thousand people stood on the Hoe for divine service, arranged by the Lord Mayor for all denominations and the congregations of all blitzed churches.

In place of the organ there was music by the Plymouth

Congress Hall Salvation Army Band. The lesson was read by a Methodist Wesleyan clergyman—the first nine verses of Isaiah xxvi. His powerful voice brought the words to thousands who knew their full meaning.

> In that day shall this song be sung in the land of Judah: We have a strong city; salvation will God appoint for walls and bulwarks. . . .

The Vicar of St. Andrews preached the sermon.

"Talking with the people while this city has been relentlessly bombed, I have heard them say that God has come very much nearer to them. . . . I have the firm conviction that what seemed to be the greatest tragedy in the world will often be found to have been the birth pangs of the greatest triumph. . . . We will look back and see that out of these troubled times the people brought something which we would never have seen had we gone on in our lazy and indolent way. . . . We shall have learned the value of fellowship and of living together in better understanding.". . .

Looking into the uplifted faces of the people of Plymouth, I saw the living proof of the Vicar's words. The men and women who sailed in the *Mayflower* must have had the same hard but radiant faces and the same proud sense of fellowship in a worthy enterprise.

And then five thousand men, women, and children stood to the blaring music of the Salvation Army band and sang:

> "Fight the good fight with all thy might, Christ is thy Strength, and Christ thy Right.". . .

These are the people of Plymouth. They and men and women like them in a thousand towns are preserving England's green and pleasant land.

XI

AFTER CHURCHILL, WHAT?

HISTORY will place Winston Churchill in the direct line of Cecil, Marlborough, and Pitt. He saved England—and with England the rest of the civilized world—in a moment when no other statesman could. From the instant when he took over from Neville Chamberlain he proved his greatness, showing himself not vindictive when he said, "If we open a quarrel between the past and the present, we shall find that we have lost the future." Political popularity, however, is a fragile thing and war leaders must hold it in steady hands if they are to keep the magic of their appeal. That magic feeds on military success in the field. Mr. Churchill may step down or he may be forced out before Great Britain sees the victory of which he has been the principal architect. Sir Stafford Cripps, formerly Ambassador to Moscow, has already been boomed as a successor to Mr. Churchill. The Marxist was pushed forward as the man to take over from the Tory. The political future of Cripps and other rivals, like that of the present Prime Minister himself, depends less upon what they and Mr. Churchill do than upon what Herr Hitler does. So long as German strength remains preponderant the United Nations must brace themselves against further and perhaps overwhelming Axis victories. Will the German *Wehrmacht* achieve those victories at the direct expense of Russia or of Great Britain? Mr. Churchill's political future stands or falls with the success of British arms. Cripps, on the other hand, has tied his future, wittingly or unwittingly, to Stalin's star.

Mr. Churchill was an American hero when he and President Roosevelt laid down the Atlantic Charter in August, 1941. The glowing approval of Americans offered an amusing contrast to the critical asperity I had just remarked in London, only a clipper's flight away. There the people said that what Great Britain wanted was a man like Roosevelt. I told Anthony Eden, the Foreign Minister, that he ought to arrange to exchange the two leaders for a year under Lend-Lease.

"There is no doubt, of course, that Winston still catches the imagination and holds the affection of the masses," said typical representatives of what is known in England as the governing, or "uppah," class. "But Winston wants to run everything himself. He won't abide criticism and turns it away with a smile or a scowl. He surrounds himself with yes men and favorites and he is guilty of flagrant nepotism. Wanting to have his hand in everything that's done, he declines to delegate authority. Production is the problem. He ought to name a Minister of Production and give him full power. He doesn't like big men around him. He talks superbly; but there's too much talk, too little action."

One influential Member of Parliament exclaimed, "Winston positively enjoys the war. It's a game to him. He is playing at war. What this country needs is a Prime Minister. Winston is a war lord, seated on a white charger, galloping hither and yon. There is no one to get on with the day-to-day business of government. He is wonderfully energetic in matters that excite his personal interest; he neglects what bores him."

A more just appraisal of the man as a popular leader was offered by one of his stanch admirers, Lady Oxford and Asquith. Widow of a wartime Prime Minister, Margot Asquith had known more about British politics and British politicians than any man or woman alive since the days half a century ago when, as a mischievous and beautiful girl, she deliberately brought Churchill's father, Lord Randolph, together with Mr. Gladstone at her dinner table because the two men disliked each other too much to meet.

"Do you know what my husband would say to Mr. Churchill if my husband were alive now?" she asked. "Mr. Asquith would say, 'I don't admire you, Mr. Churchill, for your oratory, though it is inspired. I don't admire you for your wartime leadership, though it often reflects true greatness. I don't admire you for your mastery of the House of Commons, not even for your paintings and your bricklaying. But I admire you, Mr. Churchill, for your robust good spirits when times are black.'"

This, of course, is the measure of Mr. Churchill. He is the British bulldog incarnate, the prototype of the enduring Englishman, most stanch when things go worst. That is why he alone among Britons, like President Roosevelt among Americans, looms as a world figure. He stands up against Hitler and gives buoyant hope to those who cherish democracy and freedom in the farthermost reaches of the terrestrial globe. The world listens in its millions when he speaks and chuckles when he deliberately mispronounces Naa-zee or when with calculated casualness he forgets himself and finds that the word he wants for Mussolini is guttersnipe. The reason he speaks so well was revealed to me once by his son, Randolph, who, like his father, is already making a career as journalist, soldier, and Member of Parliament.

"Given Father's extraordinary personality," said young Randolph, "our household moves smoothly. Smoothly, that is, except when Father is preparing an impromptu speech. Then books are down from all the shelves and lie over all the floors and one disturbs him at one's peril."

As even his carefully prepared impromptu speeches show, Mr. Churchill has a great sense of style. His apt quotations from the Latin are robbed of pedantry by his habit of translating them into English for the benefit of old Etonians in the House, since the men of Eton, unlike the men of Harrow, pride themselves upon their knowledge of the classics. But in the same way Mr. Churchill is stubborn and no amount of style removes the fact of his obstinacy. It is this quality which has made the governing class of Britain critical. In the moment of his greatest popularity certain of his frailties were transparent. Not unappreciative of his greatness, they had become critical nevertheless of certain of his shortcomings. Not the least of these was his stubbornness.

For instance, half a dozen of his lieutenants spent an evening trying to persuade the Prime Minister to reorganize and revitalize British propaganda services. They argued the differences in national psychologies and the necessity of preparing a special presentation of the British case for each nationality. "I don't know about that," said the Prime Minister. "I make only one speech, but people understand what I'm saying all around the world." This ended the discussion— and with it the hope of renovating propaganda methods. On another occasion certain Members of Parliament were trying to persuade Mr. Churchill to state Britain's war aims and how Britain proposed to deal with Germany in the peace. The Prime Minister felt that with the issues so complicated only mischief could result from the formulation of aims which at best could only be tentative. His interlocutors pressed him, however. The Prime Minister terminated that discussion abruptly with his usual resort to humor. "Oh, I dare say that the perfect solution for the German problem," he retorted, "would be an operation on all German males. But I am not a perfectionist in politics and I feel that I would meet with considerable opposition should I offer such a proposal in the House of Commons." And in this fashion Britain lost an opportunity to wage psychological warfare behind the German lines. Mr. Churchill was equally adamant before suggestions that all small manufacturing firms not already caught up in the war-industries effort should be drafted and organized. "The Americans organize well," he said. "That isn't the British way. If we build committee upon committee we bog down in our own red tape.

The small businessman has got to get into the war effort or become bankrupt. He will find his own way into that effort."

The most glaring instance of Churchill's stubbornness occurred about six months before he sent Sir Stafford Cripps to negotiate with India. Mr. Churchill's position on India was well known. For years he has feared chaos if the Moslems and Hindus fought among themselves. Moreover, he thought it a fundamental error of policy to cede ground under pressure. He was agreed in principle to ultimate dominion status, but he wanted certain developments in India and he wanted time. A group in the cabinet decided to flush his hand and force immediate action. As one of the men in that session later expressed it, "Mr. Amery had finished his suggestion that we should promise India dominion status at a fixed period after the defeat of Hitler. Other members of the government were prepared to support his initiative. Before they could speak, Mr. Churchill let out a roar like a wounded lion. The room was cleared as swiftly as if there had been a lion among us in very truth. As yet the subject has not been raised again." Many critics felt, months later when Mr. Churchill did send Cripps as his special envoy, that the gesture to India came too late. The movement for Indian independence is led by men like Nehru and Gandhi whose singleness of purpose and disinterestedness have thrilled liberals throughout the world. Behind them, however, are the big businessmen of India whose home industries stand to gain financially from the ejection of British rule. These men are neither simple nor disinterested. Many of them are willing to treat with the Japanese, like the equally shortsighted appeasers of Europe and America, and almost all of them are opposed to the heroic sacrifices involved in a scorched-earth policy. In the same way, Mr. Churchill has had a lively respect for the Moslem minority and a comprehension, possible to such a strategist, of what it will mean in this world struggle if the Moslems, of the

Middle East as well, are alienated from the United Nations.

Time will prove whether Mr. Churchill or his critics were right. Meanwhile his critics will remain vociferous in charging that he was reactionary and that his gesture was futile since dilatory. Equally harsh things are said of the Prime Minister's handling of two other grave problems. Carpers blame him for not overcoming with President de Valera the ancient grudge which robs the United Kingdom of the use of Irish bases and threatens the possibility of successful German occupation of the Irish Free State. Here Mr. Churchill is being visited with the sins of Mr. Chamberlain, whose generosity in restoring the Irish bases has been repaid only by an increasingly shortsighted truculence on the part of the Irish President. Finally Mr. Churchill is charged with having worsened relations with the Dominions by his cavalier manner. This is especially true, it is said, in the case of Australia, whose extraordinary people have a curiously confused attitude toward the motherland—best illustrated perhaps by the anecdote of J. B. Condliffe, the New Zealand economist, then resident in Australia, who was offered a professorship at Oxford. He called in his children's nurse, told her that the family was moving to England, and asked if she would like to accompany them. "England? Where all the convicts come from? No, sir," she said. Half-American himself, Mr. Churchill has had a gift for understanding Americans rare among Englishmen; but his critics object that this does not extend to the peoples of Australia, Canada, and South Africa. He has consistently refused to talk about post-war peace plans. Mr. Eden made speeches about the brave new world. When asked what he thought of them, Mr. Churchill said, "Mr. Eden has run the gamut of platitudes from 'God is love,' to 'Gentlemen will please arrange their dress before leaving the room.' "

Mr. Churchill has convictions on every matter of policy which Britain faces. Not least of these is the feeling that neither he nor the country should be stampeded into rash or hasty action. A born strategist, he has seen more clearly than any other man alive perhaps the true nature of this war. From the days of Dunkirk he has believed that both Russia and America would be involved. Given Great Britain's limited resources in man power and machines, he has conceived Britain's war as a great holding effort. Of an aggressive nature, he has wanted to vitalize that operation by spreading the Germans and clashing with them in what may be thought of as a world-wide guerrilla campaign. But of necessity Britain has been on the defensive and her war effort has brought exasperated criticism, first from the governing class, which is on terms of intimacy with the Churchill family, and finally from left-wing Londoners who, no less excitedly than Americans, demanded, "Why doesn't Britain invade the continent?" One wit said, and the English laughed at it themselves, "If the Americans and the Russians aren't careful they'll get the British in this war yet." But the genius of the Prime Minister has been precisely in the fact that he will not fritter away men and arms in abortive and predoomed efforts.

Starting her rearmament eight years late, Britain has never had a preponderance in arms or men to justify offensive action against the Germans anywhere. That Britain has been able to open and maintain several fronts and to prevent her own invasion is sheer miracle. The defection of France denied Britain vital naval and air bases. Consequently, to put a shell or a bomb against the Germans anywhere has called forth roughly three times the effort in money, matériel, and men required by the similar German blow. The relative strengths of the two can best be judged if one remembers that, during the year after Dunkirk, Great Britain could boast 2000 pieces of artillery against Germany's 100,000. The discrepancy was balanced by sea power (which outstays its critics); by the superior training and personnel of the R.A.F., together with quality aircraft engineering; and finally by the sheer dogged heroism of a people which "never knows," as the Berlin radio sneered, "when it is beaten." Germany has been in the center of the war theater; by rail, by road, and by air the German staff has been enabled to concentrate a sufficient superiority of guns, tanks, and planes against her enemies at any given moment, at any given front —precisely because Germany, not her foes, could choose the given front and the given moment. The gods have always smiled on generals who could keep the initiative.

Many critics of Mr. Churchill blinked at the essential and fundamental weakness of Great Britain, attributing British defeats not to the country's desperate military predicament but to the presence in the government of this individual and the absence from the government of that individual. "Too little and too late" was never the motto of a Churchill from the days of Marlborough to Winston. They are not due to the presence or the absence of the old-school-tie mentality in the service Ministries. They are the inevitable consequence of a shortage of arms and man power which always makes it inevitable that both must be spread too thin so long as the enemy maintains the double advantage of the initiative and the interior front. The sins of Baldwin and Chamberlain have been visited on Churchill. He has suffered from the want of means. And yet the efforts of Great Britain under his leadership have been heroic and prodigious.

Until Pearl Harbor, Mr. Churchill could not send the regular army abroad and leave the defense of the British Isles to the Home Guard. No British Prime Minister could gamble on a change in the isolationist sentiment of America. Since the entry of the United States into the war as a British ally, Mr. Churchill has been willing to strip down the defenses of the United Kingdom. Lord Halifax has revealed that during the first quarter of 1942 "no less than 80 per cent of our total military production and every soldier for whom shipping space was available have been sent overseas." Shipping remained the limiting obstacle, but Mr. Churchill was able, once America stood at his side, to begin the reinforcement of the "thin red line" which he himself had already extended from the Arctic Circle through western and southeastern Europe, North and East Africa, the Near East and the Far East, down to the equator. It is characteristic of the British that they should have given major credit during two and a half years to Canadian, Australian, and other empire soldiers. And yet of all the casualties suffered by the armies of the Commonwealth from 1939 to 1941, some 71 per cent were sustained by troops from the United Kingdom.

The British public is impatient for a more energetic and successful prosecution of the war—a second front bigger than Egypt and Libya. Mr. Churchill has said himself that evacuations do not win campaigns and he is associated in the public mind with this phase of the British war effort. Sir Stafford Cripps came home from a successful ambassadorship in Moscow at a moment when the Churchill government's prosecution of the war evoked impatience rather than gratitude. British enthusiasm for Russia's heroic resistance was transferred to Cripps, the man who had always believed in Russia. Indeed, Cripps had been expelled from the British Labor party in 1939 when he proposed that the Laborites should join with the Communists to form a Popular Front. The public remembered that Cripps, urging an alliance with Russia, had been opposed to the antired position maintained by Churchill, as well as by Chamberlain, in the years before the war. The public forgot the mistaken position taken by Cripps when the Moscow-Berlin pact was signed in the last weeks before the invasion of Poland. Then Cripps had declared: "A pact of nonaggression between Russia and Germany will be a great reinforcement for peace in eastern Europe. At the same time it is a lie to suggest that it leaves Germany a free hand against Poland or anyone else." The public also forgot, or never knew, that Sir Stafford had not been singularly successful as British Ambassador to Moscow. The Kremlin prefers that capitalist countries should be represented by capitalists. The Kremlin dislikes a liberal and it hates a Socialist. In short, Cripps came home to be a critic of the Churchill government in a moment when that government was encountering widespread popular impatience from the masses as well as the threat of organized attacks by the governing class.

Yielding finally to public opinion as well as to the pressure of many of his conservative supporters, Mr. Churchill dropped certain of his associates and broadened the base of the war cabinet by the inclusion of Cripps as Lord Privy Seal and Leader of the House of Commons. It was fortuitous, moreover, that Cripps, long a champion of freedom for India, had gone there in the first year of the war to talk with Nehru and other Indian leaders whose confidence he enjoyed. During that visit Gandhi, with the sure touch of the born politician, had waved Cripps to a stool and spared him the necessity of sitting on the floor. It is in the genius of British politics to produce a man for the moment. Mr. Churchill had been dilatory in a moment when the Japanese invasion of India seemed imminent and when the British public cried for something to be done. Though he had no political party, Cripps enjoyed the support of the British public and the confidence of the Indian leaders. Mr. Churchill sent him to India on the most delicate diplomatic mission which the war has yet developed. The Tory drafted the Marxist for the service of his country. In offering him this mission Mr. Churchill also gave Cripps a chance to make himself Prime Minister, though he suggested, with typical generosity, that Cripps should not go to India if he felt that failure there would weaken his political position. The failure of the negotiations was due to the Churchill government, not to its envoy, and this the public knows.

A dyed-in-the-wool red, Cripps would be the most un-British of all that country's politicians if he, like the British generally, were not a complex of contradictions. A Marxist doctrinaire, Cripps wants to make Britain socialist and damn the consequences. Like most men who are doctrinaire, he has been intemperate in his utterances. The election of 1931 was more than a conservative triumph in his eyes. He attacked it as a counterrevolution, "essentially Fascist in nature," and said that with so sweeping an electoral victory "there was no need for any formal personal dictatorship." To him Lady Astor and the Cliveden set were not mistaken appeasers but "gangsters." Interrupted in the House of Commons during a debate in the last year before the war, Cripps attacked Lady Astor with the orthodox language of Moscow rather than the urbanity of Westminster.

He said, "People do not fancy their country, as do the noble Lady and her set—[Interruption.] I apologize and withdraw the word and substitute gang. They do not fancy the future of their country like the gang of the noble Lady, as being a junior partner in a Fascist International ruling the common peoples of all countries by methods that have heretofore been reserved by their gang for native and colonial territory—methods of brutality and exploitation and the denial of freedom."

Cripps has consistently demanded the socialization of Britain and he once shocked that staid public by declaring bluntly, "We shall have to overcome opposition from Buckingham Palace."

This man who breaks so brusquely with the established British ways of looking at things was born to wealth and aristocracy. Lord Parmoor was his father, Cotswolds his family estate, and he wears the old school tie of Winchester. His father was born a conservative, became a liberal, and ended in the Labor government—Ramsay MacDonald's most distinguished convert. Sir Stafford's Aunt Beatrice was wife and partner to Sidney Webb. The writings of the Webbs, later Lord and Lady Passfield, lent respectability to Marxism. Indeed, their monumental work on the Soviet Union, unlike the earlier and more substantial contributions, has a unique and fairylike charm, their own visit to the Soviet

Union having disclosed nothing which changed the utopia of Marxism as they imagined it forty years before. Reared against such a background, Cripps went to France in the last war as an ambulance driver; but he had been educated as a chemist and was ordered back to an explosive factory of which he later became a superintendent. Characteristically, he was intemperate of his strength and suffered a breakdown from overwork which probably accounts for his vegetarian diet—and his dyspepsia. Complicated and complex as always, when Cripps became a lawyer after the war, he was not a Clarence Darrow, championing the down and out, but a corporation lawyer. His fees are said to have totaled almost $200,000 in a single year and he is probably the highest-paid barrister with the exception of Sir John Simon, now Lord Simon. The inverted class consciousness of this titled aristocrat was extended to his clients. Of the ruling class he once remarked wryly, "They pay me fabulous and fantastic sums to get them out of their difficulties. I have no hesitation in saying that the working class of this country are more capable of ruling than they." No one who has met Sir Stafford can doubt that he is a high-minded man. His sincerity is unchallenged, his brilliance unrivaled. When the Labor party ejected him in 1939 one of Beaverbrook's papers said, "Labor has blown out its brains."

Americans want to know what kind of Britain is coming out of this war—whether Mr. Churchill stays on or Sir Stafford Cripps takes over. Will the country remain Tory? Will it produce a "New Deal" leadership? Will it go Socialist or even Communist? Such questions are characteristically American and rather too direct for the complicated social and political system of Great Britain. As for relations with Russia, Cripps can scarcely take Britain closer to Moscow than the country has been from the first dramatic moment of invasion when Churchill over the radio announced all-out aid for the new ally, and subsequently signed a military alliance binding the two in peace as well as in war. No Tory Prime Minister would lessen the tie that binds the two countries together. Indeed, it was a former red-baiting Tory, Lord Beaverbrook, who went to Moscow to supervise shipments of tanks and planes. In foreign affairs during wartime the cleavage between a Churchill and a Cripps is no greater than the differences between President Roosevelt and Wendell Willkie in foreign policy.

Whoever is Prime Minister, the governing class will remain the governing class. Tories like Churchill and reds like Cripps will have gone to school together, will have belonged to the same clubs, and will have called each other by their first names. Similarly, the Ministries in Whitehall will still be staffed by the permanent members of the civil service, also drawn from the governing class—whose business it is to run England whatever the complexion of the Prime Minister, who enjoys a relatively brief tenure at Downing Street. The House of Commons will continue to remain more sensitive to public opinion than any other parliament in the world. Britain's backwardness as a democracy is social and comes from the rigid maintenance of the class system. A man is a gentleman, not because of his innate qualities, but because of his birth and breeding.

The lower classes in the past maintained the caste distinctions as jealously as the upper class and during the first World War they insisted that troops should be led by officers from the upper class, not trusting their own fellows in positions of command. The last war did much to change this, however. And in this war a British officer was relieved of his command merely for suggesting that officers should be recruited from the upper class alone. The social evolution is slow, but its principal impetus has come from the creation of the Royal Air Force. Without the pretensions of age and tradition which made the older services snobbish, the air force has recruited butchers' boys and bakers' boys and it has forced all its personnel to come up through the ranks. The air force has proved its superiority to the other services, but it is typical of the British that even when they admit this they feel that the quality of the R.A.F. could be improved if its social level were raised. The butcher boy and the baker boy, though R.A.F. officers, insist that the R.A.F. needs more young men with superior schooling, especially in mathematics. They say that too large a percentage of young men from the privileged classes have gone, because of tradition, into the navy or the army, where their educational accomplishments are wasted, whereas men with their education are needed in the air arm. They say themselves that too often one hundred thousand dollars' worth of flying machine has been cracked up by a boy whose schooling wasn't up to the complicated instrument board.

This war has brought a national awakening to the danger of class education and in many quarters there are movements to supplant the public schools—actually the private schools—by a nationwide system of education without class distinction. Whatever the complexion of the Prime Minister, this kind of social progress is likely to come out of the present war. Similarly, the fraternity of the bomb crater has brought together British civilians of every class and given each group a new appreciation of the qualities of the other. This progress will be carried farther by the leveling process of confiscatory taxes. Just as the last war destroyed the great properties of the landed gentry, this war will destroy the great fortunes of the businessmen and move England steadily toward greater social equality—a leveling down as well as a leveling up.

If backward socially, because of snobbish class distinctions, the British have long been ahead of the Americans in economic democracy. We ask if a "New Deal" in Britain will come out of this war. Great Britain had its New Deal twenty-five years before Mr. Roosevelt came to the White House. David Lloyd George challenged the bankers and the businessmen in 1907 and 1911, when he began to tax unearned increment. Spending like a Roosevelt, Lloyd George was challenged with the taunt that even in wartime no Chancellor of the Exchequer had proposed to spend so much. When his budget was described as a war budget the little Welshman admitted the charge, declaring that it was a budget to wage "implacable war against poverty." He proposed to pension the "veterans of industry." Midway in Roosevelt's New Deal I sat at Chert talking with Mr. Lloyd George.

"Yes, you're right," he chuckled. "The British Tories said I was making revolution. There wasn't a drawing room in the United Kingdom that did not predict that blood would run in the streets. My effort and Roosevelt's were the same. Just as I had to fight the House of Lords because they could not understand the economic aspect of democracy, so Roosevelt must fight his Supreme Court. You wait and see. Roosevelt must fight the Court ultimately or lose the New Deal battle."

I told Mr. Lloyd George about the preliminary rounds before the New Deal, when, during President Hoover's administration, I watched certain Senators oppose the nomination of Charles Evans Hughes to the Supreme Court. Senators Norris, Borah, Glass, and La Follette argued that the country was approaching a period in its history when economic questions would overshadow all others and when the Supreme Court, by its interpretations of the Constitution, would become more important as a lawmaking body than the Congress. As one Senator summed it up, "The struggle is on in this country to ascertain whether the government of the United States shall regulate and control these vast aggregations of capital or whether they, through the Supreme Court of the United States, are to control and run the government of this country." Lloyd George was delighted with my ability to recall these speeches no less than by my quotations of his own oratorical efforts of a quarter of a century before.

"That is precisely the struggle I had with the House of Lords," he said, "but I fear that where I succeeded Roosevelt will fail. Roosevelt is a great leader—indeed, a great farseeing statesman—but he has one almost insurmountable obstacle. That obstacle is the quality of the opposition in the United States. If at this distance I can understand America, the opposition—in his own party as well as in the Republican party—is stupid. The worst foe of social progress and peaceful change is a stupid opposition—shortsighted or reactionary. My great advantage lay in the high quality of the statesmanship of the men who opposed me." Mr. Lloyd George was right in foreseeing the defeat of the legislation with which President Roosevelt later proposed to reorganize the Supreme Court. But Roosevelt won because he was able to pack the Court and give it a liberal and progressive outlook. He carried through, twenty-five years later, the economic reforms achieved in England when Lloyd George curbed the power of the House of Lords.

Just as no one in England would have challenged collective bargaining in a moment when Americans were still wrangling over the question, so the right of a government to levy confiscatory taxes—like President Roosevelt's scheme to limit incomes to $25,000—is not now challenged in the British Isles. Many American radicals are agitated about war profits. Those who are frightened lest American "munitions makers" should grow rich are the very ones who are agitated about the Tory complexion of Great Britain. An illustration of how taxes are levied across the Atlantic was given by Lord Halifax.

Speaking to an American audience, the Ambassador said, "Most of you, I expect, have seen the Walt Disney film which shows Donald Duck paying $13 to the United States Treasury as tax on his income of $2501. You may be interested to know that if he were living in England today Donald would have paid $552 on the same income instead of $13. If Donald were a fatter duck and earned, let us say, an income of $400,-000 in England, he would be plucked to the tune of $377,000. So, you see, we are taking care that no private fortunes shall be made out of this war."

The ability of the rich to bear it with a grin, however wry, explains in part the strength of Great Britain today. It is this quality, moreover, which explains why that country weathered the reconstruction period after the last war while Germany went into an inflation which destroyed the middle class—the stable element which is the strength of any capitalistic country. In 1914 the generals took the Germans to war and they gambled everything on victory. The Germans financed the war with inflationary measures, and paid only about 4 per cent of the cost as they went along. Great Britain's defense was a people's war even in 1914–1918 and the people paid about 24 per cent in direct taxation as they went along. In the end British subjects could cash in their blue chips, but no German government could bank a game played with the reckless irresponsibility of the Kaiser's generals. British survival in this war, as in the last, depends essentially upon the character of the British people. Tribute is due the steadfastness of the moneyed families and the investing class. Their character was influenced and transformed, of course, by the educational process of Mr. Lloyd George's "New Deal." The rich learned to pay taxes twenty-five years ago. Many Americans screamed against "that red in the White House" and many Frenchmen said, "Rather Hitler than that Jew Blum." The British rich got over this colic a generation ago. They know that to whom much is given, of him much is expected. With this developed sense of social responsibility they will work to keep the Tories in power—naturally—but they will support the government patriotically whoever goes to Downing Street.

If Sir Stafford Cripps seems the left-wing choice to succeed as Prime Minister, the ablest and most powerful man after Mr. Churchill is Ernest Bevin, I believe. One can understand the power of the Right Honorable Ernest Bevin, M.P., Minister of Labor and National Service, if one imagines a John L. Lewis, less vain but equally dynamic, who succeeded in bringing together the A.F. of L. and the C.I.O. under his own rule and who then took over the position and power held by

Nelson and McNutt in Washington. For twenty years Bevin has ruled labor with a natural assumption of power that led some to call him the "workingman's Mussolini" and others to refer to Transport House, his headquarters, as the "Kremlin of labor." Confident of his control over the unions, he laughed at such talk. "Whenever I am asked about the dictatorship of the proletariat—of the Nazis or any other form of it—I always reply, 'I was born in a village and I lived under a dictatorship until I was fourteen and I will see you to the devil before I have any more.' " In this forthright way Bevin referred to his period as a farmhand from the age of six to fourteen. He disliked it so that he ran away to the city to drive a beer truck. In the city he became a union organizer and has never worked at anything else since.

In 1920 he amalgamated thirty-six unions into the Transport and General Workers' Union—the largest in the world. Thus he had been the most powerful background figure in the Labor party and he had transformed that political organization into a trade-union party—to the ineffable disgust and chagrin of the party's intellectuals from whom he wrested party control. This self-schooled man had already displayed intellectual prowess as the statesman of labor.. In 1920 he pleaded the case for increased wages to dockers and, addressing the court himself, he snarled up in their own complicated statistics the greatest legal array the employers of England could assemble. As a left-wing politician he was the man who made it impossible for the British government to arm the Poles in their war against the Bolsheviks—his first service to the Kremlin, which he lumped with Fascist tyrannies before Britain's alliance with the Soviet Union. Finally in 1926 it was Bevin who organized the general strike, the greatest effort of its kind in history, only to be bested in the end by Churchill, whom he now serves as chief lieutenant. He, as clearly as any statesman in the world, saw the threat of the Fascists and Nazis from the inception of their movements. Having failed to rally Italian and, later, German union leaders to a solid internal front which might have prevented the dictatorship of Mussolini and then Hitler, Bevin saw what these aggressive movements would mean to his own country. He stood for military action to prevent the Italian conquest of Ethiopia. This risked the destruction of the Labor party because of the pacifists under the leadership of George Lansbury. In a frontal assault Bevin reduced Lansbury to tears for "touting his conscience to one conference after another." The rough-and-tumble dockers' leader annihilated the pacifist. When Bevin was later reproached for having been too harsh with old Lansbury he replied, "George has been standing around like a martyr for too long—it was high time someone lit the faggots."

I got to know Bevin in Geneva, where he came to represent the British workers in the International Labor Office. A burly man, Bevin has the swart coloring of a gypsy and, though he gives the impression of juggernaut strength, he has gypsy nimbleness. Over a period of years we made a number of bets and I must admit that Bevin won most of them. This union organizer who was the courtroom equal of any of England's great lawyers was also an able economist and served with distinction on the Macmillan commission. A year before the London Economic Conference in 1933 I reproached him for Great Britain's having abandoned the gold standard— voluntarily, as I argued. Defending Britain's action, he predicted to the exact month America's abandonment of the gold standard—a full year before Roosevelt made the "baloney" dollar. I doubt if another economist anywhere in the world had foreseen that and other financial developments with such accuracy. During the Economic Conference I had to stand Bevin a champagne dinner for that bet.

It was in Geneva that Bevin became the friend of John G. Winant, then Director of the International Labor Office and later the American Ambassador to the Court of St. James's. One of the most discerning and courageous Ambassadors we have sent abroad, Winant did much to take away the bad taste left in the mouths of Englishmen by Joseph P. Kennedy. The day after Munich, Kennedy had shocked London by a chance encounter with Jan Masaryk, the Czech Minister and son of the great President Masaryk.

"Isn't the news wonderful?" said Kennedy.

Still stunned by the blow of Munich, Masaryk asked what news.

"The news of Munich," said Kennedy. "Since there is no war I can get to Palm Beach for my vacation."

Later, when Britain was at war, Kennedy came back to America to proclaim that Britain was beaten and that America ought to make terms with Germany. By contrast, Winant, who had fought with distinction in the last war, talked honestly with and about the British. He conceived his ambassadorship as something more than a springboard to the White House and in their darkest moments Londoners saw the gaunt Lincolnesque figure of Winant standing in the ruins of their homes while the German bombers were still overhead. Any American in London could feel proud of the cheer—"The American Ambassador!"—with which the simple people of that stricken city welcomed such a man. Lincolnesque, Winant is also shy and he cultivates a naïve manner. In private conversation or at a public dinner his voice is likely to trail into nothingness at the crucial point of his discourse, and with disarming frankness he can say "I don't know" to the most pertinent question. I asked Bevin whether Londoners found his friend Winant naïve because of the slowness and diffidence of his manner.

"Oh, Gil is all right," said Bevin. "Dinner-table conversation dragged the other evening, so someone present—I had rather not say just who—tried to introduce a note of levity. Winant was asked whether there would be home rule for Britain if America, under Lend-Lease, took over the United Kingdom as well as our island bases. He was asked how many Senators there were for each state. Winant scratched his head, looked up at the chandelier overhead, looked down at the floor by his side, swallowed his Adam's apple, scratched his head again, and said, 'Two, I think.' He was asked whether, once the Americans took over the United Kingdom, they would give us two Senators for England, two for Scotland, two for Ireland, and two for Wales. Winant did not hesitate a moment. Quick as a flash he said, 'No. If you had two Senators from Scotland, you would rule us!' "

This labor leader went into the government—though he was not even a Member of Parliament—the day Churchill took over. As Minister of Labor and National Service he has had the power to tell any man or woman in England where he would work and under what conditions—powers legally granted but as vast as those wielded by either Hitler or Stalin. It is a tribute to the English workers' self-discipline that these powers have rarely been employed. Suasion in England suffices. Indeed, both Labor and the Tories have criticized Bevin for not fully utilizing his vast powers and many Tories have attacked him, curiously enough, for not badgering employers.

"Labor is behind this war," Bevin said to me. "No, it's got nothing to do with the leadership of labor. Way back in 1934, when Austria was being crucified, the British workers saw that if the Nazis won they would be destroyed under such a tyranny. They saw that when the Fascists strike at labor nobody takes care of the workingman. They saw that politicians are willing to sacrifice them and that the business community and the Communists are too.

"Labor in England has had an advantage. Nobody ever *gave* them anything. They've won what they've got. It's better here than in America. Here nothing comes from above. We've had no Rooseveltian New Deal to give us things on a silver platter. We've won our rights ourselves, slowly over one hundred and fifty years of enlightened struggle. I always told the German labor leaders before Hitler that they were wrong with decrees and things like that. The Weimar governments *gave* labor certain rights and privileges.

Well, somebody else could give them just as well—or promise to give them—and somebody could take them away. The British Labor party grew out of the bowels of the Trades Union Congress. Just let somebody try to take our rights away.

"Strikes? Where are they? In the past two and a half years we have lost under a million working days. What's that spread over 15,000,000 workers? In the last two and a half years of the first World War we lost 12,000,000 workdays in labor disputes. Since Dunkirk the time lost in industrial stoppages represents only one day per man every fifteen years. Remember, too, that today we employ more people in munitions than in the last war. Now we have got air-force production—wholly new—and civil defense, which alone takes 1,500,000 from our population. In fact, man power is our essential problem. Germany, having conquered Europe, can draw on 244,000,000. Our industries can draw on only 44,000,000. With Canada and Australia we only reach 54,000,000. Canada and Australia are doing wonderful things; but they are only primary producers, in the main. United States labor alone can right the balance."

Bevin laughed when I discussed with him some of the criticisms leveled against his Ministry. He is a stubborn man about doing things his own way.

"I bring brains and humanity and sound personnel methods to this job," he said. "We are putting 1,000,000 women to work in munitions, for instance. I have already employed 600,000 of them with less than 100 complaints. The absence of complaints means that there aren't any misfits and heartbreaks. We talked with them, told them the various kinds of jobs we had to fill, and gave them a chance to get the ones they were qualified for and wanted. And among the men I have already employed 370,000 out of 390,000 derelict 'unemployables.' I ruled that a man who is all whacked shouldn't be given hard work which would take the heart out of him in a single day. These 'unemployables' were whacked because they had gone too long without work and their muscles were soft. I conditioned them for a month and then began to give them hard work as their muscles came back.

"I've kept a balance between denying the army the kind of skilled men it's got to have in mechanized warfare and raiding industry of skilled workers. The hell with all this talk about the problem of discrepancy between the worker's wage and the soldier's wage. The skilled worker isn't a private. He's a commissioned officer in the ranks of labor. For every 5000 soldiers in an army today, we've got 1500 officers and noncommissioned officers. Can you imagine that many supervisors [foremen] for 5000 factory workers? The factory worker's mentality isn't that of a soldier. The men who make the most demands for higher wages are not the skilled veterans of industry but the soldiers brought back into the factories. And take some of our bombings if you think a front line is worse than a factory lathe."

This statesman of labor—common-sense, middle-of-the-road, and British as Yorkshire pudding—is a more logical successor to Churchill than Cripps. But Bevin will not take the job. He does not want it. In wartime he can make labor do the patriotic thing. He thinks that labor in wartime ought to make its own ideas and aspirations second to the survival of Great Britain. He sees no future for labor unless there is a British victory. And he has had the habit over a long career of putting first things first. Once the victory is won he believes that labor ought to fight—"and fight like hell"—to put over its own ideas of what Britain ought to be.

"At the end of this war," Bevin told me, "social security must be the main motive of our national life. I say 'Begin there.' That does not mean that we should wipe out all profit or surplus. It does mean that the whole of our economy, our finance, and our science must be directed to give social security, not to a small middle class or to those who may be possessors of property but to the community as a whole."

Bevin means to be Prime Minister in the period of reconstruction. He is waiting until he can see the whites of their eyes. There is every reason to believe that he will achieve this goal and only an emergency in which he would be drafted could force him to take over Number Ten in wartime instead of waiting for what he conceives to be the supreme task of a labor-minded statesman. If he is the postwar Prime Minister it is easy to envisage the Great Britain of the immediate future. He honors Russia as an ally, not as a model. He is no narrow Marxist doctrinaire. He is too middle-of-the-road British for that. And Britain, too, would be middle-of-the-road progressive under the leadership of "Ernie."

No other left-wing leaders, except Cripps and Bevin, seem available at the moment, because the men of ability on the left have either lost their magic or never developed it. The British press is the best in the world for building up political glamour, rivaling American achievements with Wendell L. Willkie and General Douglas MacArthur. After all, the British persuaded themselves and most of the world that the Duke of Windsor, when Prince of Wales, had been an able, dutiful, and engaging young man. Even the British press would find it difficult, however, to refurbish the political reputations of Herbert Morrison, Clement Attlee, or Sir Archibald Sinclair. These two Laborites and the liberal were taken into the Churchill government, but it was a disservice to them. Admirable men, they seemed unsuited to administrative tasks and their warmest friends admit that no one of them has proved himself conspicuously successful. This is doubly regrettable, perhaps, in the case of Mr. Morrison. Born the son of a policeman, this blunt Cockney had distinguished himself throughout a long period and had been efficient as an administrator in the London city government, but after a period in the cabinet he is no longer the rising hope of the Labor party.

The conservatives might single out any one of a half dozen men. Anthony Eden has the advantage of having been consistently right in his opposition to Fascist and Nazi expansion.

He remains therefore justly popular, but he lacks the ruthlessly aggressive qualities of leadership which characterize heavyweights like the Churchills and the Bevins. Oliver Lyttelton, as president of the Board of Trade, wrestled valiantly with mining, clothes rationing, and the like. He also proved an effective administrator of Cairo, where he was sent to cut the traffic snarls and the red tape; and his party handed him the Ministry of Production upon Beaverbrook's resignation. Lyttelton represents the governing class at its best and he has the brightest Tory future of them all. Lord Halifax could always be brought home from Washington. In the past certain Tories looked to Lord Beaverbrook, but he seems to have destroyed his opportunity. Born Max Aitken, Beaverbrook is a Canadian and the owner of popular newspapers which are as irresponsible as they are skillfully edited and widely read. Having overcome the handicap of a Canadian accent and a seat in the House of Lords, Beaverbrook took on the production first of airplanes and then of tanks. Not unlike the energetic men who built America's railroad, Beaverbrook did not care about dislocations in the industry generally. When he wanted the factories, the labor, and the raw materials he did not ask his lieutenants how they got them. As a result, he produced airplanes and tanks, but he did some violence both to the war effort generally and to his own popularity. A final conservative possibility is Sir John Anderson. One of the few civil servants to go into Parliament and the cabinet, Anderson has behind him a long career of repression—repression of natives in the Far East and of Englishmen at home. His elevation would mean that the conservatives had gone reactionary and it would bring charges from men like Cripps that the country had gone Fascist.

Whoever succeeds Churchill, British policy and the British prosecution of the war will be altered but not radically. Britain changes; Britain moves forward; Britain goes toward the left. But the evolution is slow, just as it is sure. Whether the Prime Minister is a Marxist or a Tory will hasten the movement or retard it very little. Indeed, the movement may even be swifter under a Tory. As Lord Randolph Churchill pointed out, half a century ago, "There are and always have been men who believe that so long as they call themselves Tories they may blamelessly and harmlessly preach what doctrines they please." The socialization of England is one of his tenets, but if Cripps became Prime Minister overnight he would be too busy prosecuting the war to revolutionize the social structure of Britain more swiftly than this is being done by the very impact of the war itself. Stalin's state holds no more far-reaching power over industry and the workers, over banking and transportation, than has already been granted to the Churchill government.

There has been a profound revolution already, but the change will become significant and evident only in the moment of victory. For there has been a wartime revolution just as there was during the first World War. But once the Armistice was signed November 11, 1918, Great Britain returned to the ways of 1914. The demobilization was swift and complete. The state voluntarily relinquished its control over the means of production and distribution. The process, as viewed by the men in control on Armistice day, has been described by Mr. Churchill in *The World Crisis: The Aftermath*:

"The organization and machinery of which we disposed was powerful and flexible in an extraordinary degree. The able business men among us, each the head of a large group of departments, had now been working for a year and a half in a kind of industrial cabinet. They were accustomed to unexpected changes enforced by the shifting fortunes of war. . . . There was very little in the productive sphere they could not at this time actually do. A requisition, for instance, for half a million houses would not have seemed more difficult to comply with than those we were already in process of executing for a hundred thousand aeroplanes, or twenty thousand guns, or the medium artillery of the American army or two million tons of projectiles. But a new set of conditions began to rule from eleven o'clock onwards. The money-cost, which had never been considered by us to be a factor capable of limiting the supply of the armies, asserted a claim to priority from the moment the fighting stopped."

The return of the cabinet to "money-cost" as the sole governing factor wrecked the dream, and the wartime pledge, that the British Expeditionary Forces should return in 1918 to a "land fit for heroes." The heroes came back to stagnation and the dole. Today the British people eschew high-sounding phrases, but they seem determined, in their quiet grim way, that this process is not to be repeated. Already they are talking and planning how the wartime capacity to execute orders for a million tons of bombs (or a million dwelling houses) shall be utilized for a vast slum-clearing project. Already they are saying that what has been done for agriculture in an emergency can be done in peacetime. And so part of the wartime revolution will become permanent—not as much as the radicals desire, less than the conservatives want to yield, but enough to bring that compromise which is the essence of the British way.

XII

SIXTY YEARS IN TEN

THE Communists came of age November 7, 1937. That was the twentieth anniversary of their revolution—"the ten days that shook the world." It is a wonderful thing to become twenty-one, and the stripling revolutionary regime celebrated with vodka, song, and a parade. More than a million men marched for four and a half hours through the Red Square, where Joseph Stalin and other comrades took the salute. I celebrated the occasion myself by interviewing Maxim Litvinov, then the People's Commissar for Foreign Affairs, who proved remarkably revealing and frank. Things move slowly in Moscow, where even a foreign minister must tread cautiously through the bureaucracy and red tape. As a result my scheduled interview was twice postponed. I finally reached Litvinov in December after he had come back to Moscow from the farcical Brussels conference where America, Great Britain, France, and other signatories had discussed (but done nothing about) the Nine-Power Pact, involving Japan's position in the Far East. Litvinov awaited the future with profound pessimism. It was three months before the Germans were to march into Austria, ten months before they were to humble Great Britain and France at Munich.

In many talks with Litvinov at Geneva and one interview with him at Moscow in 1932 I had found him the shrewdest and best-informed foreign minister in the world. Realistic, even cynical, his personality was strangely compounded of intellectual brilliance, charm, guile, and blunt bad manners. When I saw the Foreign Commissar in his dingy, barely furnished office in the Narkomindel, I deliberately provoked him by suggesting the failure of his policies. Britain, France, and America, embarrassed by the Spanish Civil War, had cooled perceptibly toward the Soviet Union. Germany, Japan, and Italy, emboldened by Russia's isolation, had signed the Anticomintern Pact. I asked about this pact.

"Anticomintern Pact? What nonsense!" exploded Litvinov. "Can you never look at things without your cheap bourgeois prejudice? The Anticomintern Pact is no threat to the Soviet Union. It is dust in the eyes of the Western democracies. Italy took Ethiopia. What in the world does Ethiopia mean to the Soviet Union? Nothing, except that it runs counter to our program of collective security. And Spain, invaded now by Germany and Italy. We try to help the Spanish Republic because it is on the frontiers of France, with whom we have a pact and where there is a Popular Front government. But what does Spain mean to the Soviet Union, militarily? Spain is vital strategically to France and Great Britain, vital even to America, if you pretend to remain a maritime power and send your ships freely around the globe. And Japan? We remark in Moscow that the Japanese are destroying your Nine-Power Pact and tearing your Pacific interests to shreds.

"Ideologies mean little to the Fascist brigands. The Germans have militarized the Reich and are bent on a brutal policy of gangsterism. Those contemptible peoples, the Japanese and Italians, are following at the German heels hoping to share in the spoils of German conquest. It is the rich capitalistic countries which will fall an easy prey. The British and French peoples are soft under leaders who are blind. The Soviet Union is the last foe to be attacked by the Anticomintern powers. They will loot your countries, but we have the Red Army and a vast extent of territory. Our mountains are high, our rivers broad, and we are not an inviting land."

Litvinov spoke incisively, his diction precise. His cherubic face wreathed in a soft downy halo of ash-colored hair, the burly Commissar adjusted his glasses and proceeded.

"Listen," he said. "Hitler and the generals who control Germany read history. They know that Bismarck warned against war on two fronts. They know that he urged the re-insurance policy with Russia. They believe that the Kaiser lost the first World War because he forgot Bismarck's admonition. When the Germans are prepared at last to embark upon their new adventures, these bandits will come to Moscow to ask us for a pact."

Thus Litvinov anticipated by two years the Molotov-Ribbentrop agreement, which burst like a bombshell August 22, 1939, making it possible for Germany to invade Poland and start the second World War. He faced squarely the realization that his own foreign policy had failed. Immediately after the first World War and allied intervention against the Communists, the Kremlin had based its foreign policy on the meretricious and doctrinaire assumption that Versailles was an imperialistic and, therefore, iniquitous settlement. This point of view facilitated the Rapallo *rapprochement* with Germany, whose industrial organization offered compensations to peasant and agricultural Russia. After the rise of Hitler the Russians reversed themselves. The tip-off came in 1932 when Karl Radek—then the Kremlin's journalistic spokesman, later purged—wrote an article defending the Versailles Treaty on the ground that its provisions could be changed only by war, which, in its turn, would bring a worse treaty. I understood the significance of the article and predicted Russia's entry into the League of Nations. This was Litvinov's policy and, as soon as he brought Russia into the League in 1934, he labored mightily for collective security, implementing the sanctions provisions of the Geneva Covenant by pacts with France and Czechoslovakia which were designed to organize a solid front of peace-minded states. It was typical of this realist that in the last month of 1937 he faced honestly the fact of the collapse of this policy. To fail in Russia in 1937 was dangerous. Merely because of failure you could be denounced as a Trotskyist or shot as a saboteur.

Sitting in the Narkomindel, talking with me and wondering, no doubt, whether he would be included in the purge, Litvinov foresaw more clearly than any other man alive the ultimate collapse of France and the full consequences of British policy as elaborated by Baldwin and Chamberlain. I volunteered that Mussolini had come to terms with Hitler and that the Germans would take over Austria shortly. Litvinov bobbed his head and said, "In about three months—probably in March." I asked if Britain and France would oppose this with force. "Of course not," he said. I suggested that Hitler's next move would be against Czechoslovakia or Poland. "Not Poland—Czechoslovakia," he said. I pointed out that Russia was the ally of Czechoslovakia and would be obliged in that event to make war against Germany. "How do you square this obligation with a policy of isolation by Russia, as you have just outlined it to me?" I asked. Litvinov chuckled. "Don't tell me about our treaty with Czechoslovakia," he said. "I drafted that treaty. Read the text again more carefully and you will see that you are wrong. We are obliged to come to the aid of the Czechs under the League of Nations' machinery and then only if France has assumed her obligations." I shrugged my shoulders.

"Well?" I queried.

"Well, France won't fight. France is through," said Litvinov.

When I shook the Commissar's hand, I said good-by to a man who had looked unblinkingly on the ruin of his whole policy and predicted the signature of the Berlin-Moscow pact.

Quoting "informed and authoritative Russian sources," I described this radical change of Russian policy in a quaking world where the motto of diplomats everywhere had become "Sauve qui peut." I wrote: "The Russians are going in for isolation until they see the British or French pull out their own chestnuts and prove themselves capable of some policy beyond repetitious capitulation before Hitler." I concluded my dispatch, published in January, 1938, with the following paragraph: "This is Litvinov's *Realpolitik,* and Stalin has approved it with a minor qualification. The Comintern, Russia's organization of Communist agents abroad, must continue to agitate for peace and do all it can to create an impression of solidarity with victims of aggression. This is necessary to disarm Trotsky, keep Communists abroad from feeling that they have been 'sold out,' and—most important of all—'keep the sympathy of "pinks" in every country since they are Russia's friends.' "

This distinction between the policy of Russia and the policy of the Communist International was necessary. Russia was Russia long before there was Communism. Russia will still be Russia when the Communists are as dead and forgotten as the Manichaeans, those heretics who affirmed that God was a divine substance penetrating mankind with particles of light, or divinity. Communism is a dogma of class struggle invented by a radical German refugee named Karl Marx, who applied the Hegelian dialectic to the machine-age problem of production. Marx, who supported himself in London by writing long-winded articles for the New York *Tribune,* influenced the world as much as any modern man, but his dogma has been so radically distorted by the evolution of two brief generations as to be scarcely recognizable today. By contrast with this theory, Russia is a vast, sprawling geographic entity comprising one-sixth of the area of the world and an even larger proportion of the world's resources. Russia is men, women, and children—not a dogma—and they total more than 170,000,000.

Russia is a fatherland that inspires passionate devotion in its children, uniting the Stalinites and the Trotskyists, the youngest atheist Comsomol and the oldest Tsarist refugee, so that when the foreigner invades their land they cry out together, "Little Mother! Holy Russia!" The capitalist's fear of Communism is understandable, if exaggerated, but the statesman's confusion of Communism and Russia is tragic. There may have been slight choice between Communism and

Nazism as political systems, but as between Russia and Germany there was a whole world of space and several centuries in human outlook. Peace was a fundamental Russian interest, just as war was the fundamental German program. When Russia stood for peace—was willing to fight for collective security—the Baldwins and the Chamberlains drove Stalin and Litvinov first to isolation and then to the Moscow-Berlin pact. These conservatives could make no distinction between Communism and Russia.

Communism is not Fascism. Mussolini and the Fascist party seized power in Italy and then began to improvise the theory and philosophy of Fascism. A bundle of contradictions, cynically twisted to the pragmatic needs of each changing moment, the philosophy of Fascism has remained consistent only as an instrument to keep Mussolini and the party in power. Communism started with a full-blown Marxist doctrine, implemented by the writings and practices of Lenin. Private property and the profit motive were held to be the causes of exploitation and greed. A propertyless and classless society was to be established with the means of production and distribution centered wholly in the state. But the Communist party, despite this utopian scheme, moved toward absolute power as surely and inevitably as did Fascism. After the death of Lenin the Communist party turned away from the "dictatorship of the proletariat" directly toward the dictatorship of the party. Stalin became supreme as the leader of the party. Two shrewd journalists in that period, Walter Duranty and Paul Scheffer, foresaw the personal triumph of Stalin. Trotsky, a Marxist doctrinaire, believed in the dogma of world revolution. An orthodox Marxist, it was his theory that Communism could endure in Russia only if it fulfilled its world mission and spread the new religion to all the countries on Russia's frontiers and beyond. Stalin, the party organizer, remained a practical party man, rather than a Marxist theorist. He was a man of action and a realist who lived of, by, and for the party.

The distinctions between the party and the Russian masses shocked me when I first visited Russia in 1932. There were 170,000,000 Russians and less than 3,000,000 Communist party members. The masses had nothing, the party members everything. The glaring disproportion between the standard of living of an American millionaire and an American worker has never been comparable to the discrepancy between materialistic comforts and luxuries of the party members on the one hand and the want and poverty of the Russian masses on the other. The party, through Dictator Stalin's G.P.U., was ruthless, moreover, in defense of its unique and unchallenged position. The party's right to shoot without trial was accepted by 167,000,000 who cowered before less than 3,000,000. A. T. Cholerton, the ablest of the British journalists resident at Moscow, epitomized Communist practice with the classic remark, "Habeas corpus has been replaced here by habeas cadaver." Unlike Mussolini and Hitler, who were forever justifying their political murders, Stalin made no effort to defend himself. In 1931 he received George Bernard Shaw and Nancy Astor. Irrepressible as ever, Lady Astor came to the crux of the matter.

"How long are you going to continue this killing?" she asked.

"Just as long as it is necessary," answered Stalin.

This is not the kind of answer you would expect from an American businessman or farmer or worker, or from an American Communist agitator, either. And it is another kind of man who is talking. Stalin comes from Georgia, an inaccessible and wild country which grows wine and rugged men rather better in the main than the marrying Mdivanis. More akin to the Oriental than to the European in spirit though not in race, the Georgian spills blood as carelessly as he spills wine. Stalin might still be in Georgia spilling wine as well as blood if his mother had not been a devout Christian. She wanted her son to be a priest and she unwittingly made an intellectual and radical agitator of him. The sufferings of mankind became so urgently oppressive in Stalin's mind that he broke from the orthodox theological seminary and tried to find some way to do something about them. He became a Marxist. The Tsar's police were soon on his trail. He was arrested twenty times; four times they exiled him into Siberia and three times he escaped to continue his work. He worked everywhere and with everybody. Lenin knew him in exile and wrote enthusiastically, at least once, of his work and of his writings. And then after years of danger and hardship—while serving his fourth sentence in Siberia—this man suddenly saw his dream come true. He watched the outbreak at last of the revolution which was to make Russia a republic of workers and peasants. This is the "man of steel" who became secretary of the Communist party and worked quietly for years—a kind of Russian Jim Farley who aligned the factions. Lenin lies in his tomb and Trotsky—because he forgot that party organization comes first in a party regime—met death as an exile. The old Bolshevik comrades are in prison or dead. Only Stalin stands today.

Stalin rules because he was different from the rest. He believes in discipline—the kind of ruthless party discipline that shoots the man who departs from the "party line." He believes in Russia—the kind of belief that made him build nationalism in Russia while Trotsky and the others argued that Communism could live only if there were a world revolution. Discipline and nationalism, as applied by Stalin, were denounced by Trotsky as "the revolution betrayed." Certainly Stalin changed Moscow so that it would have been unrecognizable to the old Bolsheviks. Lenin used to walk into my Moscow hotel with no guard at all, and go up to the room of American journalists like Albert Rhys Williams or John Reed. Stalin not only moves in a bulletproof car under heavy guards but even bans a book like John Reed's *Ten Days That Shook the World*. The G.P.U. took it away from me at the frontier because Reed truthfully made Lenin, not Stalin, the hero of the ten days.

But if Lenin was affable and democratic where Stalin is tyrannical and inaccessible, he did not hesitate to use the "broom of steel," and Trotsky, who built the wartime Red Army, was as quick to kill. Men who came to power by intrigue, men who have lived all their lives in the atmosphere of internal strife, find it difficult to believe that there are men of any other mentality. Revolutionaries who fought to build their kind of Russia are going to fight anybody who is against their kind of Russia. No man can voice unrest or quarrel with the policies of Stalin. If he does, he is shot. The Communists, like the Fascists, have no outlet and no other technique for dealing with minority opinion. In the mentality of the party dictatorship, a man who differs with you is a man capable of plotting your overthrow and death. Stalin began to purge because he believed in iron discipline. With each new death more and more Russians were disgruntled and more and more murders became necessary. The police terror had already destroyed the capitalists and intellectuals of the *ancien régime,* and then followed the equally harsh suppression of the kulaks or small bourgeois-minded farm owners. Then the police liquidated the Trotskyists after Stalin drove Lenin's partner into exile in 1928.

As the personal dictatorship of Stalin became absolute, it was not enough to liquidate these social groups who remembered pre-Communist Russia and the individuals who had sympathized with Trotsky. Stalin had to remove the leaders who remembered pre-Stalin Russia. Under the party dictatorship one rule must prevail. The dictator must be always right. Stalin had played an important role, but he had been less conspicuous than Lenin and Trotsky in the revolution. Not only John Reed's book but even the official histories were rewritten to prove that Stalin was the lone genius of the *coup d'état.* I remember the official Soviet moving picture, first shown November 7, 1937, which portrayed Lenin as a nervous little man, afraid and indecisive, but able in every moment of danger to turn around and find at his shoulder

Stalin, who was portrayed not as the rather short man he is but as a tower of strength calmly puffing at his pipe and giving Lenin the laconic answer to every problem.

There are many explanations for the purges, but there can be no doubt that any party dictatorship is a devouring Frankenstein by definition, and that Stalin, the man at the levers, became afraid of mounting opposition. One cold day in December, 1934, a Communist named Kirov was killed in Leningrad. A death more or less under a dictatorship ordinarily means little, but this death meant much. Stalin had only two confidants and Kirov, his man of action, was one and Kuibyshev, his one-man brain trust, was the other. Stalin took a train posthaste to Leningrad. It was plain at the time that Kirov had been killed by a man who bore him a personal grudge; but the murderer had relations with Zinoviev and Kamenev, old Bolsheviks who were disgruntled. While Stalin was debating whether Zinoviev and Kamenev had possibly been in correspondence with Trotsky, Kuibyshev died. It was a natural death but a great blow to Stalin nevertheless. Stalin is a man to beat his foes to the blow, but this time he did a strange thing. He stayed the hand of the G.P.U. from December, 1934, until August, 1936. Having moved slowly and stealthily meanwhile, Stalin suddenly staged a great public trial of Zinoviev and Kamenev. Thus began the extraordinary performance of public show-trials in which incredibly incriminating confessions were volunteered by the defendants themselves. It was not until January, 1937, that the Piatakov-Radek group came to trial and then suddenly, on June 11, 1937, Stalin startled the world by executing Marshal Tukhachevsky and seven other generals of the Red Army.

Correspondents estimated that in addition to Marshal Tukhachevsky and the seven generals executed with him, some thirty thousand officers were involved in the Red Army purge. The arrests were so widespread that correspondents could estimate their full extent only by a division of labor in which we subscribed to and read all the newspapers. The Communist press never printed the nationwide totals of this mass operation and the only references made in any newspaper to arrests were those effected in the city where a given newspaper was published—arrests, in short, too well known to the readers of that newspaper to be withheld from them. We journalists bought some seventy-odd papers published over the whole of the Soviet Union and, carrying out the daily chore of wading through them all, we got some notion of the horrible nationwide nature of this purge. We knew already in 1937 that it had affected some 40 members, or alternate members, of the Central Committee of the party, 9 former members of the Politburo, 18 former People's Commissars together with 50 Assistant People's Commissars, and no less than 16 Soviet Ambassadors or Ministers. This terror was nationwide and it affected every type of Russian we knew, every city block where we had friends, and even our own staffs. All correspondents hired Russian secretaries to serve as translators. In my period in Moscow the G.P.U. arrested the secretaries of Harold Denny, of the New York *Times;* of Spencer Williams, of the Manchester *Guardian* (Williams was also head of the American-Russian Chamber of Commerce) ; and of James Brown, of the International News Service. There was one amusing incident—how rarely anything in this purge seemed amusing—involving an employee of Demaree Bess, then of the *Christian Science Monitor* and later of the *Saturday Evening Post.* Mrs. Bess had found a carpenter and she sent him on to a diplomat with a note: "This is the man I told you about." When the G.P.U. discovered this note, the carpenter passed three days and nights in grim Lubyanka Prison, where the deep cellars muffled the crackle of the revolvers. He was philosophical about his experience.

"I didn't mind," he said, "because I figured they wouldn't hurt a simple fellow like me. It was interesting too. I never had a chance before, an illiterate man like me, to talk with all the educated men I met in prison. Only it was pretty full down there and they were busy and I didn't want them to forget me."

Witch-hunting creates a unique mentality of suspicion and some of the things published in the newspapers were too naïve to be credible. For instance, there was a purge of workers in the Moscow zoo. The papers said the zoo keepers were killing animals. The Moscow newspapers said that they had thrown tacks into the squirrel cage. "It isn't credible," said the wife of one American correspondent. "If there are any tacks to be had in Russia, I'd like to know where the zoo keepers buy them. I can't find any." But none of us made facetious remarks when Russian friends said, "I can't sleep any more at night. I just lie awake, waiting to hear the knock on the door. I haven't done anything, but then lots of other people haven't done anything." You didn't like it when a friend said, "I keep a razor and toothbrush wrapped up under my pillow. If they ever come for me I'm going to jump from the window and make a run for it. I'd rather get away or die on the spot. No torture for me." Right and left they arrested everyone with whom we foreigners had any contact.

Joseph E. Davies, the American Ambassador, whom I found to be friendly, energetic, and shrewd, has recorded his feelings as he watched the prisoners in the box during one trial. "There was Krestinsky, under-Secretary of State," Davies wrote, "to whom I had presented my credentials a year ago; Rosengoltz, former Commissar of Trade, with whom I had lunched just a year ago this month at his country home; Dr. Pletnov, the heart specialist who had treated me professionally, and whom I knew quite well; and Grinko, the Secretary of the Treasury." Davies also records how he entertained for the high command of the Russian armed forces. "Within nine weeks of this dinner," he observed, "eleven of the principal officers of the Army and Navy were tried by court-martial and shot. Among them Marshal

Tukhachevsky and four other generals of High Command, who were among our dinner guests." Ekay Davies, the Ambassador's charming daughter who had studied Russian, told me that she found conversation with Tukhachevsky difficult. One can well believe it.

It has been suggested that Stalin carried out this purge to stamp out fifth columnists in touch with Germany, Japan, and Italy. The liquidation of the Russian fifth column well in advance of a war, it is argued, explains Russian success against Hitler. This seems to me to be an absurd explanation of why Stalin conducted the purge, which was in the nature of a preventive civil war, not an attack on foreign agents. The result of the purge, of course, has served that purpose. It is the congenitally opposition-minded individual in any country who gives Hitler a chance to create a fifth column. The man who is defeatist, the misfit who searches about him for a "wave of the future," and the obstructionist who hates his own regime and government more than he hates Hitler is always a potential fifth columnist. And it is true that such men in Russia were liquidated by the purge. But it must be remembered that Stalin was killing when Russia's relations with Germany were excellent, that he began to stage the great public show-trials long before the second World War, and that while Kirov was killed in 1934 it was not until 1937—late in the purge—that Stalin struck at the Red Army leadership and charged that Russians were conspiring with foreign governments.

The purge had already reached its height, with the arrest of not less than 1,000,000 Russians in three years, before Stalin turned his attention to foreign consulates and swept foreign experts from the Soviet Union after 1937. In the great trials the defendants always said what the prosecution wanted them to say. They had been in prison for periods varying from three months to a year. They were promised escape from the death penalty if they came in and confessed to the elaborate conspiracies worked out by the prosecution.

Those who were unwilling to do this were shot by the thousands, a revolver held to the back of their heads in Lubyanka Prison. Those who were willing to confess found that when their public testimony departed from the carefully worked-out confession of guilt the court was promptly recessed; the treatment they received in the interim sufficed to make them amenable when court reconvened. It is significant, therefore, that Marshal Tukhachevsky and the other generals were executed with no effort to stage a public trial.

To understand the execution of Tukhachevsky let us look at the background and understand the system. Recurrent purges are inevitable under any party dictatorship. No minority of 3,000,000 can control 170,000,000 without iron discipline. And there was real opposition to Stalin within the Communist party. Stalin undertook to do for Russia in ten years what capitalism did for America in sixty. The building of heavy and light industries under the Five-year Plans was harsh and the people grew weary. They were always being promised the good things of this life, but for the future. There was general disgruntlement. Thus the purges not only served to remove important Communists—of the thousands of old Bolsheviks around Lenin, only Stalin, Kalinin, and Voroshilov remained—but also to provide an excuse before the public for the hardships and continued poverty of the people. The Communist bureaucracy, like the Fascist bureaucracy, was a monstrosity of favoritism and inefficiency. This as much as the backwardness of the lumbering Russian masses explains the shortcomings of the Russian production effort. Such a result was the natural and inevitable consequence, as Ambassador Davies remarked, "of the drive to re-establish party considerations over the ordinary considerations of efficiency and good judgment which the administration of a business properly and usually would employ." To have a job which enabled you to eat and live well, you had to be a party member; and to get such a job you had, as often as not, to denounce the ordinary skilled Russian who was not a party member.

That vast turnover caused by the ejection from good jobs of many individuals who had no pull with the party machine was partly responsible for several Soviet phenomena such as the sale of hats in the summer but the absence of them in the winter, or a glut of shoes in one town when they could not be bought in the next town. Naturally the Russian masses resented abuses by Communist ward heelers. When Stalin started purging the party the masses believed hopefully at first in the propaganda which held the party members being purged responsible for all the graft and inefficiency. Similarly Stalin's popularity with the peasants was increased rather than diminished when he purged the G.P.U., which represented to them an oppressive group. And yet all this killing shook Russian morale—not enough to overthrow the regime but enough to cause profound and nationwide distress.

I believe that the Red Army was purged because of widespread alarm among its leaders lest the party, devouring the masses, should also destroy the fatherland. The purges were necessary to keep the party in power and Stalin supreme. But to many a Russian general, fearful of Germany's military preparations and intentions, it must have seemed that the purges would bring a collapse of the Russian industrial effort and of mass morale. In short, Russia, because of its party dictatorship, had come in June, 1937, to the same deadlock reached in Germany in June of 1934. In Germany the army won when Hitler struck down Roehm and the other party leaders and, from then onward, Germany became a military state, in which the ultimate decisions were based on military needs and considerations. In Russia, Stalin struck down Tukhachevsky and the generals. The party proved itself supreme.

It is understandable that generals, charged directly with the defense of the fatherland, should have been alarmed at

the dislocations caused in the Soviet economy by the purge
and especially by the repercussions on industrial production
and national morale. It is also understandable that Stalin
should have been blindly furious at Tukhachevsky or any
other generals who may have reproached him for the low
agricultural and industrial yield. For it is precisely in these
fields that Stalin's achievements had been most impressive
—so impressive, in fact, that, whatever may happen to Communism, history will probably record him as the first great
Russian builder after Peter the Great. It was Stalin who
carried through the Five-year Plans immediately after the
1928 exile of Trotsky—plans which embraced the agricultural collectivization as well as the industrialization of the
Soviet Union. "We are from fifty to one hundred years behind the advanced countries," Stalin said, "and we must
run through this distance in ten years." The collectivization
has been denounced as one of the harshest programs ever
undertaken by a government. The government is believed
to have starved 2,000,000 peasants to death. But by this
program it socialized 99.2 per cent of the agricultural land
and 92.4 per cent of all the peasant households. Who is to
judge the brutality and ruthlessness of this policy, Stalin
must have demanded, against the benefits which it has conferred on Russia?

Harsh though his policy was, Stalin destroyed the greatest
of all the Russian bugaboos—famine. When I was last in
Russia, in 1937, the grain yield for that harvest was estimated at 111,384,000 metric tons (4,451,360,000 bushels).
That compared favorably with 80,100,000 tons, the best
yield of Tsarist Russia, in 1913, or with the "all-time" high
of 89,800,000 tons already achieved by Stalin in 1933. "One
good harvest," said Catherine the Great, "makes up for five
bad years," and Stalin might have added that a succession
of good harvests makes up for the purging of peasants who
stubbornly opposed collectivization and slaughtered half the
nation's livestock in sabotage. While multiplying the grain

yield, Stalin made Russia first in Europe and third in the world in the production of cotton. He gave his country world primacy in sugar beets and flax. There were 12,000,000 head of cattle again by 1927. The Russian peasants began to take a deservedly glowing pride in this progress, but no one should think that the Communists had succeeded in producing the impossible—a contented farmer. The peasant was still in a position of class inferiority to the industrial worker.

Until the adoption of the new 1936 constitution, the farmers had been entitled to a political representative for each group of 125,000 as compared with a delegate for every 25,000 workers. The farmer suffered more than any other member of the community from the peculiar intricacies of a planned society. Some 74 per cent of the budgetary revenue in 1937 was derived from a turnover or sales tax. Directly or indirectly 60 per cent of this tax came from agricultural products. The government owned and, therefore, took outright the produce of state farms. It also took outright 58 per cent of the produce of the cooperative farms. Workers on the state farms were paid wages whereas the cooperative farmer was paid for his grain in cash and grain, handed back for his personal consumption. After charging the farmer for the use of tractors and the like the state paid him only twenty-nine kopecks, or scarcely more than a quarter of a ruble per "workday," or, if he preferred grain, roughly one kilogram of grain per "workday." Then, when the state sold the grain to the miller, it slapped on an exorbitant turnover tax. When the miller sold to the flour maker, there was another tax. When bread reached the consumer, its basic cost had been quadrupled and it was completely out of the reach, of course, of farm workers, who could live only because they got grain as well as kopecks for their labor. The turnover tax levied on grain was levied on almost everything else produced in the Soviet Union. The basic cost of sugar, for instance, was increased sixfold. In short, there was practically nothing in the way of consumers' goods which was not prohibitively priced. When the farmer got to town occasionally, he saw things in the windows; but he could not buy them. Except for his faith in Communism, his situation was comparable either to that of a convict laborer, if he worked on a state farm, or to that of the lowest level of a sharecropper, if he worked on a collective farm. He could better his position only if he proved a capacity for party organization, whereupon he might cease to be a farmer in order to become a ward heeler. This was the price of the forced industrialization and of the preparation against a Fascist war.

The first Five-year Plan (1928) started the expansion of heavy industry. Stalin built tractor works at Kharkov, automobile and truck factories at Gorki and Moscow, tractor factories at Rostov and Stalingrad. The great Dnieper Dam was completed, steel furnaces were put up in the valley of the Don, and fertilizer works in the Urals were the beginning of the creation of a vast industrial setup beyond those mountains which was to prove so important and so farseeing after the German invasion. Despite the inefficiencies caused by Communist party methods, the Five-year Plans were successful in the main and by 1937 some 75 per cent of the country's industrial output rolled from factories built since 1917. Stalin's accomplishment has been summarized by Ambassador Davies.

"Measurably the Five Year Plan had justified itself," he wrote. "The outstanding fact in the situation, however, is that it was not *because* of government operation of industry, *but in spite of it.* The enormous wealth of the country practically assured, quantitatively, a large measure of success, despite the enormous inefficiencies, wastes and losses which such a system must necessarily entail. What the regime did do, however, was to conceive the plan and drive it through."

I wrote in January, 1938, of the visible change in Russia since I had last been there:

"Since I saw Russia five years ago incredible progress has

been made. You see it all around you in warmly clad people in the streets, wearing woolen overcoats and rubbers. The long queues of breadlines I used to watch are abolished and there are actually plate glass show windows with delicatessen foods and perfume and women's clothing on display. You have to wait under street lights for Russian-built automobiles to pass.

"The first Five Year Plan, which gave Russia heavy industries, was nearing completion in 1932. It was increasing Russia's share in the world's industrial output from four to fourteen percent, moving the Soviets up from fifth to second place. It was twenty years' work done in five, and without foreign capital. It was a great accomplishment, but you did not see its results on the streets or in the show windows.

"Now the second Five Year Plan is nearing fruition. The light industries have been developed and the people are promised consumers' goods at last. This is what you see in the streets and in the show windows today. It looks too good to be true—and it is! Only half the things the people need are in the windows and the prices on them are prohibitive.

"For instance, take the shoes you see in the show windows. The only pair of men's shoes you could possibly wear are the quality of a $3.00 pair in America and they are priced at 220.5 rubles. If you figure the dollar at the official rate of $1.00 to 5 rubles, this makes them cost you $44.10. There is a pair of women's shoes which an American would shake her head at, but which she would buy if she were a Russian and could afford them. They cost 252 rubles, or $50.40.

"I saw the following typical prices in a clothing store: Astrakhan fur coat, 4,158 rubles; bad quality sable, 2,843 rubles; man's fur hat, 613. The articles are not like the coats pre-depression business men in America were buying for blondes. They were just ordinary serviceable goods.

"The trouble with the Russians and these prices is that fully a third of the workers are still in the bottom bracket, for which Stalin last month (December, 1937) set a minimum salary of 110–115 rubles a month. This means that a pair of good shoes would cost one of these workers two months' salary. The best paid workers in heavy industry draw only a little more than 3,000 rubles and the average for all workers is 231 rubles per month. That fur hat would cost the average man three months' salary. He could not buy the fur coat with a year's salary.

"Why are prices so high for good shoes or anything else that is good quality? The answer is that, while the two Five Year Plans have enabled the state to provide enough second- and third-rate goods for the people, they have not been able to produce quality goods. If the prices of good shoes were cut, the whole supply would be exhausted in a few days, it is explained."

I found that the Russian workers wanted consumers' goods and wanted a wage which would enable them to buy such goods. I talked with the workers who were building the Moscow River bridge. They told me that, whereas the average worker is paid 231 rubles, they received 350 rubles ($70) a month, which sufficed with cheap rent and state insurance. This does not look bad if you remember that at the height of the depression in 1933 the average income of the American worker was exactly the same—seventy dollars a month. But in Russia seventy dollars in rubles did not buy 70 dollars' worth of food and clothing. Prices were too high in Russia. The real wage of the Russian worker was a fraction of the American's wage. Seventy dollars in rubles would not buy twenty dollars' worth of food. I asked the worker on the Moscow River bridge if 350 rubles a month was enough.

"It is too little to support a family on," he said. "I pay fifteen rubles a month for a room," explained the worker, who had no family. "Food cost me seven rubles a day, which makes 210 rubles a month. That leaves 125 rubles for everything else. I can't buy many clothes with that, but I don't complain. I get on all right since I haven't anybody to support. But most of these fellows here make 150 or 200 rubles a month."

When they talked about food they did not mean American meals. They meant cabbage soup and black bread, with little meat and fish.

I talked with the crack man in the welding crew working on the Moscow streetcar line. He made 350 rubles a month, lived in a room ninety feet square with his wife and daughter and two other families.

"It's pretty crowded, and unpleasant, living like that," he admitted.

He paid forty rubles a month for his third of the room. Meals averaged fifteen rubles a day for him and his wife and daughter.

"That's all very well, but fifteen rubles a day come to 450 rubles a month and you make only 350," I said.

"Yes, but my wife makes 200 rubles a month and my daughter makes 150," he explained. "I also get my working boots and my padded overalls free of charge."

The woman who hung up and gave out coats in a check-room made 150 rubles a month. She lived with her mother and little brother. Neither one worked. Three persons could not eat enough on what she made. She lived in the suburbs in a hovel and pinched every kopeck, but the three were hungry. She was a good Communist and an intelligent woman. Before I could give her the check number she remembered my coat and had it ready for me. I remarked this and she said proudly that she could read and write.

"I would like to get some eggs, milk, and chicken once in a while," she said rather wistfully. Then she began hastily and quite sincerely to explain how much Stalin was doing for the country and how someday, if they were patient, "the Communists will surpass America." But then it was pretty hard.

Against this standard of living one must cite social insurance. The woman who handed out keys in my hotel was a widow with four children. She did not make enough to support them and I expressed my sympathy, especially since her husband had been sent abroad by the Soviets and she had known the real comforts of foreign lands.

"Oh, don't forget," she said, "that each of my children gets one hundred rubles a month insurance and that their schooling and the like is entirely free. The oldest of them, my fourteen-year-old daughter, studies music under such masters as not the richest child in America could have."

Nevertheless, the hunger of the checkroom girl who made 150 rubles a month was probably more representative of the standard of living. Under Stalin's wage increase 115 rubles a month was the minimum for salaried workers and 110 rubles the minimum for those on piecework. Fully a third of the workers were in a bottom bracket, paid over the minimum, and yet not more than 200 rubles a month.

L. E. Hubbard, one of the trustworthy economists who has studied Russia, thinks that "the average Russian can buy as much food with a week's wages as a Londoner can buy with nine shillings," or $2.25. Sir Walter Citrine, who was a worker himself as well as a trade-union leader, estimated the average real wage of the Russian worker at twelve dollars a month. But to this one must add health insurance, free education, and paid holidays.

This situation reflected a vicious circle. Communism sought to increase the productivity of the Russian worker. But the standard of living of the worker remained low and he did not produce enough to make it possible for the state to offer consumers' goods cheap enough for his wage level. Russia had the resources and the factories, but the production problem remained unsolved. American engineers told us journalists that on any job in Russia twice as many workers were employed as on a similar job in the United States and that even then it required twice as long to finish it. In their own discussions of industrial production the Russian newspapers wrote: "With a third the number of workers Americans have an output three times higher than ours." I think there were two reasons for this situation.

In the first place, the Russians were evolving from a semi-feudal economy where less than a hundred years ago Russian peasants were still serfs. During the years 1928–1932 industry absorbed 12,500,000 peasants. These unskilled individuals, drawn from the steppes, were lummoxlike. For generations they had said, "Work is not a bear; it will not run away into the forest." It takes more than three Five-year Plans to do away with a century of "Nichevo." That Russian word for "Never mind" makes the Spanish "Mañana" sound like an urgent call to arms. I could see the truth of this merely by leaving my typewriter and stepping out into the street. Two women were holding a ladder for a bricklayer. The foreman told the women that one could hold the ladder and that the other should busy herself with something else. "Da, da," they said in unison, and went right on talking together.

The second reason is equally important. Communism, like Fascism, is essentially a wartime economy. Without the complete mobilization of the nation, without the urgency and hysteria of a war atmosphere, neither Communism nor Fascism is able to compete against democratic production. The party dictatorship which substitutes "party regularity" for competence and efficiency as the test of promotion causes daily dislocations to industry which become glaringly evident in each sporadic outburst of purging. Moreover, the absence of the profit motive, while relatively unimportant in wartime or while an artificial wartime psychology obtains, becomes a positive factor once the atmosphere of urgency is dissipated. When Stalin introduced the first Five-year Plan the Russian people responded with an enthusiasm which was both inspiring and thrilling. The production effort was dramatized so that quotas became "objectives" on the "industrial front" in the "battle" of this, that, and the next thing. The state proposed the program of "Saturdaying" and millions voluntarily gave up their rest day. The state suggested the formation of "shock brigades" and competition between factories so that millions worked overtime without compensation in order to complete schedules or to surpass rival brigades. But after each of these inspirational drives the enthusiasm of the workers sagged and production fell back.

In 1931 Stalin swerved radically. He did away with the system of equal wages and introduced piecework throughout all the factories. Draftsmen were paid by the square inch of work done, regardless of quality, and iron puddlers on how much, not how well, they puddled. This shifted the emphasis to the individual, who was given a profit motive. Once the individual was paid on the basis of a norm—the quantity of output which entitled him to his basic daily wage and premiums —Stalin introduced the idea of the *udarnik*. A man who passed his production norm and earned a premium became a *udarnik,* but even then there was the inevitable and perhaps inescapable sagging of enthusiasm. Communists who remembered pre-Stalin literature reminded their fellows that Marx himself had written: "Piecework wages . . . offer [the capitalist] many opportunities for making deductions from wages and practicing other forms of cheating while they bring the worker only physical exhaustion as a result of excessive efforts to raise the level of wages, efforts which, in fact, tend rather to lower wages." Few workers read Marx, but all of them knew about the exhaustion and the unimproved standard of living which had followed Stalin's introduction of the piecework system. Production fell off again and Stalin looked for a new technique.

The speed-up, or Taylor, system had been bitterly decried by workers throughout the world as a capitalistic trick to make men automatons, cogs in machines, brutes who after a few years of much high-pressure work were thrown exhausted onto the human scrap heap. In Russia it was hailed as the Stakhanovite movement, thanks to masterly Communist propaganda.

In 1935 the Don Basin was rich in coal. The miners, moreover, had the latest pneumatic drills and equipment. But they could not get the coal out. Production was half what it is in American mines. There was some progress under the *udarnik,* or piecework, system, but again production fell back. The Communists picked out a healthy young nobody named Alexey Stakhanov and made him the best-known man in Russia after Stalin. Our begrimed hero, young Alexey, had an idea. He turned to his comrades in labor. "One of you pull away the coal, one of you load the cars and the like, and I shall keep the pneumatic drill going all day," he said. The comrades fell to with that Bolshevik alacrity which is said to shame the enslaved workers of capitalism. At the end of the day they were astonished. Instead of having mined seven tons of coal per man, the usual production, young Stakhanov's team had mined thirty-five tons per man. By sheer coincidence the comrades of the press and radio happened to be down in the mine pit on that glorious occasion. They were in a position to disseminate the new gospel with the admonition to go out in true Communist spirit and do likewise. In this fashion the *udarniks* were organized into teams or shifts called "Stakhanovites."

"What a coal digger can do, I can do too," said a man with the unlikely name of Busygin, who was a foreman in the Gorky auto plant. This worthy ally of Stakhanov organized team play among his workers too, and an equally surprised press, standing by with pencils in hand, carried the good news that Comrade Busygin had increased the production of crank shafts from 674 per shift to 1146.

Marie Demchanko, twenty years old and pretty enough to be a heroine with young Alexey or even sober Comrade Busygin, would not be outdone in Communist fervor by any mere man. It was her job to grow sugar beets. Very well. She and her fellow workers weeded and watered the fields as no fields have ever been weeded or watered before. Working as a team, they got twice the normal yield in beets. A pretty girl, Marie could also turn a pretty phrase and, according to the Soviet press, she said, "We want to powder our beloved fatherland with sugar."

These charmingly ingenuous youngsters not only became overnight the aristocrats of Soviet Russia—the folk one sees in the Bolshoi Opera or in the restaurants buying champagne and caviar—but also gave the emotional stimulus to Stalin's speed-up plan. Seventy per cent of the workers were already on a piecework basis in 1935, so that it was easy for the Stakhanovite movement to add a further profit incentive for shifts as well as for individuals who surpassed the norm. Production mounted again. Then suddenly the Communists swindled the workers once more. Within a year of the speed-up achieved by the Stakhanovites, Stalin announced in November, 1935, that the old goals were too low and he increased the norms of what a man should do in a working day. By April, 1936, norms in all industries were so high that only the best workers could surpass their daily production quotas and earn premiums. In April, 1937, Stalin not only raised the norms again but also lowered the wage rates per piece. The worker produced more units per day, but he received less pay. Thus there were ups and downs in production following each new intervention by the state. Even the Communists themselves found it difficult to understand just what was happening in production.

Never modest about Communist accomplishments, *Pravda*, the country's leading newspaper, carried the headline "The Stakhanov Movement Grows and Wins." The article said in the beginning, "The Soviet worker is three times more productive than the worker before the revolution. During 1936 alone the productivity of labor in our large-scale industry increased 21 per cent." Just as the reader got caught up in the swing of the thing, there came a snag—the following paragraph: "The growth of the Stakhanov movement is impossible without overcoming hostile counteraction. The spies and hirelings of Fascism, the Trotskyite-Bukharinite wreckers manifest a beastly hatred of Stakhanovites. There is no

crime, however base, to which they will not stoop to bring disorder in this powerful movement." Which paragraph was
one to believe? I tried to break down the official Soviet
statistics to get the answer. Reading the official figures, one
found proof that men and machines alike were breaking
under the strain of the speed-up. In 1937 the production of
coal, coke, iron ore, pig iron, and petroleum failed to equal
production figures for 1936. The metal-cutting machine-tool
industry, the combine, cement, locomotive and freight-car
industries, were behind 1936 production. Only the steel,
rolled-metal, and copper industries showed increases over
1936, but even they lagged behind planned production for
1937. I tried to break down the figures into single typical
industries. The automotive industry was behind the production figures planned for 1937 and had surpassed 1936
production only because a change of model in 1936 had kept
the plants idle for many days. In the first eight months of
1937 the conveyor at the Moscow truck plant was idle 23 per
cent of the working time. On November 14, 1937, I visited a
plant as big as anything Ford has got and found that on that
day it produced only 80 automobiles and 425 trucks, which
indicated no increase in output in almost two years. Soviet
production was equally unsatisfactory from the point of view
of quality. As official publications themselves revealed, synthetic rubber tires designed to do 25,000 kilometers were no
longer serviceable after runs of from 500 to 800 kilometers.

What was the explanation for these production setbacks at
a time when Stalin had resorted to both the profit motive
and the speed-up process? The explanation lay in no small
part in the paragraph *Pravda* devoted to "wrecking" and
"sabotage." Plant managers, engineers, and foremen had
been frightened half to death by the purges and were unwilling to take initiatives. The workers had been swindled under piecework and speed-up processes which had increased
neither their real incomes nor their standard of living. The
machines were breaking down under more shifts than they

were designed to take. Morale was being badly shaken by a purge in which slovenliness and inefficiency were synonymous with "Fascist wrecking." How steady would you be while trying to speed up a loom if by racing it too fast you broke it and risked arrest? The failure of Communism to rival in peacetime the efficiency of capitalism could be seen in statistics. Russia's per capita production of pig iron was scarcely three-fifths of Britain's, while if Russia were to equal America in per capita production she would have to produce not 15,000,000 tons of pig iron but 60,000,000 tons annually. The failure could also be seen in the attitude of the workers. There is obvious dissatisfaction when workers begin to shift jobs, going from one factory to the next and from one town to the next hoping that the grass will be a little greener over the hill. Was it possible to find statistics on this? I found official figures for the migration of labor during 1935 and 1936. The following table indicates the percentage of men leaving their jobs during the year in comparison with the total number employed at any given time over the yearly average:

	1935 Per Cent	1936 Per Cent
All industries	86.1	87.5
Coal industry	99.1	112.7
Food industry	149.2	141.1

By the end of 1935 Stalin was thoroughly alarmed at the social discontent reflected in this labor turnover. He introduced the principle of bonuses for seniority of service. Wage increases varying from 10 to 20 per cent were ordered in 1938 in certain industries for men who had worked for several years in the same factory or farm. The Soviets admit that every year three-quarters of all their workers have shifted jobs in spite of every effort of the state backed up by the G.P.U.

It seemed plain to me when I was in the Soviet Union that

Communism had not proved equal to capitalism in its own vaunted field of production. Often it seemed to me that the problem of production could not be solved efficiently under Communism, but of this I was not certain then and I am not certain now. Any study of state socialism as it operates in Russia must be qualified by the extraordinary and special considerations which obtain in that vast, rich, and yet backward land. I believed that the Soviet Union had many weaknesses; but I never believed that the Stalin regime faced collapse, for the Russian people saw as clearly as Stalin the ultimate danger of invasion by Germany and Japan. This is why they accepted such peacetime sacrifices as no other people made.

In spite of the inefficiencies of Communism and the crippling effects of a party dictatorship, Stalin, thanks to the Five-year Plans, had made gigantic forward steps in this rich land, and he placed primary emphasis upon preparation for defense. By 1936 he claimed Soviet primacy in world production of harvester combines and beet sugar; second place in the production of machines, tractors, motor trucks, iron ore, and gold; third place in the production of steel and fourth in coal. Among Europeans he claimed first place in total industrial output; in machine-tool production; in the manufacture of tractors, harvester combines, motor trucks; and in the production of gold, beet sugar and superphosphates; as well as second place in steel and third place in coal production. In the years immediately preceding Hitler's invasion of Poland, Russia's national income could be estimated at about $27,500,000,000. This was roughly the equivalent of Great Britain's national income, though the per capita income of the Soviet Union was barely one-third that of Britain. Hitler came to power in 1933. In 1934 Stalin was able to devote only 3.3 per cent of his total revenues to defense, but by 1937 the percentage had been raised to about 22. The official statistics available indicate a total military expenditure in 1937 of 22,431,000,000 rubles, which at the bootleg ruble rate

would be about $2,200,000,000. (The United States prom-
ised in 1942 to ship Russia $3,000,000,000 in arms.) Despite
its vast preponderance in national resources Communist Russia could not' match the arms production of Nazi Germany in
the years preceding the war. But Stalin was able during those
years to double Great Britain's expenditures and dwarf the
efforts of France. A trustworthy British source, the *Bulletin
of International News*, offers an interesting comparison in
pound-sterling purchasing power. The Royal Institute's
Bulletin compares the three powers as follows:

Military Expenditures in Millions of Pounds

	Germany	Russia	Britain
1935	520	230	122
1936	730	415	172
1937	840	490	251
1938	1470	760	391
	3560	1895	936

It is understandable that Marshal Tukhachevsky and his
fellow generals may have been dissatisfied during these years
with Russia's production of arms. Their military espionage
system kept them informed of daily developments in Germany. They knew that their potential foe, though scarcely
half as rich in natural resources as Russia, was outarming the
Soviet Union two to one. They knew, moreover, that they
were being outpaced qualitatively as well as quantitatively.
It must have impressed them, as it impressed foreign correspondents, that Soviet trucks and tanks were stalled along the
roadways and that Soviet synthetic rubber tires wore out at a
fraction of the mileage for which they had been designed.
They saw with distress the dislocations caused to industry
by the recurrent purges. They saw, because they lived cheek
by jowl with it, that the revolution devours its own children.
They saw that these purges were the inevitable concomitant
of unbridled party dictatorship. They saw that the graphic

line of industrial production zoomed between purges. They saw the weariness on the faces of the millions, tired of being promised a letup and frightened of the next purge, which always seemed imminent. It is understandable that these men, the leaders of the Red Army, charged with the defense of the Fatherland, may have felt that the security of Russia depended upon a cessation of purges and of Communist party interference with defensive efforts. And it is understandable that Stalin and the party would not abdicate before Red Army opposition.

Stalin, nevertheless, did himself irreparable harm before the world at large, diminishing the prestige of the Red Army and the confidence which Great Britain and France ought to have had in that army. Because Stalin had "cut off the poppy heads"—striking down the flower of Red Army leadership—Stalin's allies thought that he had destroyed the army. Certainly the complexion of the army leadership was changed. I talked with observers from the succession Baltic states who were privileged to watch the maneuvers of an army sadly bereft of leaders above the rank of colonel and plainly inhibited by the self-consciousness and fright of youthful commanders suddenly promoted to the highest ranks. The assistant French military attaché was one of the few foreigners who believed that the purge had not crippled the Soviet military machine.

"After all," he said to me, "we executed two hundred French generals during the World War and, believe me, the French army was much stronger for every one of these generals purged."

"What do you mean?" I exclaimed. "You never shot any generals in France during the World War."

"Of course, we didn't shoot them," he replied. "We relieved them of their commands. Whenever a French general proved incompetent, he was sent to Limoges. We said such a general had been 'limogé.' In France we don't shoot men for incompetence or for insubordination. Here in Russia they do."

I found confirmation for the view that the Red Army was shaken but efficient in such illuminating information as I could pump from two Russian generals I was able to see, because they were interested in what I had learned at the Spanish fronts and were willing to risk the dangers of contact with a foreigner in order to discuss the relative performance of tanks and planes in Spain. Most important of all, I was convinced that the man who knew more about the Red Army than any other in Moscow, Russian or foreign, was Colonel Philip R. Faymonville, the United States military attaché. Like his colleagues, George Strong, Raymond Lee, Truman Smith, Horace Fuller, John Magruder, "Barney" Legge, Norman Fiske, and other American military attachés I have known abroad, Faymonville was a credit to his country—extraordinarily able and shrewd as well as an indefatigable student of European armies. The quality of our military attachés in the past ten years has been very high indeed.

Faymonville had been with the American Expeditionary Forces in Siberia; he had learned Russian as well as Japanese. He had won the confidence of hundreds of Russian officers in a period when most attachés had only the most formal contact with them. Faymonville knew that the Russian army was not fully equipped and that it had not mastered the problem of supply, but he believed that it would give a good account of itself in any defensive war. Its deficiencies would prevent effective offensive action beyond its own frontiers, he thought; but the Red Army on the defensive would surprise the world, he predicted. Other attachés were too much impressed with these deficiencies and with Stalin's decision to reintroduce the system of commissars or political agents of the Communist party, who would keep an eye on the military commanders and share responsibility with them.

Faymonville agreed that in any other army this would bring indecision and prove disastrous, but the Red Army, he argued, was not like any other army. It was, in fact, a Communist army which depended to a remarkable degree upon unorthodox tactics for its defense in depth and upon *partisan,* or guerrilla, actions behind the scorched earth of enemy lines. In such an army party discipline and party enthusiasm were important. I became convinced that this was a correct picture of the Red Army. The Russian Embassy in Washington was not pleased with what I reported of the purge and of production, but Ambassador Oumansky said that no foreign correspondent had written more favorably of the Red Army.

I was also impressed with the growth of Russian nationalism. I was struck in 1937, as in 1932, by the feeling that nationalism was a greater force in modern Russia than Communism. This Slav people, a race of poets and musicians, believed in its destiny. It had begun, moreover, to take a naïve and childlike pride in its superiority—imagining that superiority over the old Tsarist Russia meant superiority over the capitalist countries too. One hundred years ago the Russian people had been serfs. They were scarcely free under Communism, but their lot had been improved and they believed passionately in progress. This is a national mood out of which a great leader—and Stalin is certainly that—can fashion an unbreakable wartime morale. I did not pretend to know what Russia's morale would be in wartime. I felt certain that if the American people had lived under the ruthless discipline of a dictator like Stalin they would use the occasion of war to make revolution. But I was persuaded by men like Faymonville that Russians were not to be judged by the standards of other peoples.

The picture of Russia and of Communism offered by its agents abroad was absurd. For the American, British, or French peoples, life under Stalin would have proved unsupportable. There was no utopia of the sort described by the propagandists. We would have been revolted by the Russian standard of living and the suppression of civil liberties. But the Russians celebrated the twentieth anniversary of their revolution with unmistakable enthusiasm. They knew, as no American could know, that Stalin had improved the conditions which obtained under the Tsars. The fear of famine had been removed. The backward land, dependent upon the export of raw materials and foodstuffs, had been industrialized. Education and public health had become universal. The Russians read new editions of their poets in literally millions of copies. The people were frightened by the purges, discouraged by the harshness of the production program, and bowed down under the weight of taxation. But they believed in Russia for the Russians.

Stalin's program meant to the simplest man that Russia would never become an easy prey to Fascist conquest and a colony of the Germans. Here again they could not be judged as one would judge business-as-usual Americans, because they saw war, thanks to Moscow's propaganda, as an ever-present threat. It was not to be escaped ultimately and preparation for it was the justification for every sacrifice. Finally, they believed in the 1936 Constitution. To foreign observers like myself this document was a cynical mockery. It guaranteed to all Soviet citizens "the right to work," "the right to rest," "the right to education," "the right to material security," and freedom of speech, press, assembly, and demonstration. Article 124 recognized freedom of religious worship. Private property was sanctioned if it did not involve the "exploitation of the labor of others." To me these guarantees were not worth the paper they were written on. To the Russian millions this constitution was the charter of their freedom—the promise of their future. They were persuaded that Stalin meant ultimately—as the situation permitted—to extend democracy to the Russian masses. I watched them vote for the first time under their new constitution. I was struck by the fact that the Communist candidates were unopposed. The Russians were struck by the fact that they were learning how to exercise the ballot.

That is why I believed that, in spite of the purge, the Red Army would give a good account of itself when Russia was invaded. On the twentieth anniversary of the revolution I saw more than an indifferently trained army marching through the Red Square. I saw the mighty Slav race, the clear blue eyes, the squared shoulders, and the forward surge of millions upon millions of young giants, six feet two or three. I felt that the children of backwardness can be heirs too. They are heirs to the future—the future of their own imagining, the future of their faith. And so I felt profound distress when Maxim Litvinov said to me in 1937 that the failure of the democracies to cooperate with the Soviet Union had forced this mighty people to turn toward isolationism and a pact with Nazi Germany. I stood that night before the Kremlin, its battlements bathed in moonlight and St. Basil's Church looming up like a dream from the Arabian Nights. The temperature was forty degrees below zero and I could hear the crunch of a boot on the snow a mile away. I have never felt such sadness. I wanted the Slavs on our side in the coming war. I thought that we Americans, thanks to our own isolationism, had lost a mighty ally against Germany and Japan.

XIII

THE NATURE OF MODERN WAR

THE German invasion of Russia was dictated by strategic, not ideological, considerations. Over the opposition of Nazi party leaders, the German General Staff, overriding the apprehensions of General von Brauschitsch, persuaded Hitler to undertake this campaign—the most ambitious and impressive military operation in modern history. The logic of the German generals seemed inescapable and Hitler was quick to appreciate it, though many Nazis, including Marshal Goering, argued against the campaign in Russia until the fourth week before the actual attack.

Hitler and the generals recognized that there had been serious miscalculations in the German war plan and they foresaw, as a result, their own ultimate defeat unless the strategic initiative could be regained. *Blitzkrieg* in Russia offered a solution—without it Germany might lose the war. What were the complexities of the situation which the generals confronted?

In the first place, despite the collapse of France, Great Britain declined to negotiate peace because she preferred the destruction of the British Isles to capitulation; and, when Germany attempted to reduce Britain by frontal assault, the Royal Air Force proved so superior to the *Luftwaffe* that plans for invasion were abandoned until British resistance could be worn down by a period of submarine and aerial attacks. In the second place, the United States, alarmed after Dunkirk, was hastily improvising a two-edged program of rearmament designed to bolster Great Britain with Lend-Lease aid and to prepare America for the moment of her own intervention. The second of these considerations was vital. It persuaded the Hitler generals that the ultimate issue lay between Germany and the United States. To the German military mind—as distinct from Nazi thinking, which held the United States in contempt—American industrial might and American armed intervention had proved decisive in the first World War. Thus the generals saw suddenly that history might repeat itself. They feared that, at worst, America would tip the balance of power or, at best, force Germany to fight a long and protracted struggle. Confronting these realities, both of which had resulted from the German genius for miscalculating the national psychologies of the peace-loving and democratic Anglo-Saxon peoples, the generals were perturbed by a final danger, more general, and yet more urgent, than British stubbornness or the slow awakening of the young giant across the sea. The generals saw that Germany might lose the strategic initiative. This had been the greatest of her advantages and the surest promise of her victory.

Creating armaments and training soldiery while her future victims remained on a peacetime footing, Germany had gained the political initiative during the preparatory period when she annexed Austria and Czechoslovakia and subjugated Spain. From the moment of her attack at Danzig she had taken and maintained the military initiative, selecting the time and place for each of the subsequent and crushingly victorious operations. This control of the initiative—both political and military—was one of the secrets of the preponderance of German power. Just as its further utilization offered the surest promise of victory, so its loss threatened the very foundations of a totalitarian state. In the course of a long war the democracies, though they start more slowly, have greater resources of spiritual strength, the capacity to endure reverses and defeats, the willingness to fight on when victory seems remote or even illusionary. Not so the totalitarian state. Pragmatic in conception, and dedicated to the political formula that nothing succeeds like success, the totalitarian state cannot endure a static situation. The dictator is always a man on a bicycle. Against these background considerations the German generals, reasoning from the general to the specific, projected three urgent arguments for an immediate conquest of Russia, the largest item for expansion catalogued in *Mein Kampf*. They proposed that Germany should:

1. Obtain direct access to the petroleum, minerals, and foodstuffs of Russia because their exploitation would remove Germany from the category of have-not powers and enable her to fight a long war, even of attrition, against the United States.

2. Secure her exposed flank against Russian attack, which in a long war with America would force Germany to fight simultaneously on two fronts. Here time was essential, since the Germans reasoned, in the first place, that the Russians were rearming at an increasing rate and, in the second place, that Russia ought to be knocked out before America and Britain were ready to fight.

3. Persuade Japan to carry out the stipulation of the Tripartite Pact, whereby she was to act as one with Germany and Italy against American intervention, and demonstrate that in so acting Japan need fear no Russian attack from Siberia.

I have outlined the considerations which inspired the German General Staff, according to information which reached me in Lisbon, Portugal, in the last months and weeks before June 22, 1941. If this summary seems unconditional, indeed almost didactic, it is because my news sources, though for obvious reasons I cannot cite them, were individuals who enjoyed the confidence of the German General Staff and because they kept me informed before the event. America has been subjected to sensational reports that Hitler, Rosenberg, and other Nazis forced a reluctant General Staff to attack Russia for ideological reasons. These came from individuals who have predicted semiannually since 1933 the internal collapse of Germany and who have exaggerated rifts with the generals—rifts which take place in any war and any system. However well intentioned, such reports are mischievous for they reflect a basic incomprehension of modern Germany—an incomprehension which explains why the authors of such reports are refugees in America while the champions of a scientifically articulated plan for world conquest are the masters of the destiny of the Third Reich.

The first concentrations of German troops along the Russian frontiers began almost ten months before the actual invasion. By Christmas of 1940 it became clear that Germany was massing a great army in eastern Europe. Trustworthy sources from the Balkans kept me informed of these developments and German officers and diplomats in Rome, indiscreet in the extreme, confirmed not only these reports but the approximate date for a showdown between the uneasy partners of the Moscow-Berlin pact. Three stories cabled to the Chicago *Daily News* from Rome eight months before the invasion brought two warnings. The brilliant *Daily News* correspondent in Berlin, Wallace R. Deuel, was warned by the authorities there about my "revelation of military secrets" and simultaneously I was threatened by German embassy officials in Rome either with arrest as a spy or with expulsion from Italy. I wrote nothing more during the fall and winter about my increasing certainty that Germany was mounting a colossal offensive against the Russians for the coming spring. Subsequently I was expelled from Rome by the German authorities there for other reasons (their suspicion, ungrounded of course, that I had a hand in the ubiquitous British espionage from Italy and their certainty that I had urged on Count Ciano and certain Italian generals the advantage and possibility of a separate peace by Italy).

Immediately upon my arrival in Lisbon in April, 1941, I began to build news sources among the representatives of

Nazi satellite countries who would be in a position to keep me informed of developments in German plans. It became plain to officers of the Portuguese and Spanish General Staffs in liaison with the Germans, for instance, that an abandonment or delay of the *Blitzkrieg* against Russia would mean the invasion of their own countries by the German *Wehrmacht,* which, as an alternative blow against America, would have occupied the Iberian peninsula, North Africa, and such key strategic points as the Azores and Dakar. We were equally excited, therefore, when, during the month of May, 1941, some two thousand German Gestapo and propaganda agents were withdrawn from Spain and Portugal, creating the presumption that action there had been vetoed. My old friend Quo Tai-Chi, former Chinese Ambassador in London, came through Lisbon on his way to Chungking, where he was to serve briefly as the Chinese Foreign Minister. Our information—from wholly different sources—indicated the preparation of an army of nearly two hundred divisions for an invasion of Russia between June 15 and June 30. Shortly after Quo's visit I learned from another diplomatic source that Mr. Churchill expected the attack before the end of June, that he had so informed Joseph Stalin, but that a British suggestion for the coordination of defense had been unwelcome. Thereafter confirmation for the story came from several sides and with precise details, after the last opposition within Germany by Marshal Goering, Dr. Clodius, and the German Ambassador to Moscow collapsed; for then the generals were able to fix the date.

On June 4, in a fifteen-hundred-word cable to the Chicago *Daily News* and its fifty-odd client newspapers, I predicted the invasion categorically. In a subsequent dispatch I fixed the time as before the end of June. On June 10 I wrote that Germany would conduct no diplomatic negotiation with the Kremlin and that Stalin could offer no concession which would delay or prevent the military invasion of his country on the date fixed by Hitler and the generals. Subsequently

I learned that Stalin had misjudged the situation. He knew that a crisis approached; but he believed that the Germans would try for a diplomatic bargain, demanding direct exploitation of Russian resources, so that he expected a period of delay even if an accommodation could not be arranged. Not only was Stalin warned by Churchill. I learned some months later that Sumner Welles, as early as January, 1941, also conveyed a warning message to the Kremlin. The accuracy of the information received by President Roosevelt, Secretary Hull, and Mr. Welles received categoric confirmation ten days before the invasion when one of the American military attachés in Berlin flew to Washington to report the day and hour of the attack, his message having been considered too important for transmission through the normal channel of coded cables. My newspaper dispatches were a world beat and the New York *Post,* among other client newspapers, reproduced photostatic copies of them when the invasion began. They were not exclusive, however. Three days before the invasion William H. Stoneman, the London correspondent of the Chicago *Daily News,* broke the story from England. There is no better newspaperman in the world than Stoneman.

Confident that the *Blitzkrieg* could follow a carefully synchronized timetable, the Germans marched into Russia with the greatest army in history. About 180 German divisions, 20 of them armored, had been concentrated at the frontier, and to this mass of trained, expert soldiery, there were added 40 Finnish, Hungarian, and Rumanian divisions; for, like Napoleon before him, Hitler impressed the man power of his satellites. To comprehend the magnitude of this force it is necessary to recall that in 1914 Germany opposed a total of only 123 infantry divisions to the combined armies of France and Russia. Russia was beaten in the first World War by 11 German and 38 Austrian divisions. Enjoying the initiative in 1941, so that she was free to concentrate superior forces in the sectors of her own choice, Germany organized her 220 divisions into three major and three lesser groups. The major armies took the center of the front, General von Leeb driving toward Leningrad, General von Reichenau toward Moscow, and General von Rundstedt toward Kiev and the Ukraine. The minor groups were disposed as follows: General Falkenhorst, the conqueror of Norway, drove toward Murmansk, the Arctic port of entry for British and American supplies; the Finns, under their own Marshal von Mannerheim, attacked north of Leningrad; and in the South the Rumanians, under their General Antonescu moved along the Black Sea. What was the Russian strength and how was it disposed? At the time of the invasion—pending full mobilization—the Russian army probably stood at between 160 and 170 divisions as against Hitler's 220. Before Leningrad, General Voroshilov commanded, in the center General Timoshenko, and in the south General Budenny.

The success of the German advance was overwhelming. Never in the history of armies have soldiers fought with greater *élan* than did the Nazis who brought to the East a superior confidence and morale gained from their easy victories in the West. Staffwork, logistics, and the quality of the commanders in the field were worthy of such soldiers. Though slowed in the North around Leningrad, the German armies under Reichenau and Rundstedt advanced steadily in the center and South, pushing forward in four brief weeks from two hundred to four hundred miles in several points. The Stalin line in many places was pierced. And then, as one week succeeded another, the Russians were driven back across the Dnieper; Odessa fell, with the resultant threat to the Crimea and the Black Sea; and the invaders marched into the highly industrialized Donets basin. By the end of September, Smolensk and Kiev fell, which meant the loss of the Ukraine and the near annihilation of Budenny's army. Hitler then announced that there would be but one more decisive battle. October 17, the Russian government, except for Stalin, moved from Moscow to Kuibyshev, and with German shells falling into the suburbs of Moscow the Russians at the end of October saw Kharkov fall. Two weeks later they were to brace themselves to the loss of Rostov, gateway to the oil of the Caucasus. In less than six months the German arrows had been driven 550 miles into Russia; Hitler had conquered 500,000 square miles of Russian territory.

The Germans had pondered for years General Karl von Clausewitz's classic study of Napoleon's campaign of 1812. They accepted as fundamental, of course, his dictum that "the destruction of the enemy's armed force is the leading principle of war." They also appreciated Clausewitz's argument that Russia must be struck so that she sues for peace quickly, otherwise anything short of total conquest becomes total failure. *Blitzkrieg* showed the way to the accomplishment of both. To make each battle a battle of annihilation —the militarist's dream of classic Cannae—the Germans modified *blitz* tactics. In Poland and France the *panzer* divisions had pinned their enemies against the natural barriers of the Pripyat marshes and the Channel. In Russia the ground of maneuver was too vast for the Germans to roll up the Communists against comparable barriers. Accordingly *blitz* tactics were revised for the given terrain and the given foe. The Germans continued to concentrate fire superiority in tank units supported by dive bombers in order to achieve a break-through; but when the break-through came, the Germans used it for encirclements in the field, destroying surrounded Russian units piecemeal. This was called *Keil und Kessel* ("wedge and kettle"); for after the tank forces had driven a wedge, the German infantry, motorized and foot, closed round like huntsmen to beat the surrounded game toward the center. Once the battle opened, the Germans searched for the Russian weak spot; having found it, they concentrated tank forces there for the break-through— which enabled German tanks to fan out in the rear of the Russian army, cutting communications and crowding the

Russians together. Surrounded and isolated, the Russian army faced dwindling supplies of food and ammunition, the loss of airdromes and, consequently, of the possibility of reconnaissance. Then the Germans alternated their system' of attack, first pouring destruction from motorized artillery and bombers into the entrapped Russian army, then initiating new tank attacks to knife through again and disrupt divisional communications.

The success of these tactics was facilitated by the absence from the Russian ranks of Marshal Tukhachevsky and the two hundred-odd fellow officers killed by Stalin in the purge. One commentator has said that their ghosts led the initial German assaults. Writing anonymously in the quarterly *Foreign Affairs,* he declared: "It is only now possible, in the spring of 1942, to appreciate fully the constructive imagination and the strategical genius of Tukhachevsky and his fellow officers of the General Staff, diluted or perverted as their plans have been in execution by the lack of equal imagination on the part of troopers like Marshal Budenny and other amateur commanders." This commentator, like military and journalistic observers generally, was able to learn the details of Tukhachevsky's defense plan because it was made available to Russia's French allies. A French general wrote in *Le Temps* over a period of years of the preparation of the Stalin line. German espionage also made known the Soviet defense strategy.

Tukhachevsky saw that it was vital to prevent a rupture of communications between Kharkov and Moscow, the life line of Russia, until the whole of the Russian forces could be mobilized and concentrated west of that line. He saw that Kiev was the pivotal defense point. Having purged the army of the military genius who had prepared a sound defense, the Communists thwarted Tukhachevsky's grandiose scheme in execution. Stalin had expected at least six weeks of diplomatic negotiations before the German attack and was just as surprised as we Americans were at Pearl Harbor. As a result large Russian forces were concentrated far west of the Kharkov-Moscow line and of Kiev. Tukhachevsky planned to meet the German invasion with only small covering forces, selling space for time. Stalin met the initial assault with large armies. Consequently his losses were already too heavy when the Germans were in a position to breach the Kharkov-Moscow communications system and the Stalin line before Kiev, where it was strongest and where large Russian reserves, had Stalin saved them, could have crushed the German forces according to Tukhachevsky's plan. Because Stalin modified this plan in execution (just as the Schlieffen plan was modified in 1914) Rundstedt made an easy crossing of the Dnieper at Cherkassy; Bock and Rundstedt joined forces east of Kiev, and the two were able to annihilate the Russian forces protecting the most vulnerable part of the entire system of defense—the railways linking Moscow and the Ukraine.

Marshal Budenny was a Communist ward-heel politician rather than a general. In peacetime he had been the man on horseback at parades in the Red Square and he liked to drink whisky with American correspondents. But the near annihilation of his army was a costly blunder. Russia's first-line European army was broken, because of it, after four months of war. Equally important, Russia had been compelled to bring reenforcements from the Far East and, as a result, Hitler had achieved the second of his objectives as well, for he could persuade Japan that if she went to war against the United States she need fear no attack from Siberia. As for direct access to raw materials, Hitler controlled the Ukraine and the Donets basin while the oil of the Caucasus beckoned. The most daring military operation in history seemed almost accomplished and Hitler announced that there would be one more battle and then victory. In mid-October, German arms seemed to have triumphed.

This was the moment when Hitler and his generals should have reread Clausewitz. They should have seen that he never wrote for the Prussian mind, which plans wars of conquest, but for those who would liberate the masses from the Napoleons and the Hitlers. They should have seen that Clausewitz, who wrote more than a hundred years ago, understood, as with uncanny and prophetic vision, the invasion of Spain in 1936 and the invasion of Russia in 1941. For what Clausewitz wrote of modern war—specifically of Napoleon in Spain and Russia—Hitler and his generals should have pondered before they attacked the masses in those two lands. Writing *On War* in 1831, Clausewitz declared:

"War, as it is actually made [that is, modern, total war between whole peoples], has a great influence upon all plans, especially strategic ones.

"All former methods were upset by Napoleon's luck and boldness [or Hitler's]. First-rate powers were almost wiped out with a blow [France]. By their stubborn resistance, the Spaniards showed what the general arming of a nation and insurgent measures on a grand scale can effect. By the campaign of 1812, Russia taught us, first, that an empire of great dimensions is not to be conquered, which might have been easily seen, second, that the probability of final defeat for the invader does not, in all cases, diminish in the same proportion as battles, capitals, and provinces are lost—which was formerly an incontrovertible principle with all diplomats, and therefore made them always ready to enter into some ineffectual temporary peace.

"Russia also showed that a nation is often strongest in the heart of its own country, when the enemy's offensive power has exhausted itself, and the defensive then vigorously springs over into the offensive. In 1813, Prussia showed that sudden effort may increase an army sixfold by adding the militia, and that this militia is just as fit for service abroad as in its own country.

"All these events have shown what an enormous factor the heart and sentiments of a nation may be in the production of its political and military strength."

The first year of the German invasion was a Russian victory, and Clausewitz—writing a hundred years before the event—is the only commentator who offers a completely convincing explanation of the German failure. Hitler's *blitz* army was a professional force, specialized and highly trained, but Russia proved the validity of Clausewitz's assumption that modern war is fought between whole peoples—not between the professional armies of monarchs. Most important of all, Russia proved in 1941, as in 1812, that "an empire of great dimensions is not to be conquered." Blitz, or lightning, war is predicated upon the ability of a highly trained army to exploit the time factor, but in Russia space was added to time. How this came to be decisive is readily understood by anyone who accepts Gneisenau's definition of strategy as "the calculation of space and time." A sixth of the globe, three times the expanse of the United States, Russia is forty times the size of continental France. There the *Blitz* operated under the optimum condition—time with a minimum limitation by the space factor. And yet even in preparations for the Polish and French campaigns the more conservative of the German generals had been seriously preoccupied by the problem "How long can an offensive action last?" Writing under that title as late as 1939 in *Militaerwissenschaftliche Rundschau,* the official organ of the German high command, Generals Geyer, Muff, von Sodenstern, and Colonel Baentsch and Major Westphal indicated that German officers were by no means unanimous in believing that *Blitzkrieg* offered a short cut to sure and certain victory. Moreover, Germany's great transportation expert, General Groener, predicted before the invasion of France that a lightning German advance would have to stop at the River Loire because men and supplies would have become exhausted. Military observers are now convinced that he was right and that the German advance could not have been continued for another week. What General Groener did not foresee, of course, was the collapse of the French politicians and generals under the influence of defeatists like Pétain and Laval.

Stalin was not Reynaud or Daladier—he was a Russian Clemenceau—and if there were defeatists in the Soviet Union they were either shot or intimidated into silence. Events justified Clausewitz's assertion that in total war the winning of battles and the capture of capitals and provinces is not decisive since modern diplomats represent a whole people fighting for survival—not a monarch. Certainly the loss of battles and provinces did not destroy Stalin's confidence in the possibility of ultimately defeating the invader and there is no evidence that he even contemplated peace negotiations. It is axiomatic, of course, that a nation is often strongest in the heart of its own country. Clausewitz proved profoundly modern—more modern than the Chamberlains and the Daladiers—when he suggested "what an enormous factor the heart and sentiments of a nation may be in the production of its political and military strength."

For in final analysis the victory of Russia in the first twelve-month period was the victory of a people wholly heroic in their hearts and in their sentiments. It was the spirit of sacrifice of the Russian masses which upset the German timetable and it was the delay in the timetable which took the lightning out of *Blitzkrieg* and bogged down the mightiest army in history. Inspired by such heroism, many observers abroad have concluded that Communism was as white as they had once thought it black. Overnight they lost reader-confidence in the American journalists who had reported the ruthless starving to death of 2,000,000 kulak and peasant farmers, the wholesale slaughter or exile of more than 1,000,000 men in the purges, the cruel denial of consumers' goods to the masses. Stalin was suddenly pictured as a man who loved children and dogs, a genial host who gave the lie to the Communist antireligious crusade by toasting President Roosevelt with the words "May God help him in his task." The journalists have given us a false picture of Russia, they said, because otherwise the masses would not have been willing to die for the regime. This lack of realism is as unhappy as the previous tendency to view foreign and internal affairs as a struggle between the forces of Communism and Fascism, a tendency which persuaded millions to the view that Mussolini and Hitler were saving the world from Communism.

Nationalism has always been a greater force in contemporary Russia than Communism. Stalin recognized this. From the moment of 3:00 A.M., June 22, 1941, his propaganda made this war the struggle for the defense of the homeland. He has not talked to the Russian people in terms of preserving or extending Communism. He has talked of driving out the invading foe. The Russian loves his homeland and through the whole of his lengthy history he has fought to defend it with a valor excelled by no other people. The contemporary Russian is tough. He has to be. He fought a murderous war against Germany and Austria, then a bloody revolution, and finally a protracted civil war. He suffered two famines in the period which followed. Then he bore up under the Five-year Plans as Stalin from 1931 onward poured more than half of the national income into the construction of the industrial plant essential to war—denying himself not merely auto tires and sugar but food and clothing. Communism did not win the Russian; it scourged and hardened him. Out of the suffering and travail came the maturity of the Slav. One hundred years ago when Napoleon invaded Russia the Slavs fought as heroically as they are fighting today.

Then most of them were serfs. Today they may not be free men by American standards, but they are no longer serfs. And the homeland for which they fought had been transformed. Its collective farms offered the promise that the Russians would never suffer famine again; its power dams and factories opened the vision of plenty for all. Stalin's 1936 Constitution was a pledge that someday they would enjoy what we in America call the four freedoms—a pledge given by a man who has ruthlessly suppressed them, but a pledge which the Russian masses believe that he will some-day honor. And this is the measure of Russian heroism—they fought, not to conserve an agreeable way of life, but to build the future. The Russian is childlike and naïve in his idealism, if you like; but that he is profoundly idealistic no one can deny who has traveled through Russia or who has read the masters of the world's greatest literature. The French fought to save their property; the Communists voluntarily set the torch to theirs like Kutuzov before them. The Germans fought to loot the wealth of the world; the Communists could look forward to famine and plague. The godless Russian masses fought for a religion which they do not practice merely on Sunday mornings. They fought for their dream of a future—a future which has little to do with Communism. Except for the British, no people has behaved so magnificently in seemingly hopeless adversity since the dark days of Valley Forge.

For the Russian willingness to die broke down the German *Blitz* in the end. Entrapped by the "wedge and kettle" tactic, one Russian army after another fought stubbornly even after it was completely isolated. The Germans, with understandable satisfaction, pointed out that large Russian units had lost all ability to operate strategically and that the headquarters from which they had been cut off sent general orders that they were to stand independently—checkers which the high command could no longer move about the checkerboard. Hemmed in, unable to replenish their supplies of food and ammunition, denied either air reconnaissance or instructions from headquarters, these isolated units stood under withering German bombardments, knowing that when Germans came within range they were to fire. As more of these units stood instead of surrendering, the German satisfaction soured. It became increasingly difficult for the overworked German infantry to press in closely. Russian units began to break through the encirclements. With this development Russian morale improved—probably in the moment of the Battle of Smolensk when Marshal Timoshenko first proved his greatness.

Annihilating many units, forcing the surrender of others, and yet finding that the Russians increasingly broke through the encirclements, the advancing German infantry came to feel that its task was endless and that Russia was an all-absorbing sponge. It had come up at last against the fundamental principles laid down by Marshal Tukhachevsky—defense must be defense in depth, it must concentrate on antitank measures, and it must be skillfully camouflaged. In the first World War defense extended generally thirty miles in depth, with strength concentrated in the last five miles. The Communists deployed for a depth of roughly ninety miles; a Red Army corps of 60,000 men held a narrow front of from five to twelve miles, but its strength extended ten times that distance in the rear. This defense in depth, the Germans found, fell into three zones, each a fortified island whose fire interlaced with that of the next island to cover every foot of ground where tanks or infantry might pass.

In honeycombing western Russia with collective farms the Communists had seen to it that each was an armed camp, especially designed to offer opposition to tanks. The Russians skillfully hid their defenses to bring the enemy upon them unexpectedly. I remember having seen an example of Russian cleverness in the Ukraine near Kiev in 1937. Forts which were being built then were not like those I saw in the Maginot and Siegfried lines. They were far inferior to the French and German preparations except that they were less obvious. In a collective farm settlement, or village, concrete pillboxes for several types of artillery would be encased in thatched-roof log buildings. When the Germans came upon such a settlement, or village, they were surprised with withering fire and, since they could not determine the source of this fire, it was necessary to halt and destroy the whole village, house by house, in order to silence guns from only three or four houses. Not these forts but the willingness to die of the men who manned them slowed the German advance.

Similarly the Germans came to rue the Soviet system of mobilization. At the commencement of hostilities each district sent its quota of divisions to the front, but the district was not denuded. As the Germans advanced they encountered the sudden mobilization of reserve divisions with the skeleton organization for a whole army. Thus the *Blitzkrieg* in Russia, like any other military operation ultimately, came to be a contest of infantry. The task set for the German infantry proved too great—because of the willingness of the Russians to die and because they were encountered over and over again in the millions. Exhausted foot soldiers attempted to carry out encirclements for which there were not enough motorized infantrymen. The field commanders began to feel the want of trained reserves—one of the few Versailles handicaps from which Germany could not recover. It became clear simultaneously to the Germans and the Russians alike in mid-October, as Hitler proclaimed his victory, that the invincibility of the German army was a myth. No army is invincible.

Hitler proclaimed victory (after one more battle) precisely, in my opinion, because he saw in that moment that the *Blitzkrieg* had failed and that Germany could only reorganize for the defensive until the spring of 1942—not too alarming a prospect since America was still paralyzed by isolationism and had not even comprehended the purpose of his campaign in Russia. This is the only explanation of a pronouncement of victory at this moment by such a master of the use of propaganda as a primary instrument of war, unless we are to believe that Hitler was not informed from day to day of developments and that he was elated by past successes. This is not like Hitler. It is interesting to note that as Hitler grabbed the front pages of the world press with a claim to imminent victory his military spokesman in Berlin was revealing (for publication with the classified ads) that Germany had failed in its primary task—what Clausewitz called "the destruction of the enemy's armed force." The Berlin spokesman estimated in the third week of October that the Russians still disposed of 1,500,000 men around Moscow, 1,600,000 in the South, and 400,000 in the North. Thus, while the Germans claimed that the Russians had lost 6,000,000 casualties, they admitted that Timoshenko still outnumbered the Germans since he fought with an army of 4,000,000 men. This statement of Russian strength on October 21—twelve days after Hitler's announcement of victory—is the more impressive if one remembers that Hitler and his generals had proved themselves the best weathermen in the world and were already in that moment anticipating, with an announcement of snowstorms, the Russian winter—which proved the most severe in 150 years.

There is every reason to believe, consequently, that Hitler did not blunder into the attack on Moscow but that he undertook it as a demonstration for the political purpose of bringing Japan into the war against the United States. The Japanese were already impressed that German operations had forced the Russians to withdraw divisions from the Far East. Would Tokyo hesitate to go through with the Tripartite Pact if it learned that the German *Blitz* had spent its force, that Hitler could not reach the Volga as promised, and that the Russians held intact in the West an army of 4,000,000 men ready for counterattack? Certainly the German field commanders would have preferred falling back immediately to winter quarters. Certainly they dreaded a demonstration against Moscow which was to cost them, as they must have foreseen, the loss of 130,000 officers and men. It is absurd, however, to accept the conclusion that Hitler and the General Staff fought. The problem embraced political and strategical considerations of a higher order. The General Staff certainly appreciated that Japan's entry into the war was worth the risk of such a demonstration and the loss of 130,000 men. In one of his few generous actions Hitler, later in the winter, accepted the resignation of certain generals and himself assumed direct command. Hitler thus spared the generals responsibility before the German nation for a decision which had transcended purely military considerations.

This theory is confirmed by the nature and conduct of the operations against Moscow and by the disposition of the German troops. A precedent for the demonstration is found in Napoleon's attack on Kaluga, October 23, 1812, at the very moment when he issued orders for the withdrawal from Moscow. Clausewitz has pointed out that "it was most important for Bonaparte to begin his retreat by a sham offensive toward the south." That Hitler understood Napoleon's operation seems clear from the troops he concentrated against Moscow. Twenty-two German infantry divisions were massed in the center, with only eleven in the two attacking wings. The right wing had no less than four *panzer* and two motorized divisions, while the left wing had three *panzer* divisions. Thus there were no tanks in the center, where the terrain offered them an opportunity to maneuver, and there was an insufficiency of infantry in the wings—which required heavy infantry weight if the Russian flanks were to be turned in any seriously fought battle. This disposition of troops makes it plain that Hitler approached Moscow with his army skillfully arranged not for attack but for retreat.

The writer in *Foreign Affairs* confirms my assumption when he concludes: "The withdrawal of large masses of troops began when tank divisions north and south of Moscow —especially the latter—were still pressing forward. Rearguard actions were fought by comparatively small forces. The whole vast retreat, involving thirteen tank divisions and about a million men, probably began about the third week of November. Control over its schedule was never lost." It is interesting to note the virtual absence of details from the Moscow front in the German communiqués in the last days after the attack at Pearl Harbor had been planned but before it had been executed. Then on December 8, the day after that attack, the German statement became frank, when it said, "In some places positions are being occupied which will make defense in the winter easier. Where far-advanced units of certain attack wedges are in unfavorable positions for the winter, these positions are now being brought back to a certain line." It was no longer necessary—after the day which will live in infamy—to pretend to be attacking Moscow. The *Blitz* had failed, the Germans everywhere had already begun to fall back to winter quarters, and there was no longer any reason for pretense. It was necessary only to find an excuse before the German people for the German defeat. Hitler blamed the weather.

The fact that the momentum of the German armies had spent itself by mid-October should have enabled Stalin to crush the Nazis. The time had come for Russian counter-attacks along the whole front. Here was the opportunity at long last to destroy German arms in a series of overwhelming battles which might have brought the end of Hitler. The Russians failed and for two reasons. In the first place, the Germans had shattered Russia's first-line army and Timoshenko's reserves were not up to their opportunity either in quality of troops or in armaments. Stalin could not recover from his losses in the Ukraine. The near annihilation of Budenny's army before and around Kiev had proved too costly. In the second place, the Germans devised the "hedgehog" system of defense. This enabled them to withdraw the bulk of their armies hundreds of miles from the Russian forces into commodious winter quarters. The Russians were held off by "hedgehogs" of relatively insignificant covering forces. During the first World War, General von Falkenhayn, and subsequently Ludendorff, organized machine-gun and sharpshooter squadrons. Picked men specially trained against tanks and low-flying planes as well as infantry, these troops were attached to general headquarters and they were independent of field commands. They were sent into the front to hold it in depth as the Germans retreated into the Hindenburg line. They had been organized as sacrifice troops; but, to the astonishment of general headquarters, a single squadron of three hundred men was able repeatedly, by surrounding a village like the quills of a porcupine, to hold up three or more tank-accompanied divisions and to perform this "impossible" feat with light losses. In Russia the "hedgehog" system was attempted on a vast scale. Thanks to the possibility of supplying each "hedgehog" by air, this outer defense proved too strong for the Russian counter-attacks even when the "hedgehog" was as far as two hundred miles in advance of the main German armies nesting safely in their winter quarters.

Russian casualties through the first months of the war had been too heavy. Russian strength was too exhausted. Stalin was well advised under the circumstances to accept the situation and to use the winter months in an effort to reorganize his armies, reestablish his own armaments industry, and train his men in the use of weapons coming in from Great Britain and America. The opportunity was at hand to destroy the German army, but Stalin was not in a position to exploit it. If Russian propaganda persuaded millions of Americans that the Germans were being ruthlessly pursued and wiped out in the deep snow and the freezing temperatures, that is less a reflection on the Communists than on the American public and the mass of undiscerning picture-magazine journalism which it devours. In the Communist regime propaganda is vital and Stalin's was designed essentially for the home front. The destruction of the Dnieper dam was not announced officially to the Russian people. How by Communist standards could such a loss have been announced? The retaking of Rostov became, under the treatment of the Communist propagandists, one of the great and decisive operations of the war. Why should it not have been so treated in Russia? Why should the Russian public have learned what foreign observers could learn by a careful scrutiny of both the Russian and German communiqués—namely, that the Germans held Rostov with only two S.S. divisions when the Russians counterattacked?

The Russians have been spoon-fed under Communism and anyone who tried to go beyond the official headline got shot for his pains. The American—since he is free to do so—might be expected to show more discernment. Official Moscow communiqués have proved over a period of time to have been sufficiently trustworthy; the difficulty came in the fact that the great American news agencies had to send something more sensational. And yet it might have been presumed that the more thoughtful American editor and reader would have remarked the discrepancy between the numbers of the German dead and the amounts of German equipment captured. By studying the communiqués against my background knowledge of the Russian and German armies, I think I can guess the relative casualty totals. I believe that in the first twelve months Russian casualties must have totaled at least 6,000,000 dead, wounded, and prisoners. I believe that German casualties have totaled well under 2,000,000. The thrill of headlines which proclaimed the defeat of Hitler's troops made too many of us lightheaded. The German armies retreated, but in no instance were they routed. Their withdrawals were orderly, their rear-guard actions stubborn, and they left very little booty to the Russians.

That is why the Germans were able to renew their attack in the spring of 1942. Coming out of winter quarters with their morale unimpaired, the Germans drove for the Don River basin, the Volga, and the oil of the Caucasus. They had reorganized their armies and changed their tactics. *Blitzkrieg* "wedge and kettle" methods were abandoned. The Germans sent forward massed armies, tanks serving now as infantry accompaniment. The efficiency of their military machine and of their new tactics was proved by the fact that they could still outmaneuver and outnumber the Russians on local fronts. With the Ukraine and the Donets basin already occupied, the Germans concentrated their strength against two objectives: first, the Don River basin—80 per cent of the Russian coal, 75 per cent of the pig iron, 60 per cent of the iron ore, 85 per cent of the sugar, and 95 per cent of the manganese—and, second, the Caucasus—source of 400,000 of the 593,000 barrels of oil a day produced in peacetime by the Soviet Union. If Germany could seize the Caucasian oil, she would cut Russia off from 85 per cent of its peacetime production of the raw material upon which much of the farming and transportation, as well as the war machine itself, depends. For the defense Russia had an army of not less than 4,000,000 men, reorganized and reequipped through the winter months, and this army held forth the promise of counterattacks. Did it have the necessary armaments? Had production around Leningrad and Moscow and east of the Urals been sufficient? Had Great Britain and America helped with arms?

The answer came haltingly. In the spring Timoshenko attacked in the Kharkov area. His advance was arrested, but his diversion caused the Germans serious inconvenience. Then came the heroic defense of Sevastopol, which upset the German timetable and seemed to have saved the Caucasus. And still the Germans advanced, the superlative quality of their troops, equipment, and staffwork making it possible for them to achieve local superiority wherever they attacked. When Hitler reached Maikop and Novorossiisk it no longer looked as if the Russians were falling back deliberately, extending German communications against the moment of a counterattack. It looked as if they could not stand against the invaders. Finally the Germans launched their major offensive against Stalingrad, planning, no doubt, to winter in that great city which could offer shelter against the blizzards that blow across the open steppes. But Stalingrad did not fall. The Russians defended it street by street, house by house; the

Germans were compelled to record their gains in yards, not hundreds of miles. Days passed and weeks, and still the city did not fall. Observers spoke of a second Verdun and the Communists answered with understandable impatience that there was no comparison. And then in the seventh week of the most heroic defense in history—after a boast by Hitler that he would take the city—the Berlin radio announced an "important change in the character of the battle." German objectives at Stalingrad had been achieved, the Berlin radio announced. Then the world suspected that Hitler had failed in 1942 as in 1941 and that he was preparing to withdraw his armies against the winter of his discontent.

It was in this moment that Stalin, in a letter to Henry C. Cassidy, the Moscow correspondent of the Associated Press, remarked: "As compared with the aid which the Soviet Union is giving to the Allies by drawing upon itself the main force of the German Fascists, the aid of the Allies to the Soviet Union has so far been little effective. In order to amplify and improve this aid, only one thing is required: that the Allies fulfill their obligations fully and on time."

Stalin referred, of course, to the engagements negotiated with Great Britain and the United States in the spring of 1942. Russia subscribed to the four freedoms as laid down in the Atlantic Charter and promised to make no separate peace with Germany. In return Great Britain signed a pact with Russia whereby the two allies "will after termination of hostilities take all measures in their power to render impossible the repetition of aggression and violation of peace by Germany." The United States limited its formal engagements on paper to an iteration of Lend-Lease stipulations and Mr. Hull's well-known views on freedom of trade. But more important than the formal paper were the conversations between President Roosevelt and Mr. Molotov, the People's Commissar for Foreign Affairs. "In the course of the conversation," said the two in a joint communiqué issued by the White House on June 11, 1942, "full understanding was reached with regard to the urgent tasks of creating a second front in Europe in 1942." This is the obligation which Stalin wanted fulfilled fully and on time.

Germany had failed again in 1942 to defeat Russia. Paraphrasing Pitt's great tribute to England, Stalin could have said, "the Soviet Union has saved itself by its exertions and may yet save the world by its example." For though his losses were severe, Stalin still had an army in reserve. He not only felt that he ought to try to redeem his promise to his own heroic people that the war would be won in 1942; he also saw the possibility of crushing the German army if Great Britain and America could invade the continent.

Great Britain and America could not invade the continent. They lacked the shipping and the seasoned fighters required to penetrate German defense in depth. But they opened a second front. Montgomery thrashed Rommel, and American troops landed in Africa. This did not seem to many Russians comparable to their mass fighting where they were bleeding and being bled by the millions. But strategically it was the most important Anglo-Saxon contribution to Hitler's defeat—the surest guarantee of Russian, as well as our own, ultimate victory.

XIV

JAPAN SELLS AMERICA SHORT

REPORTING to the nation by radio after Pearl Harbor, the President tried to tell us the truth. "The news is all bad" he began. The public grasped immediately the extent of the surprise blow in Hawaii, probably because we have been a naval power for most of our history and because we can visualize the big gray ships of war pounded atilt and set aflame as they lay at anchor in Pearl Harbor. What the Japanese did to us at Manila we failed to comprehend, though it was equally decisive. We had massed air strength at Manila and the other flying fields of Luzon. The Japanese —several hours after Pearl Harbor and in broad daylight— caught our planes like sitting ducks.

Those planes had been sent to the Philippines in mid-November because their presence there made it possible for us to win a war in the Pacific. It had been the fashion among naval strategists, who underestimated the role of the modern airplane, to suggest that the Philippines were not defensible. In anticipation of Japan's entry into the war Washington had come to the conclusion, nevertheless, that it was possible to defend the islands with strong forces of modern aircraft, and for that purpose we had built a ring of bomber bases. Accordingly our best ships and men were sent out—and in considerable force. Pearl Harbor lies only 2400 miles from the California coast, but the Philippines are 7500 miles away. They are situated between Japan, 1500 miles distant, and Hong Kong and Singapore. Similarly they afford natural protection for the Dutch East Indies, New Guinea, and Australia. Thus we moved out Flying Fortresses and the like in advance of hostilities and in sufficient force to pound Japanese invaders to pieces. Once our planes were aflame, however, the Japanese could land tanks, guns, and effectives at isolated points in the Philippines with virtually no opposition.

We lost the islands, therefore, in the first two days of the war, though the Japanese, proceeding methodically and at their leisure, were in no haste to reduce Corregidor and our gallant forces in Bataan. The surprise attack not only burned our planes but also destroyed our airdromes. Even if we could have organized convoys to move reenforcements of aircraft 7500 miles to Manila against superior Japanese naval strength and island-based aircraft, we would not have been able to put them into the air. The American public wanted planes and other reenforcements sent to the heroic men who called themselves "Battling Bastards from Bataan— no Mama, no Papa, no Uncle Sam." But there could be no relief. That was plain within a few days of the Japanese blow which destroyed our planes and our airdromes as well as our fleet at Pearl Harbor.

If we had not lost our aircraft in this initial disaster, the United States could have fought with a strategic plan for the defense of the Far East. Repelling Japanese landings in the Philippines, we could have shuttled our bombers between American, British, and Dutch air fields. It would have been possible to concentrate our forces for superiority at local fronts. Operations for the defense of Hong Kong, Singapore, Java, and the like could have been planned and naval actions could have been assisted by land-based aircraft. We would not have been victorious everywhere, but Japan could never have made a clean sweep of the rubber, oil, and tin which the United States wants now more badly than does the Axis. We would not have lost face throughout the Far East with the danger that India will go the way of Burma.

The American public seemed unable to comprehend that we were responsible for the disaster in the Pacific. We shook our heads gravely as the British lost Hong Kong, Singapore, and Burma and as the Dutch lost the East Indies. We forgot that they could be defended only by a joint strategy and that they had been lost because of an American Dunkirk. We exulted in the heroic resistance of the men under General Douglas MacArthur. Reading the headlines in the American newspapers, one might have believed that MacArthur was at the outskirts of Tokyo. The Japanese, however, were not impressed by American headlines. The point of view of the Japanese military was summed up by Major General Kenryo Sato in a report to a committee of the Japanese Diet. General Sato said that the fall of Gibraltar, Suez, India, and Australia were "only a matter of time." He promised war to the finish with no "halfway peace." He declared that the weakness shown by Japan's chief opponents had "not been paralleled in recent history." In both diplomacy and military strategy, said this spokesman for the Japanese war lords, the Anglo-American camp "has been the victim of gross miscalculation, the like of which has seldom been witnessed."

Hindsight is cheap and it can be used as a shabby trick by the journalist, the politician, and the armchair strategist. Hindsight is better, however, than no sight at all. When I read General Sato's statement shortly before we had to fly General MacArthur out of the Philippines, I tried to examine the reasons for our own weakness and for our gross miscalculation of our enemy. Japan's intentions should have been plain to us all. I am no Far Eastern expert, but I had understood the Tripartite Pact signed in September, 1940, by Germany, Italy, and Japan. I had also understood the implications for us and for Japan in Hitler's invasion of Russia. Lecturing over America in the fall of 1941, I had predicted categorically Japan's entry into war against us. I was wrong about the date. I thought Japan would attack us in early February, 1942. I was also wrong about the strength of Japan and about our own ability to cope with her. I never dreamed that she would so completely outclass us in the initial stages in fighting power and brains. How was Japan able to measure us in such unflattering terms? How was she able to surprise us?

Japan's long-range plans were disclosed in detail in 1927 in a document known as the "Tanaka Memorial." Circulated by the Chinese, who gave me the first copy I ever saw during the invasion of Manchuria in 1931, it was denounced as a forgery by the Japanese. When Baron Tanaka, the leader of the aggressive militarists, became premier in 1927, the Japanese civil and military authorities in Manchuria and Mongolia met for eleven days in Mukden to discuss the policy of Japan in face of China and the world. According to the Chinese a program of positive policy was formulated which Premier Tanaka presented to the Emperor on July 25, 1927. The memorial runs over many pages. Americans are interested in such general observations as the following:

"For the sake of self-protection as well as the protection of others, Japan cannot remove the difficulties in Eastern Asia unless she adopts a policy of 'Blood and Iron.' But in carrying out this policy we have to face the United States which has been turned against us by China's policy of fighting poison with poison. In the future if we want to control China, we must first crush the United States just as in the past we had to fight in the Russo-Japanese War. But in order to conquer China we must first conquer Manchuria and Mongolia. In order to conquer the world we must first conquer China.". . .

It must be remembered that in 1927—when this program was adopted—relations between Japan, Great Britain, and the United States were excellent. They had already been stabilized for some years by the Nine Power Pact and the disarmament treaty which came out of the Washington Naval Conference of 1922. Few settlements have been more statesmanlike. The naval ratios made Japan safe from attack in Japanese waters and she in turn had engaged herself to respect the Open Door in China. The Open Door, together with the Monroe Doctrine, was the great achievement of American diplomacy—our most successful venture in power politics. Power politics is the normal interplay and rivalry of capitalistic states. That is why war in an unorganized world is often, and accurately, defined as an "extension of diplomacy." In power politics you appropriate your neighbor's watch by a fair exchange or by threats and table pounding. If these alternative methods, which are the essence of diplomacy, fail you, then it is necessary to ask yourself how badly you want your neighbor's watch; whether, in short, you care to fight for it or not. America and Britain were pacifist and satisfied powers. Under their Open Door policy no country was to steal China's watch. Instead China provided a great clock in the market square which Uncle Sam and John Bull and all the rest could see when they were working in the rear of their own houses. Access to the China market with its great clock had saved both John Bull and Uncle Sam the necessity of spending money for a kitchen clock, and both of them had grown fond of what was almost a landmark. Both had assumed that Japan would appreciate and respect the great clock which served a purpose useful to all alike. Neither believed that Japan would prefer to build an arsenal and barracks around the China market place, shutting the clock out from John Bull and Uncle Sam. The "Tanaka Memorial," however, carried this revealing argument:

"The Nine Power Treaty is entirely an expression of the spirit of commercial rivalry. It was the intention of England and America to crush our influence in China with their power of wealth. The proposed reduction of armaments is nothing but a means to limit our military strength, making it impossible for us to conquer the vast territory of China. On the other hand, China's sources of wealth will be entirely at their disposal. It is merely a scheme by which England and America may defeat our plans. And yet the Minseito [the liberal party in power during the Washington Naval

Conference] made the Nine Power Treaty the important thing and emphasized our trade rather than our rights in China.

"This is a mistaken policy—a policy of national suicide. . . . If we merely hope to develop trade, we shall eventually be defeated by England and America, who possess unsurpassable capitalistic power. In the end we shall get nothing. A more dangerous factor is the fact that the people of China might some day wake up. Even during these years of internal strife, they can still toil patiently, and try to imitate and displace our goods so as to impair the development of our trade.". . .

This is the mentality most difficult for Americans to comprehend, for we cannot conceive of people who never believe that trade can be mutually beneficial and who freely choose war as a preferable way to their monopolistic goal. The German Junkers and the Nazi champions of the master race have it. It grows out of the spirit of conquest. It is based on the war lords' notion that it is more honorable to fight than to work. In the savage state the bucks have always been the warriors, disdaining work as fit only for squaws. In America we can scarcely credit the idea that modern peoples had rather loot than build. We cannot believe that any people would prefer the methods of war to the methods of peace. Americans have been willing to fight, but we fought for ideas rather than for loot and even when we conquered a continent we felt that we were fighting in order to have room for our idea—our idea of freedom. Our greatest struggle—the Civil War—was a conflict of ideas. Consequently we are bewildered and incredulous before the Japanese dream of world conquest just as we are unable still to comprehend economic monopolism, which is the submerged base of the Nazi theory of the master race.

And yet the Japanese for more than three hundred years have revered Hideyoshi because, by his invasion of Korea and his plan for the conquest of China, he sought to make the Emperor of Japan the emperor of the world. This idea had not been forgotten in 1854 when Commodore Perry opened Japan to foreign trade and Townsend Harris negotiated the first treaty. Carl Crow, in *Japan's Dream of World Empire,* points out: "A little reflection shows that Japan could not accept any other theory of world relationship without doing violence to her idea of an emperor who was an omnipotent god. To admit that his divine rule extended only to Japan would be a denial of his omnipotence and the whole theory upon which Japan was governed would fall to the ground." This was explicitly recognized when Japan negotiated with Townsend Harris the first treaty with the outside world. In presenting this treaty to the Emperor for his approval, Lord Hotta, the Prime Minister, wrote in a memorial:

"Among the rulers of the world at present, there is none so noble and illustrious as to command universal vassalage, or who can make his virtuous influence felt throughout the length and breadth of the whole world. To have such a ruler over the whole world is doubtless in conformity with the will of Heaven. . . .

". . . and in establishing relations with foreign countries, the object should always be kept in view of laying a foundation for securing the hegemony over all nations."

Commenting on the "Hotta Memorial," with its precise and unmistakable promise of world conquest, Tyler Dennett, in *Americans in Eastern Asia,* writes: "This same idea appears at regular intervals in the literature of Japan throughout the remainder of the nineteenth century."

The literature of the nineteenth flowered into the deeds of the twentieth century. Japan worked to a schedule that might have exhausted a less determined people. She first made war on China (1894–95), forcing her to yield Formosa and give up her claim to Korea. She fought Russia (1904–05) and gained economic control over Manchuria. She annexed Korea (1910). She tried to gain control of

China as a colony by the famous Twenty-one Demands, against which the powers stood successfully (1915). She fought in the first World War and, though she failed to retain Germany's Far Eastern holdings, she won the strategically valuable mandated islands (1919). She invaded Siberia until an American Expeditionary Force saw her safely out (1918–19). She conquered Manchuria and set up the puppet state of Manchukuo (1931–32). The wars against China (1937–) and the United States (1941–) followed inevitably and, it would appear, according to schedule.

It is something of a surprise to us—for we in America are not a history-reading people—that through the whole of this period our own country has placed one obstacle after another in the way of Japanese expansion. To the Japanese militarists we have seemed their implacable foe. For we had a positive policy in the Far East long before the opening of the Panama Canal made us a Pacific power or before rubber and tin became vital to our national defense. Commodore Perry, in writing of the opening up of Japan, said that "the interests of commerce and the honor of the country demand it." The British then were our principal rivals for the China trade and, as Perry sought to beat them to coaling stations and trade concessions in Japan, he said that it was necessary for the United States "to anticipate the designs of that unconscionable government, the British government, whose cupidity was limited only by its capacity to satisfy it." In other words America's China trade was endangered by the threat of a British monopoly. So long as that was true we opposed our policy to that of the British. When the Japanese threatened our interests we were equally strenuous and enterprising in our opposition to them. And we resolutely resisted European efforts to partition China as Africa had been partitioned.

Our policy was influenced, of course, by the new school of American imperialists, but the spirit of America was neither imperialist nor expansionist. As George E. Taylor puts it in *America in the New Pacific,* "The only way to keep a foothold in that area, if everyone else was taking colonies, was for the United States to take colonies. The seizure of the Philippines, therefore, cannot be dismissed as an accidental consequence of the Spanish-American War. There is a very real sense in which the United States carried over to the old world of Asia the same attitude that it had towards European empires in the New World of the Americas. A Pacific empire was acquired, that is, not so much for its own sake as to neutralize the spread of other empires."

Our entry into Hawaii and the Philippines was paralleled by the Boxer Rebellion of 1900. The Chinese themselves rose against the foreigners. As a result the foreigners agreed to an international control over China. The United States pressed this opportunity to secure the agreement of the powers to its Open Door policy, which held the China market open for joint exploitation instead of the monopolistic domination of any single power. How ill-suited this was to the purpose of the Japanese military can be seen in the vigor with which Japan protested our annexation of Hawaii rather than in her attitude at the time toward the principle of the Open Door. For there was a fundamental cleavage and rivalry between the Japanese and the American civilizations. We did not think of ourselves as anti-Japanese and, indeed, by our own definitions, we were not. We strengthened Japan—whenever Russia seemed too strong. Like London, which was in alliance with Tokyo until the 1922 naval conference, Washington looked forward to the day when Japan could serve as a policeman in the Far East. What we wanted was an opportunity for American ideas to flourish in the Pacific. By the circumstances of our birth as a nation we were opposed to imperialism with its system of colonies and monopolies. We thought of ourselves as antiexpansionist and antiwar.

But it was the essence of our program which alarmed the Japanese. We were not trying to colonize China; we were trying to modernize it, to westernize it, to Christianize it. As we elaborated the notion of the Open Door at the turn of the century, our spokesmen talked about "the world-, quickening forces of Christianity, Civilization, and Commerce." Taylor quotes a British educator in China as having said:

"The Americans realized long before the war [1914] that the conquest of a nation may be made by the most beneficent and benevolent processes, and with the consent and cooperation of the nation or people itself. Schools, colleges, and universities are far more effective and lasting in the influence they wield than the military colonies the Romans established." A League of Nations commission held that the teaching programs and methods of the United States were abruptly substituted for the centuries-old wisdom and learning of China, and Taylor comments: "The prestige of America was so high that the officials for public education in China simply identified American education and the modern educational system."

Stealthily pressing our program of westernization, we had become the dominant power in the Pacific by 1922. At the Washington Naval Conference we persuaded the British to abrogate the Anglo-Japanese Alliance, the Japanese to renounce rivalry in naval construction; and the powers generally to accept the Open Door. The industrialization of Japan, largely influenced by America, had made it possible for that country to double its population in sixty years and to raise at the same time the standard of living. This accomplishment had given a new respect and dignity to business elements. Japan was emerging rapidly from military feudalism. It seemed that there were responsible political and business leaders in the country with whom the United States could negotiate. The militarists, like their feudal system, seemed to be slowly transformed by the westernization of Asia.

Meanwhile China, too, was evolving. Immediately after

the Washington Conference, Sun Yat-sen, the Chinese revolutionary, struck against the imperial regime at Peking.
Sun Yat-sen and his Kuomintang party had won the support
of Communism. Moscow had signed the Rapallo Treaty with
Germany and, withdrawing from Europe, the Comintern
carried revolution to the East. America was opposed to the
spread of Communism in China, though there was much
sympathy for the "westerners" around Sun Yat-sen. The
Chinese revolution raged from 1922 to 1927, creating a
nationalist army and overthrowing the war-lord system. Ultimately the nationalist revolution split under Anglo-American pressure; the Chinese Communists were driven into
Kiangsi province, the Russian agents were ejected, and the
Kuomintang was able to set up at Nanking the government
which ultimately, under Chiang Kai-shek, fought so stubbornly against the Japanese, even after it was driven to
Chungking. American ideas were threatened during this
revolution, but when Chiang Kai-shek and the Kuomintang
turned against the Communists they shot thousands of stu-
dents who preferred the Russian to the American way.
American liberalism won because it was represented by
Madame Chiang Kai-shek, T. V. Soong, H. H. Kung, and
the other "westernized" Chinese, and also because the wrath
of the people was turned against British imperialism. America was considered the lesser of the evil alternatives and this
led in turn to a decade of Anglo-American rivalry.

The Chinese revolution gave the Japanese military their
excuse, and the Anglo-American rivalry offered them their
opportunity. The militarists had chafed under the trade
and peace policy of the liberal Minseito party. "This is a
mistaken policy—a policy of national suicide," the generals
declared in 1927 in the "Tanaka Memorial." "England can
afford to talk about trade relations only because she has India
and Australia to supply her with foodstuffs and other materials. So can America because South America and Canada
are there to supply her needs. Their spare energy could be

entirely devoted to developing trade in China to enrich themselves. But in Japan her food supply and raw materials decrease in proportion to her population." What the militarists wanted was the antithesis of the American way. They wanted to conquer the Asiatic peoples and, as military rulers, dictate all economic as well as political and social life. They thought of themselves as what they were—war lords—and they thought of the Chinese as what they might be under the rule of the Japanese militarists—the drawers of water and the hewers of wood. The Japanese had arrived, independently of the Germans, from whom they were separated by much water, at the same notion of the master race. Their Co-prosperity Sphere, like Hitler's New Order, provided that the conquered countries should be the producers of food and raw materials. The Americans and the British, at worst, forced health and sanitation measures on reluctant backward peoples; the Japanese militarists were planning to force the use of narcotics on whole peoples, to bomb their cities, set fire deliberately to their universities, and make their women fair prey to rape.

Japan had the industrial plant and the national discipline for such a program. Long before Soviet Russia inaugurated the first of her Five-year Plans, in 1927, Japan had laid down a centrally directed national economic development. The feudal nature of Japan lent itself to state planning—a kind of 1776 mercantilism. Without state intervention the country could never have emerged so rapidly from its isolation as a country without ships, without railroads, without financial institutions. Thanks to the remarkable expansion of industry between 1906 and 1926—stimulated by state planning —Japan was able to absorb her increasing labor supply and even to raise the standard of living. Planning had served the Japanese well. But when the militarists decided in 1927 to return to an aggressive policy, they exploited the unrest and social discontent inherent in the swift transformation of Japan. The period of quick profits seemed at an end. The militarists could argue that conquest was the easier way and, indeed, many Japanese businessmen—they had been through a financial crisis—feared that the country's suddenly expanded economy was reaching the point of diminishing returns. Shortly before the Manchurian "incident" Harold G. Moulton, of the Brookings Institute, published, in 1931, *Japan, an Economic and Financial Appraisal.*

He concluded that, "whereas the rate of population has been accelerating, the rate of industrial growth has been declining since the fortuitous and temporary factors of the boom era have spent their force. Moreover, if employment is to be provided during the next fifteen years for the oncoming workers born during the last fifteen years, the number of jobs must be increased at the rate of approximately 500,000 annually.

"In view of certain factors affecting Japanese trade possibilities there is no assurance that such a volume of employment can be provided. Agricultural expansion is definitely limited. Silk culture has practically reached the margin of profitable extension; the growth of oriental markets for manufactured goods is dependent upon political and social and economic factors beyond the control of Japan, and markets elsewhere are subject to the tariff policies and fallacies of other countries. With such uncertain and uncontrollable elements in the situation, the rate of economic growth in the next fifteen years is a matter of conjecture, but one may safely conclude that it is likely to be less rapid than has been the case in the last fifteen years when an exceptional conjuncture of factors resulted in a phenomenal industrial expansion."

The military leaders saw in this economic situation their last opportunity to regain control of the country. The heroics and saber-rattling of military expansion might appeal to the nation more than the sober facts of economic reality. Recruiting from the land, the army knew the plight of agriculture. While the population had increased 12 per cent in a decade, the land under cultivation had increased only 5 per cent. If the price of rice went up, the urban dwellers suffered panic; but if rice went down, the farmers suffered despair. Only a small group had been enriched by the factory expansion, and the masses were confused by the political and social ideas which bubble in the wake of industrialism. There was widespread distrust of the industrialists and of their liberal politicians. As for the popular attitude toward foreigners, there was anger with the Western World for its restrictions on Japanese emigration, its shortsighted and irresponsible Smoot-Hawley tariff, its diplomacy which denied Japan an opportunity to expand in China. The expansionists thought that the Japanese people—frightened by the modern problems of a modern economy—would be willing to choose reaction; that the country would turn back to military feudalism and the Emperor, yielding to a mumbo-jumbo emotion based on the mass suffering and the mysticism out of which Napoleons and mighty warrior peoples are made. Accordingly the militarists filled the newspapers and magazines with pictures of the South Manchurian Railway and other Japanese ventures in the northern provinces. When the nation was China-minded again the militarists created the famous Manchurian "incident" at Mukden, September 18, 1931. They made the war which destroyed the League of Nations; ushered in the decade of Fascist aggression; and led to the attack on Pearl Harbor, December 7, 1941.

Manchuria was the part of China extending north from the wall and it was ruled independently of Nanking. Marshal Chang Hsueh-lian was its war lord and he had established a close cooperation with the Kuomintang government of Nanking under Marshal Chiang Kai-shek. The young Marshal Chang Hsueh-lian wanted this cooperation because the Russians and the Japanese had special treaty rights in connection with the Chinese Eastern and the South Manchurian railways—rights which either might invoke for further penetration. The "incident" was staged on the latter railway, which the Japanese controlled. According to their account, part of the track north of Mukden was blown up by Chinese between 10:00 and 10:30 on the night of September 18. Using this "incident," without a declaration of war, the Japanese troops moved from Korea into Manchuria with swift precision. They were over the frontier by midnight. By dawn, September 19, they had captured the Chinese arsenal and barracks at Mukden and were fighting from Dairen to Changchun. Within four days they had occupied southern Manchuria. The Japanese Foreign Minister, Baron Shidehara, had been confronted with a *fait accompli* by military leaders who looked on him much as they looked on the Western powers.

I read the announcement of the Mukden "incident" in the *Journal de Genève,* three sentences in a Swiss newspaper. The paper had been handed to me in the corridor of the League of Nations building by Vladimir Romm, the correspondent of the Soviet Tass Agency. "Where is Mukden?" I asked him. One of Moscow's ablest journalists and diplomats, Romm had just come to Geneva after a period of several years in China and Japan. He had come because Moscow anticipated the Japanese attack on Manchuria and believed that its success or failure would be decided by the diplomatic struggle in Geneva. Romm was one of their aces; they wanted a man of his ability and background on the spot in Geneva. The Americans, the British, and the French were caught with no Far Eastern expert at Geneva among their journalists or diplomats. "Mukden will be more important for your country during the next decade," said Romm, "than any other place name on the maps of the world." Romm took me into the League of Nations Library and suggested that I begin a rather late education in Far Eastern affairs by reading MacMurray's treaty series. And Romm told me about Mukden. He had just been there.

Nevertheless, this gunplay in a provincial Manchurian

capital seemed unreal. I was full of the power and promise
of the League of Nations. War? Why, war was outlawed.
The Japanese would not fly in the face of the conscience of
the civilized world. The League of Nations in the long
evolutionary process of history was giving a new dignity to
mankind. Man had won over the lower animals, not because
he was stronger in physical combat, but because he could
stand and act together with his fellows. Man had conquered
the beasts of the jungle. Man had conquered fire. Man had
conquered flood and tempest and plague. No one of these
phenomena any longer could destroy man. War alone had
remained beyond the control of man—a flood, a tempest, and
a plague in itself—but now man had learned how to conquer
war, just as he had conquered the other forces of destruction,
by standing against it with his fellows in a solid front.

The League stood as the symbol of human progress and
before its promise of international cooperation even the
world depression—then beginning—seemed not quite un-
surmountable. I had been thrilled by the speech a few days
before of Viscount Cecil of Chelwood, who spoke for the
British delegation to the League Assembly. Heir to the
ministers who have counseled the Crown since the reign of
Queen Elizabeth, Lord Cecil spoke with authority when he
stressed the hope with which the world awaited the forth-
coming Disarmament Conference. "I know the danger of
prophecy," he said, "but I am sure that no one in this vast
assemblage will rise to contradict me when I say that war
was never more remote, nor peace more secure. I think we
may congratulate ourselves upon what we have accomplished
in eleven brief years of the League of Nations."

Cecil concluded in language comprehensible to the business mentality of the democratic peoples of Great Britain,
France, and the United States. The dominant need of the
moment, he said, was to revive international investment in
order to bridge the gap in the balance of payments between
creditor and debtor countries, stop the drain on gold which

threatened a number of currencies, and provide capital for economic enterprises without which recovery and employment for the "involuntarily idle" (one of his phrases) would be impossible. The revival of business confidence would come with disarmament, he thought. What Cecil said seemed to make sense. A journalist in the gallery, I felt privileged to look down on the parliament of man. There sat the delegates of fifty-odd nations, every civilized country in the world except the United States, the Soviet Union, Brazil, Costa Rica, and Afghanistan. Who could doubt that these countries, too, would participate soon, and that mankind would stand in solid phalanx against depression and war—the twin evils left to scourge our civilization?

Mukden came within a week of this speech and all the world now knows what the Japanese did to the League of Nations and to the dreams of millions who, like me, put their hope in the organization of peace. The League failed for two reasons: the absence of the United States and the Soviet Union from its membership and the lack of teeth in its covenant. True, the United States attempted cooperation. President Hoover and Henry L. Stimson, Secretary of State, were exhausting every measure short of war. Both saw the danger that independent action might involve the United States in war—and alone. Both longed for the anonymity to be found in a seat at the horseshoe table of the League Council. A formula to get America to the Council table was worked out by Prentiss B. Gilbert, who had been sent to Geneva as a special consul to deal with League affairs. (Gilbert had been a boy-soldier in the Philippines, a mining superintendent, a globe-trotter, a playwright, and an expert in military intelligence before he turned his vast talents to diplomacy. Later, as *chargé d'affaires* in Berlin, he was to die at his desk from overwork because of his singular sense of duty—a distinguished, if unsung, diplomatist who has left the mark of his extraordinary personality and example upon a generation of colleagues who deserve better of the nation than the nation knows.) Gilbert sat as the representative of a signatory of the Briand-Kellogg Pact. The world has forgotten today the thrill it experienced then as the tall American strode across the Council room, and old Aristide Briand, hunched over the table with his straggling mustaches and unlighted cigarette, preened himself for one of the little speeches which made him the premier orator of Europe. Beginning huskily in a low tone, to make his listeners strain forward, Briand raised his voice almost imperceptibly, choosing his words with painful precision, until that voice suddenly rang through the room like a silver bell.

"The nations of the world that watch the progress of every work of peace," said Briand, "will not see without emotion the ranks of those anxious to prevent war strengthened by the presence of noble America, supporter of justice and peace."

Japan was not such a nation and she knew that a generation of American isolationism had not been swept aside by Gilbert's taking a chair at the Council table. Mr. Hoover had come to Geneva not in order to organize a world coalition which would mobilize overwhelming naval and air strength to drive Japan out of Manchuria or destroy her. Mr. Hoover had come to Geneva to sink the United States into the inky and innocuous obscurity of a League of Nations resolution. He came to Geneva because the League Covenant, with its threat of economic sanctions, offered the machinery for mobilizing world opinion against Japan.

Economic sanctions of the sort outlined in Article XVI of the League Covenant cannot restrain a determined aggressor. The very act of going to war, with troops mobilized and the national spirit aroused, hardens the soul of a people. A nation which is already belligerent is not likely to be intimidated by neighbor nations who agree on "measures short of war." This was to be demonstrated five years later by Italy—a power much weaker than Japan. When fifty-odd League members decreed economic sanctions, Italy was not deterred from military operations in Ethiopia and, indeed, sanctions served to unite the Italian people behind their dictator. The aggressor can be restrained only by those who are willing to outbid him in determination. They must be willing to pay the price of peace, and that price paradoxically is the willingness to fight. In short, an effective League of Nations can never be a pacifist organization. It is dedicated to peace, not to pacifism. Its purpose, like that of the policeman, is to maintain the peace and, as surely as the policeman, it must be able to and willing to shoot. An effective League can serve to localize wars so that they do not become world-wide or world-exhausting; it can crush the aggressor under the overwhelming weight of a world coalition. Having demonstrated once or twice that no aggressor can stand before the combined might of the organized world community, such a League would become, by the authority thus gained, a deterrent to war. League membership is like fire insurance; you have got to pay for both. Peace can never be cheap.

It became the fashion after the Manchurian "incident" to lay the blame for failure on Great Britain or the United States—depending upon whether you were an Englishman or an American. This is too glib. Mr. Stimson has shown in *The Far Eastern Crisis* that Great Britain did not double-cross us, and Prentiss Gilbert, in private conversation, bore him out categorically. Mr. Stimson worked energetically and with great courage. He could not persuade the British that we would go to war—if it came to that—any more than the British could persuade us that they were willing to go to war. The reason is plain. Neither *was* willing to go to war. The personality of Mr. Hoover played a part. No man ever tried harder to be a good President than Mr. Hoover; but, seen from Tokyo or London, he looked like the sort of man who is forever putting his hand to the plow and turning back. He had lacked the force—that indefinable quality of leadership found in Lloyd George or Clemenceau or Churchill or Roosevelt—to control his own Congress. He had condemned the Smoot-Hawley tariff bill and then signed it.

(Americans have never understood that this tariff measure impressed the world as a disastrous excess of nationalism, comparable in its disruptive results to a war of aggression.) Mr. Hoover would blow hot and then, reading the Hearst and other isolationist newspapers, he would blow cold. Europeans came to mistrust him—mistakenly but instinctively —just as Americans came, for the same reasons of personality, to mistrust Sir John Simon, the British Foreign Secretary, whom journalists came to loathe as the special pleader and advocate of expediency. It must be remembered, moreover, that Europe generally labored still under the shock of the United States Senate's rejection of the Versailles Treaty and, more specifically, the clause creating the League. Having ministerial government, the Europeans could not understand our system of balance between the executive and the legislative. Our failure to ratify the Versailles Treaty looked like sharp practice, if not treachery, to most Europeans. Japanese diplomacy exploited in skillful fashion the general want of confidence, alternately offering the British a favored position in the new Far East, reminding France of the dangers to her vast holdings in Indo-China, and whispering to American finance that it would enjoy special privileges in the development of Manchuria.

We were maneuvered into the false position of asking Europe to pull our chestnuts out of the fire. We were the dominant Pacific power. Our Open Door was being scrapped. Naturally we wanted Europe to stand up to Japan. France thought that America's new policy of cooperation with the League was too sudden to be a real conversion. France knew that the Covenant, with its absence of teeth, had been predicated upon military guarantees. The men who drafted the Covenant had also drafted a British and an American treaty of mutual guarantee for France whereby the Anglo-Saxon countries would come to the immediate military assistance of France if she were attacked by Germany. But what had come of those military alliances? The Anglo-

Saxons had declined to ratify them. America wanted France to risk war with Japan, but America formally declined to risk war with Germany. Great Britain, too, had misgivings. What was America's policy in the Pacific, asked the British. Did she mean to continue to support China in driving British capitalists out of China, where they had a $1,250,000,000 stake—five times the investment there of the United States. It was all very well for America to talk about equal access to the China market, if that was what Washington meant. America had a balance between agriculture and industry so that overseas trade represented merely a margin of profit. The British Isles were dependent, however, upon industry alone; they had to ship manufactured goods—and capital— abroad for vital foodstuffs. If Japan were beaten and China freed, would America join in driving British imperialism out of China at a moment when the British, like the rest of the world, were suffering already from the Smoot-Hawley tariff? The British, like the French, concluded that America was an immature and unpredictable power. Was there any reason to assume that Americans were capable of rising above their shortsighted isolationism?

The success of the Japanese militarists in Manchuria made it impossible thereafter for either the democracies or the liberals within Japan to stop them. Only military defeat could crush them. They had prepared the "Tanaka Memorial" in 1927. They had carried through the first phase of General Tanaka's program when they invaded Manchuria in 1931. Thereafter they brooked no contradictions from the business-minded liberals. They dealt with peace lovers summarily by the direct method of murder. They had already murdered Hara, the liberal Prime Minister who had prepared the way for the Washington naval treaty, and Hamaguchi, the liberal Prime Minister who had insured the ratification of the London naval treaty. Flushed with Manchurian success, they murdered in the single year of 1932: Inouye, the former Finance Minister; Baron Dan, of the business house of Mitsui; and Prime Minister Inukai, who counseled moderation toward China. Instead of moderation toward China, there was to be a new war there in 1937 in preparation for the subsequent steps in world conquest. Had the "Tanaka Memorial" not been specific? Had it not said, "In the future if we want to control China, we must first crush the United States just as in the past we had to fight in the Russo-Japanese War"? Accordingly, the military radicals struck at Tokyo, February 26, 1936. They killed the more conservative elements among their own expansionists: Admiral Viscount Saito, Lord Privy Seal and former Prime Minister; General Jotaro Watanabe, Inspector General of Military Education; Korekiyo Takahashi, probably the most popular man in Japan. Twenty-four other leaders—the most distinguished men in the land—were wounded or barely escaped with their lives.

Like Hitler's purge of June 30, 1934, this, too, made war inevitable. July 7, 1937—after another staged "incident"—the Japanese launched the third of their wars against China —a struggle now entering its sixth year. In preparation the Japanese had signed with Germany, the previous November, the Anticomintern Pact. A year later, November, 1937, Italy joined the Anticomintern Pact. The Fascist International had been cemented—ostensibly against Russian Communism, actually against the rich capitalistic democracies. Japan and Germany were both expansionist; they were opposed to communism and capitalism; they had each deified a leader—the Emperor, in the one case; the Fuehrer in the other—and left the destiny of the nation wholly in the hands of their militarists. Using the excuse of the Anticomintern Pact, Germany flooded Japan with a fifth column. Mr. Wilfrid Fleisher, of the New York *Herald Tribune,* has described penetration of the Japanese ministries and agencies by German "experts" and "advisers" on the scale which I remarked in Italy. It was well-nigh inevitable, therefore, that Japan, September 27, 1940, should have signed with Germany and Italy the Tripartite Pact. This was a military alliance directed against the United States. Though we were described merely as "a power at present not involved in the European war or the Sino-Japanese conflict," the published text made it clear that the pact was not against Russia, with whom Germany was not yet at war. The signature of a military alliance against America was softened by appropriate remarks from Yosuke Matsuoka, the Foreign Minister—with whom I had drunk many a bottle of whisky before discovering the contempt in which he held Americans. But it was an alliance and it meant war. Count Ciano, the Italian Foreign Minister, laughingly told me that it meant the defeat of America, because, he said, it would become operative when Germany's submarine preparations had reached a stage where Hitler could sink ships faster than we could build them. "You will be rendered a have-not power in a matter of weeks," said Ciano.

In the years before Japan signed the Axis alliance against us we had been supporting China—our natural ally—with words. We had been "restraining" Japan with shipments of scrap iron, oil, and the like. For all the elements of greatness in the man, Cordell Hull, our Secretary of State, found it difficult—because of his patience—to bring a rupture with the Japanese. Mr. Hull seemed to cling to the belief that the German and Japanese policies were policies of desperation rather than of choice and calculation. He seemed to hope that their leaders, if given equality of economic opportunity, might ultimately embrace the notions of Mr. Hull's own liberal world. He was also influenced by advisers who rightly believed that if we denied Japan oil her navy would immediately invade the Dutch East Indies in order to seize oil. Mr. Hull knew that our navy, building a two-seas fleet, wanted time—every navy always does. He was concerned, moreover, because Hitler's strategy was one of trying to embroil us with Japan in order to prevent arms shipments to Great Britain, because, if Britain fell, Hitler felt that the conquest of America would be easy. Mr. Hull was determined not to play Hitler's game. The well-balanced, if cautious, policy of the State Department can scarcely be condemned by a people who were partially isolationist and wholly unwilling to declare war against either Germany or Japan. The nation can condemn the President for not telling the country frankly that a collision could not safely be avoided—for avoidance meant one American Munich after another.

Mr. Hull had to work out a policy short of war. There was, of course, almost no possibility of such a policy being successful. Mr. Hull had to play Machiavelli—amateur Machiavelli against total Machiavelli. His blood boiled as dispatches came over his desk reporting the rape and the butchery. He knew that the world could not endure half aggressive and half law-abiding. He knew that every bright page in American history had been paid for in American blood. He knew that ultimately war alone was likely to resolve the problems between Japan and the United States. But neither he nor the President would put the issue to the public in those terms. How could they, they asked themselves, when the Congress of the United States agreed to extend the draft period by the margin of one vote—when the isolationists had declined to fortify Guam?

In anticipation of Japan's entry into the Axis the United States gave notice at Tokyo that it would denounce the commercial treaty between the two countries. The treaty was to lapse January 26, 1940. To the Japanese this meant that we intended a strict boycott which would make it exceedingly difficult for Japan to prosecute her war in China. The Japanese were frightened and the fate of their government was in our hands. And then we hesitated. Public opinion in America was divided and Washington could not decide whether a boycott would keep Japan from entering the Axis or drive her toward it. Washington behaved like London before Munich.

After the Japanese entered the Axis alliance, the United States speeded aid to China over the reopened Burma road, strengthened the defenses in Hawaii and the Philippines, increased embargoes on Japan, and consulted with Great Britain and the Australian and Netherlands governments on the joint use of bases such as Singapore. There was a new note of realism which enabled Mr. Hull, for instance, to warn the Cabinet of imminent war even when he was negotiating with Saburo Kurusu, the special envoy. The public contempt for Japanese strength was not shared altogether in Washington. Many officials there knew that Japan was not exhausting herself in China. Ever since her entry into the Axis alliance Japan had reduced the scope and scale of her operations on the Asiatic mainland. The Chinese communiqués described battles which sometimes did not take place, or which, properly speaking, were not battles at all. It was understandable that Chungking—like Moscow later—should use mass propaganda with regard to its results rather than its essential accuracy. They were not fighting for the benefit of American spectators. Similarly it was not strictly true that Japan was a "have-not" nation. Exploiting Manchuria and a considerable part of China, Japan was the first nation in the world in exports of textiles, first in rayon, first in silk, first in the manufacture of plate glass. She stood third in shipping, fourth in hydroelectric development, fourth in chemicals. She was self-sufficient in food, graphite, sulphur, and minor metals, and she produced 95 per cent of her coal. Where she was deficient—cotton, petroleum, iron and steel, lead, zinc, aluminum and copper—she had stocked reserves. We also knew that she had greatly exceeded the tonnages by categories laid down in the Washington and London naval treaties and that her aviation industry was being reorganized by her Axis allies.

What the American people lacked in face of Japan was that simplicity of character which comes from high purpose rather than soft living. This alone would have enabled us to recognize the war as inescapable, to undertake immediate sacrifices, to assume the initiative, and to resolve in our hearts to crush an insatiable and treacherous foe. This lack of a national feeling that there are some things worse than war characterized even Mr. Roosevelt in August, 1941, when he discussed the Atlantic Charter with Mr. Churchill. At that meeting the British Prime Minister asked what the United States would do when Japan struck next. Mr. Churchill said that as for himself he could promise that Britain would stand by America within the hour—even if Japan's war was not made against Great Britain. Mr. Roosevelt felt compelled to reply that America would do nothing. He assumed that Japan would strike at Singapore or Java. He hoped that this blow would awaken and arouse the American people to intervene when Japan struck next after that. The President reflected the mood of a people which had been wondering how to get back to the standard of living to which it had been accustomed rather than how we were to save our civilization.

It is this mentality on the part of the whole nation, it seems to us now, which explains why the Japanese surprised our ships in Pearl Harbor and our planes on the airdromes of Luzon. The soldiers and sailors, the generals and admirals, of a democracy can rarely rise above the mood and mentality of the people they serve. America, in the period of reaction from Versailles, had lulled itself to sleep. We had learned nothing from the Manchurian experience. We had not faced up to the meaning of the collapse of France, of the Tripartite Pact, or of the German attack on Russia. Consequently our military men were asleep too. Neither commander at Pearl Harbor—there was not even unity of command—seems to have heeded the warning of the Navy Department. Bowed down, after his own optimistic speeches, by the enormity of the failure of the navy, Colonel Frank Knox flew promptly to Pearl Harbor to cut through service red tape and reorganize the defense of that vital base. Seemingly unaware that the Secretary would be obliged to recommend his court-martial, the American admiral met Knox's plane and invited the Secretary to be his house guest! And though there was unity of command in the Philippines, and no excuse for the loss of our planes there, the isolationist press embarrassed General Douglas MacArthur by their plaudits.

Happily for the nation, the courage of the men of the army and navy in Hawaii and the Philippines left nothing to be desired, and the United States Marines showed a comparable morale at Wake Island. They took pride in the fact that they were expendable. Our fleet shattered and our planes burned out on the ground, we set to work to retrieve the most difficult military situation with which the country had ever been faced. The navy fought, and won, two magnificent defensive operations in the Coral Seas and at Midway. The navy organized the long convoys to Australia and moved out the bomber aircraft. Within eight months of Pearl Harbor it undertook a land-sea-air offensive five thousand miles from the continental mainland, the invasion of the Solomon Islands—unprecedented in American history and the surest promise of our ultimate victory over Japan.

XV

CAN THE ISOLATIONISTS LEARN?

I REMEMBER little Francesco, the Italian soldier who drove my truck in Ethiopia. "Signor, tell me why we fight?" he asked. "Mussolini says that war is good, but the priest says that war is bad." He was a sturdy little peasant from the mountains of the Abruzzi, where, as he said, the snow makes everything clean at Christmastime. They turned him into a Fascist; but he felt no hatred against the Ethiopians, only pity for them. Though brave, he was as reluctant a soldier as Prince Camillo Caetani, who hated Fascism but died in the high mountains of Epirus fighting against the unoffending Greeks.

"What would you do if you were a German?" asked my friend Count Karl von Pueckler. I watched him oppose the Nazis at first and then applaud Hitler in the end as a greater German than Frederick or Bismarck. He died, according to dispatches, fighting bravely before Smolensk. He felt trapped by our times as did Captain Roland von Strunk, who served the Nazis out of desperation—a killer shot down in his own turn by the Gestapo just in the moment when he had bought a cottage on the lake, hoping to live quietly for a while at least with his wife and child.

I listened night after night to the songs and the dreams of Mischa, war correspondent for the *Red Star*. Six-feet-two, this hulking Slav would be moved to tears by the beauty of the folk music. "The Russians will give the world," he said, "love and the simple knowledge that we are all brothers." Mischa could not be a brother to Vladimir Romm, the third of our convivial trio, when Romm was caught up in the purge. Communism had taught both the brutal discipline which made Vladimir confess his "guilt" and Mischa denounce his friend.

I remember Sugimura, the Japanese Ambassador who believed in the League of Nations and worked for peace. Unlike the little men of his race, he was a giant and a wrestler. "I know you journalists and how you get big stories," he said. "You find a black feather and you make the crow. Technique! Well, that is the way with a Japanese who hates war. We must construct peace in spite of the militarists and out of almost nothing at all." Sugimura died of a broken heart. Peace has not yet had its victories, but it, too, can list its casualties.

There are the Britishers like O'Shaughnessy, the silver-haired surgeon who died serving a Bren gun at Dunkirk; and the Frenchmen like my friend Albert, who fought gallantly but got the slow shame of Vichy instead of death; and the Austrians I knew, and the Czechs and the Yugoslavs and the Spaniards and all the rest. Now begins the long roster of the Americans. Already there were those who died as noncombatants, though truly they fought this war—the two dearest friends of them all—Prentiss Gilbert, in Berlin; Webb Miller, in London. Already there are the college mate shot down in the bomber and the friend missing at Bataan. But the long lists are yet to come. They will be compiled when the youth of America begins large-scale operations in the spring of 1943.

It seems to me that these Americans are the most splendid young men of them all. What did my brother write me of the American soldiers in Australia? He had to serve for many months as a shy and self-conscious censor for their mail. He hated the job. "But in reading some 17,000 letters," he wrote, "I have yet to find a complaining or a cowardly note. There is a deep and simple idealism running somewhere through every letter that I have read. They are only concerned for the comfort and welfare of the folks back home. They are willing to make any sacrifice themselves. If you could read these letters you would be humbled by their cumulative effect. These boys are the finest in the world."

It will take such boys to defeat our foes. We are fighting for our very survival against a combination of powers which undertook this war aggressively and confidently. Victory will be possible only after the heroic and prodigal sacrifice of hundreds of thousands of these young men. It is this tragic realization which has brought a revolution in American thinking. The people of this great country are agreed today that we must win the peace as well as the war. There no longer appears to be any serious debate on that point. The nation almost unanimously rejects the notion that we must have another world war every twenty-five years. The people seem determined to organize peace and to put force behind it. If we can carry this wartime mood over into the period of peace, the young men of America will not have died a futile and a meaningless death. The graves they must share with our allies and our foes can be turned into a common grave uniting mankind in the end. There we can bury the reasons for this war as well.

We Americans, together with the British and the French, permitted the creation of the monstrous systems which prepared the attacks against our own peace-loving lands. Democracy abdicated. We offered the peoples of Italy, Germany, and Japan no persuasive example and no practical alternative to the vicious programs urged by their own leaders. The promise of democracy as a world system seemed a hollow thing when it failed to organize world security. Why vaunt individual liberties when they must be suspended for a war every generation? To many Europeans that seemed like boasting that religious freedom exists in a community where, in the streets around the church house, men are murdered and their wives raped so that no citizen dares to venture out on Sunday morning. If in the world community there was to be no international police force and no arbiter but military power, then each country was well advised to forget individual liberty and undertake its own rearmament, said the leaders of these countries, and their peoples agreed. Democracy merely offered luxury freedoms, they argued. And when our system sentenced millions to unemployment in the midst of plenty it seemed to vindicate the dictators' jibe that it was outmoded. The masses can scarcely be expected to starve in meek acceptance of a traditional system. They prefer to rise in bloody revolution or to surrender their political liberties to any demagogue or clique of generals who promise to satisfy their economic want by conquest. Modern man, in his desperation after the first World War, became pragmatic. He wanted his form of government to be capable of maintaining order and of generating economic expansion.

The Fascist and the Nazi systems, like the Japanese militarists, created for millions the illusion that they could do both. That is why they stirred mass idealism. Order was maintained, however, by violence and at the price of individual liberty; economic expansion, at the expense of neighbor states brutally invaded and ruthlessly pillaged. These two systems were neither sure of themselves nor constructive. The traditional rulers and the traditional systems of Italy, Germany, and Japan had lost the power to create sufficient wealth for populations rapidly increasing as a result of their own emigration and demographic policies. The Fascists and then the Nazis made counterrevolutions. They protected the traditional vested interests from the consequences of their economic failure by rooting out those who challenged their traditional privileges. The Fascists and the Nazis used revolutionary techniques for this purpose. But their movements were reactionary, not revolutionary. It was inevitable that Mussolini should murder Matteotti, the Socialist leader, and that Hitler should strike down his German counterparts in the purge of June 30, 1934, just as the Japanese militarists murdered that country's liberal statesmen. It was equally inevitable that each of these counterrevolutions should embark upon war. In no other way could they fulfill to the Italian, the German, and the Japanese peoples their false promises of economic expansion.

Communism also created for millions the illusion that it could maintain order and evolve an era of economic plenty. It maintained order by methods of violence which in no way differed from those of the Fascists. But Communism was a true revolution. It did not turn the clock back or try to play Canute. The economic welfare of the whole nation was made paramount over the interest of any vested group. As a result Stalin developed a continent-wide economic expansion, industrializing the backward country of the Tsars and ending the threat of famine with the collectivization of the farms. Because Communism was able to create this economic expansion the Soviet Union desired peace and was under no compulsion to conquer and loot. The democracies could deplore the nature of the Communist regime, but they had no reason to fear that it wanted or would make war.

In face of these dynamic world movements the democracies retreated, led back by the American isolationists to the "normalcy" which brought the failure of our system in the peace of 1919, the depression of 1929, and the war of 1939. If we had built a strong League of Nations we could have defeated Japan swiftly when she defied the peace-minded coalition. We could have warned Germany against unilateral denunciation of treaties and if she persisted in her rearmament we could have advised German civilians by radio to evacuate the areas and then bombed out German heavy industry before Goering ever completed the *Luftwaffe*. If we had acquired the habit of international cooperation we could have made a success of the London Economic Conference. But we went our separate ways, attempting collaboration timidly and too late. The procrastinations of our statesmen were outstripped by the inexorable march of events. French democracy remained static, its social revolution embarrassed, postponed, and finally made impossible by the threat across the Rhine, so that ultimately when the French went to war after the invasion of Poland they fought largely with the weapons, the industrial plant, and the ideas of 1918. British democracy proved equally reactionary in the hands of business-as-usual industrialists whose final bankruptcy was made plain to the world at Munich. The absence of leadership in Great Britain —together with the isolationism of the American public— explains why the initiatives in world affairs were left to the dynamic dictators. They were able to achieve the momentum of going concerns and the illusion that they represented "the wave of the future."

Of the great democracies we alone were fortunate in our leadership during the last decisive decade. When the militarists, the industrialists, and the landowners of Germany brought Hitler to office in 1933, the American people declared for more, not less, democracy. Under the leadership of Franklin D. Roosevelt we renewed our faith in progress as the mainspring of a people's government shaped by Jefferson, Jackson, Lincoln, Roosevelt, and Wilson; we held that democracy, too, could be made dynamic, and we proposed to find modern solutions for modern problems. In his inaugural address, March 4, 1933, the new President declared bluntly what the masses felt in their bones. "The rulers of the exchange of mankind's goods," he said, "have failed through their own stubbornness and their own incompetence, have admitted their failure and have abdicated. . . . The measure of the restoration lies in the extent to which we apply social values more nobly than mere monetary profit." Thus, from the moment he assumed office, the new President declared that the interests of the whole nation were superior to those of any traditional group or class. The laissez-faire system had operated for more than a century on the theory that competition and the profit motive would increase production and thereby automatically assure abundance. Modern advances in technology, however, had solved the problem of production. Distribution had replaced production as the problem of the twentieth century. We live in a consumption era where millions can starve in the midst of plenty unless we find a modern incentive in place of the no-longer-adequate theory of the profit motive.

Mr. Roosevelt proposed to substitute general welfare for the profit motive as the main concern of a country in crisis. He undertook governmental interference and regulation in order to protect the "forgotten man." This governmental intervention led to charges by his opposition that the President aspired to be a dictator and that he planned to saddle "Fascism" or "Communism" on the American people—his critics could never decide just which. These charges did not turn the masses against the New Deal. They knew that in our age an individual is not free, even to walk across the street, until the light goes green. They knew that this sort of regulation is the measure of the complexity of modern life and that it has nothing to do with a totalitarian versus a democratic regime; for the test of the regime remains the answer to the question "Where does ultimate sovereignty reside?" Our constitution and our elective system remained intact and both proved admirable checks on the abuse of power. When the Supreme Court invaded the field of the lawmakers, time itself struck against "the nine old men." When Mr. Roosevelt went too far against the Supreme Court in his turn, he was voted down by the Congress. When he abused his prerogatives in an effort to purge the independent Congressmen, he was voted down by the sovereign people. There was nothing wrong with our system and we proved it.

Having lived abroad during Mr. Roosevelt's occupancy of the White House, the author has been spared the day-by-day annoyances of manner and method—what strong president has been without them?—which have prejudiced so many against the only man in our history to be three times elected to our highest office. From the distance of Europe it has been possible perhaps to regard my own country with historical perspective. President Roosevelt was able to keep pace with his times, it seemed to me, and by that fact he renewed faith in democracy. He made it work. In Europe and South America I found millions who saw in Mr. Roosevelt's dynamic democracy the answer to Hitler, Mussolini, and Stalin. To freedom-loving peoples everywhere, Mr. Roosevelt proved that neither Fascism nor Communism was necessarily the pattern of the future. He made millions believe that democracy can be a going concern—not of the horse-and-buggy epoch but of our own times. If the President gave the world at large a new faith in the future of democracy, he also restored the confidence of Americans in our own destiny. The bottom third— and they stand behind the guns, the tractors, and the lathes— had been dealt a hand once again by the New Deal. Hitler began in 1933 to prepare the Germans for war, creating the greatest army and armaments industry in history. Consciously or unconsciously Mr. Roosevelt began to prepare us for war in the same year. He restored the people's confidence in a people's government. On Wake Island and in the foxholes of Bataan, American youth proved their faith in democracy. They were willing to die for it.

If we emerge victorious, thanks to the faith of our fighting youth, the United States will command such prestige as no other single power in modern times has ever known. Enjoying a balanced economy, and supplying most of our needs in raw materials and foodstuffs, we can boast already that our industrial production is greater than that of any two combined powers. We have lived under our own constitution for a century and a half. Our political philosophy is respected—not for the lip service paid it by Fourth of July orators but because it works again. We enjoy throughout most of the world a large measure of good will. Equally important, the opportunity will be at hand to shape the conquered nations to our own pattern. Our first task in the moment of victory will be to rehabilitate the hungry and homeless millions throughout the war-ravaged continents. For, having freed them, democracy cannot abandon these nations to starvation and plague. Consequently the American and allied occupation forces can minister to the needs of the conquered peoples in the same moment that our summary courts mete out justice to their leaders—the men who bombed women and children in Nanking, Guernica, Warsaw, and Rotterdam; the men who murdered innocent hostages from Saint-Nazaire to Lidice. And we can help these peoples reestablish peacetime industries and world trade in the same moment that we enforce their disarmament for a period of time sufficient to guarantee their political evolution—because there must be an interim of force, but there must also be recognition that a peace of domination cannot endure.

It is possible to organize peace and put behind it the force of the permanently united nations because our allies, too, have learned the lessons of the past. They see as clearly as we that the humanitarian approach, represented by such diverse efforts as loans to Germany or disarmament conferences or adhesions to the Kellogg-Briand pact, is now irrelevant. Subsidies to gain good will and treaties to renounce war equally missed the point. We did not want peace; we wanted peace pacts. A pact can be had for the price of the paper and the transportation of silk-hatted delegates, but the organization of peace, like fire insurance, is costly. We did not want disarmament; we wanted disarmament conferences. We did not mean to disarm, because it is unreasonable to strip your defenses in the chaos of an unorganized world. The only pertinent comment on why the governments kept attending disarmament conferences was Salvador de Madariaga's anecdote of the Jewish boy. He went to one shop and changed his dollar to quarters, in the next the quarters to pennies, and in the third the pennies back to a dollar. He repeated this in store after store until a shopkeeper to whom he had returned asked what he was up to. "Someday," said the boy, "somebody is going to make a mistake and it won't be me." As a journalist I covered most

362 WE CANNOT ESCAPE HISTORY

of the disarmament conferences, and the governments came in the spirit of that little boy. The French alone made sense, it seemed to me, when they said that countries could disarm only if there were a collective guarantee of the security of each. This is now plain to our allies.

Great Britain has learned already during the first years of the present war the true extent of her dependence. After 1918 the British smiled indulgently, and with some reason, at the suggestion that America had won the war—they gave a million dead; we gave sixty thousand. Today the people know that the British Isles have been saved by Russia and America, and even a Tory government was quick to sign a twenty-year alliance with the one and the Atlantic Charter with the other. Profoundly grateful, the British public would follow no government which proposed after the victory to end the wartime cooperation of the United Nations. Such a proposal could come only from the Chamberlainite reactionaries and they are too discredited to rule again in our time. British imperialism must evolve and the British know it. In extending India home rule and in modifying her financial influence in such countries as China, Great Britain must suffer a profound economic transformation. Depending on world markets for her manufactured goods, she must have economic and political cooperation with the major powers or she will sink to the level of Belgium, Switzerland, or the Netherlands. Thus the British people are prepared psychologically, and of necessity, to abandon the habit of framing their policies without regard to the needs and interests of other countries. And that is what is required—not a League Covenant or Union Now, for they are juridical solutions, but the simple determination that no industrialists, no trade unions, or no farm bloc will prevent international cooperation.

Russia's heroic struggle against the Germans has made it possible at last for the peoples of America, Great Britain, and China to look at the Soviet Union without prejudice.

It was ridiculous and almost disastrous in the period 1919–1939 to attempt to drop from the world view any country with the man power, the resources, the geographic position, and the incentive for peace of the Soviet Union. But many statesmen feared the spread of Communism. It must be plain by now that Stalin, and the Russians generally, are realists. They have known—even if our alarmists have forgotten—that Communism comes, not because of pressure from without, but from collapse within. After the victory of the United Nations, Russia, whether victorious in her own right or prostrate, must be preoccupied again with internal reconstruction. This task, in the future as in the past, will continue to have a sobering effect. The Communists were revolutionary like the Americans who startled the world with the Declaration of Independence. But the Russians decided, as we did before them, that their mission lay in opening up their own vast territories rather than in an attempt to spread their revolution throughout the world. Stalin has given his people a model constitution which can transform Russia ultimately into a true democracy. That way lies the future of this great people. The speed of the process of democratization, as well as the general measure of their cooperation with us, depends upon the sincerity of our helpfulness.

Like all revolutionaries, the Russians feel themselves outsiders, they are grateful for the friendship of more established peoples, and they repay it in kind. This fact and the realism of Stalin are fortuitous but auspicious. Moscow can prove the most effective member of the coalition if our victory, as I fear, plunges Europe and the Far East into violent and bloody revolutions, contained and controlled only by the occupying forces of the United Nations. In that event Russia can provide a stabilizing discipline until the revolutionary process shakes down. The United States must look, therefore, toward the Soviet Union for collaboration whether our attention is directed across the Atlantic or the Pacific. Misunderstanding and rivalry will come, in my opinion, only if the mind of the American people is poisoned against cooperation with the Soviet Union. We can refuse visas to Communist agents or deport them, if that becomes desirable, without breaking with a realist like Stalin, but we cannot decline to cooperate with the Kremlin economically, politically, and militarily unless we propose to plunge the two hemispheres into chaos again and prepare the third and bloodiest of the world wars.

The Chinese Republic, like the Soviet Union, is still in the stage of "temporary dictatorship." Her emergence into full democracy requires, and depends on, international cooperation. Without the understanding and help of the United States, Great Britain, and the Soviet Union there is a danger—and Chiang Kai-shek is certainly not unaware of it—that the military agrarians within his wartime coalition will ape the notions of the Japanese military. For the white man deservedly has lost face; the whole of the Far East will be in ferment as a century of imperialism is swept aside and, whether we like it or not, the impelling idea will be the "Far East for the Orientals." If, in the moment of victory, the great powers fail to work in close collaboration with the Chinese government, we will create an oriental Fascism which will give a horrendous meaning to old-fashioned notions of the "yellow peril." If the United Nations maintain their alliance we can count on the sympathetic cooperation of China in handling the problems of India and Japan. Chiang Kai-shek is surrounded by the "western" school of whom his wife, Madame Chiang, and his Foreign Minister, T. V. Soong, are typical. They honor American democracy and, if we make it possible, they will prove our loyal allies in peace as in war. But they must have equal status and sincere collaboration, for they are no longer a semicolonial nation.

Freedom from recurrent war depends ultimately, therefore, upon the maturity and political wisdom of the American people. If we can turn our backs resolutely on a century of isolationism—after the war as well as now—we can create an enduring peace. We have loyal allies. They are disposed psychologically to join us in the great experiment. More important still, it is to the self-interest of each. The alternative to an unorganized world community—a century of ideological, racial, and nationalistic wars—is frightful to contemplate. No oceans would offer a sufficient barrier against the modern—and future—weapons of destruction; no single nation could mobilize the industrial production and man power to stand isolated against the shifting coalitions of a war-mad world. To conjure up a single specter of chaos in the future, imagine an effort, thirty years from now, of the Western Hemisphere to stand against a Germano-Russian alliance backed by a Communistic and industrialized Far East.

We cannot maintain stability even in our own hemisphere without the postwar cooperation of the major European and Far Eastern powers. Our diplomacy has been singularly successful in the Americas to the South during the past decade. Mr. Cordell Hull and Mr. Sumner Welles have been the great architects of continental solidarity and no single Secretary of State has ever served the country as well. After the war, however, these countries must find normal markets and the means of their own industrialization. The United States cannot continue its present economic policy. Similarly, in country after country there is likely to be social upheaval involving revolution or counterrevolution. We shall need the most cordial relations with Great Britain and the Soviet Union if we are to see this period safely through.

Our own system of government in our own generation, consequently, faces a problem and an opportunity unique in history. With British imperialism and American isolationism cast off, democracy can be made safe for the world. After an era in which it seemed incapable of undertaking any initiative, democracy in the future can be made a dynamic force for peaceful economic expansion. Whatever mistakes we may make this time, let us hope that they will not be the old mistakes of the timid and the unimaginative who robbed democracy in the past of its inherent promise that out of a people's war and a people's system there must come a people's peace. Modern techniques of production can usher in an age of plenty, and the theory of political equality can be projected into the economic and social fields—that theory of equality of opportunity which, though essentially American, is secure even within our own frontiers only when its acceptance becomes universal. Thus our democratic system has an opportunity to free the world from the chaos of recurrent war and recurrent depression. The attempt alone would create an era of expansion not equaled since the great explorations which opened up our own continent. If we win this war, we can face the prospect of a century of peace and a new renaissance of mankind.

The issue of survival will be decided by the men in uniform. These young Americans glory in war no more than Francesco or Prince Caetani. They were trapped by the past decades as truly as Pueckler and Strunk. They could rise above the consequences of their country's isolationism —as individuals—no more effectively than Mischa and Vladimir could rise above the exigencies of Communist discipline. They dreamed of world peace as sincerely as Sugimura. They offered their lives as gallantly as O'Shaughnessy and all the rest who went before them. But are they not different? Are they not the youth of the most powerful country in history—the country which evolved the revolutionary concept of equality of opportunity, the country which, by applying that concept, can show the world the way to peace and plenty? Are they not the heirs to the founding fathers who said that "it is part of the American character to consider nothing as desperate, to surmount every difficulty by resolution and contrivance"? Survival depends on them, but the peace will be the measure of the enlightenment and courage of the whole nation.

It seems to me that the young men who are willing to die

have the right to say to the nation, in the words of Mr. Lincoln, "Fellow citizens, we cannot escape history. . . . The fiery trial through which we pass will light us down in honor or dishonor to the latest generation. . . . We shall nobly save or meanly lose the last best hope of earth."

INDEX

CPSIA information can be obtained at www.ICGtesting.com
Printed in the USA
LVOW010954020513

331776LV00004B/559/P